To Jerry Murphy,

With warm regards,

Don Warwick

# A Theory of Public Bureaucracy

# A Theory of
# Public Bureaucracy

## Politics, Personality, and
## Organization in the State Department

### Donald P. Warwick

*in collaboration with*
Marvin Meade
*and*
Theodore Reed

Harvard University Press
Cambridge, Massachusetts
and
London, England

Gift

Copyright © 1975 by the President and Fellows of Harvard College
All rights reserved
Printed in the United States of America
Second printing 1976
*Library of Congress Cataloging in Publication Data*
Warwick, Donald P
    A theory of public bureaucracy.

    Bibliography: p.
    Includes index.
    1. United States. Dept. of State. 2. Bureaucracy—Case studies. I.
Meade, Marvin, joint author. II. Reed, Theodore, joint author. III.
Title.
    JK851.W37        353.01        75-4907
    ISBN 0-674-88181-8

August 24, 2009

# Preface

This is a book about why bureaucracy grows and stays in the United States federal government. Its point of departure and central focus are the Department of State, but the analysis spreads from there to the executive system more generally. Our goal is to uncover what Noam Chomsky might call the "deep structure" of public bureaucracy—the underlying footings, alignments, cleavages, interactions, and motives that account for the surface outcroppings of hierarchy and rules. In digging for this substratum and later piecing it together, my colleagues and I have drawn on the tools of several disciplines, principally the sociology and social psychology of organizations and public administration. Our methodology, which is reviewed in the Appendix, might be termed Baconian. The research began as a careful sample survey of the State Department, but subsequent events led us to abandon rigorous methods and statistical tables in favor of whatever evidence we could lay hands on. The interpretations thus are based on a mental sifting and sorting of disparate kinds of information rather than on machine tabulations of questionnaire responses. Readers who are accustomed to setting analytic interpretations in their methodological context, or those who would simply like an initial overview of what was done in this research, would be well advised to begin with the Appendix. The book as a whole is written for the general reader, although Chapter 10 is addressed primarily to professional students of organizations and bureaucracy.

We confess at the outset that we do not know how accurately our theory of bureaucracy can be generalized to agencies beyond the State Department. We have quite deliberately extrapolated our conclusions beyond the solid core of data at hand in the hope of stimulating further research on the sources of bureaucratic growth and persistence in federal agencies. Every effort was made to incorporate comparable materials on other executive organizations, but these proved to be in exceedingly short supply. Quite likely an analysis having the Department of Agriculture or the Department of the Interior as a starting point would have produced a different constellation of explanatory factors, or a different weighting on those reported here. In Chapter 10 we lay out some of the crucial differences between the State Department and other executive agencies, and speculate on what they might mean for a general theory of public bureaucracy. Ultimately, however, the only sure way to know if the model developed in this book applies more broadly is to test it with a series of case studies involving a representative sample of federal agencies.

The research reported here is limited also in time. For the most part, the analysis of the State Department stops in 1973 at about the time that Henry Kissinger became Secretary of State. In addition to his accession, which does not seem to have greatly altered the internal structure of the department, there have been several other developments in Washington that may portend future changes in the federal bureaucracy and in the State Department. Congressman John Rooney, who for years has held an iron grip on the department's finances, has left the House; a revamped Congress shows signs of rebelling against the entrenched seniority system in assigning committee chairmanships; and the public recoil against the executive branch abuses associated with Watergate is prompting legislators to keep a closer eye on the behavior of federal agencies and their employees. Some of these changes may lessen the surface foliage of bureaucracy, but there are no signs to date that anyone in Washington is about to attack its deeper roots. The reader should thus be skeptical of comments, from the State Department or elsewhere, to the effect that everything is different now. Having watched the attempts made to reform foreign affairs agencies over the past decade, I am reminded of the adage, "The more they change, the more they stay the same."

A brief word is in order about our reporting policy. The study is based on essentially two kinds of information: a survey of several hundred employees in the Department of State, including personal interviews with about 150 senior managers and executives; and a variety of other sources, including congressional hearings, agency memoranda, newspaper accounts, the observed behavior of departmental officials, and previous research. With a few exceptions, the survey data were collected with the understanding that individual responses would remain confidential. Those guarantees have been scrupulously observed. For the rest, we have followed the standards espoused in the Freedom of Information Act and generally observed in the field of public administration. We take it as axiomatic that the public behavior of government officials as well as the actions of those who try to influence them should be open to scrutiny and review. We have therefore made no attempt to conceal the identity of the State Department, not only because this would be virtually impossible ("large federal agency entrusted with U. S. foreign policy"), but because we saw no reason to do so. Our original research contract with the department stipulated that the results would be made public and contained no restrictions on identification. We have also mentioned several senior officials by name, particularly when their motives and actions were of considerable importance in understanding the sources of bureaucracy. The individual mentioned most often, former Deputy Under Secretary of State for Administration William J. Crockett, had no objection to this practice, and in fact insisted that quotations from his interviews by openly identified. In most other cases the actions cited are already a matter of public record. Our policy, in short, was to treat the public organization as public unless information was protected by express or implied promises of confidentiality.

The preparation of this book involved extensive collaboration between myself and the colleagues noted on the title page. The interdisciplinary character of the analysis reflects the confluence of sociology, social psychology, and public administration in the research team. Throughout the project Marvin Meade served as our principal resource for the materials from public administration, a contribution that infuses many sections of the book. He also prepared several early drafts on the distinctive features of the public organization, and is co-author of Chapters 9 and 10. Theodore Reed carried out detailed background research on the history of the State Department, much of which is summarized in the first part of Chapter 2, and also provided a highly useful analysis of the department's organizational structure.

Both contributed as well to the collection and analysis of the survey data summarized in Chapter 3. In the end it fell to me to weave the disparate strands into a single book. The writing throughout is mine. In addition, I took responsibility for developing the model of bureaucratic growth and regeneration presented in Chapters 4 through 7, for the research and report on the Hays Bill in Chapter 8, and for the introductory sections as well as most of the conclusions. Though the final burden of writing was mine, the thought that went into this effort is the product of a fruitful and friendly collaboration extending over eight years. I also gratefully acknowledge the early contributions of a fourth collaborator, Dr. Allen Hyman, and regret that the press of other duties did not permit him to continue with us.

In conducting the research, we incurred many more debts than we can hope to acknowledge fully here. First thanks must go to William J. Crockett, whose openness to outside research during his tenure as Deputy Under Secretary of State made this study possible at the beginning and whose continued assistance helped to bring it to a conclusion. We are especially grateful to Mr. Crockett for the many hours he spent in preparing detailed responses to our questions—and for his willingness to have us use them without restriction. As scholars it is our sincere hope that other governmental administrators will follow Mr. Crockett's example in opening their agencies to outside scrutiny, and will show his good grace when the results are more muddy or less flattering than they might have hoped. The original survey in the State Department was also greatly facilitated by the generous assistance and support of John E. Harr, Richard Barrett, and especially Walter Hobby and Raymond Walters, our most immediate contacts. Our thanks, too, go to the several hundred departmental employees who took time to fill out questionnaires and rating scales, and particularly to the forty reorganized program managers, many of whom spent six hours or more in activities related to this project.

The initial study was made possible by a grant from the U. S. Department of State to the Institute for Social Research at the University of Michigan. The later stages of analysis received generous support from the James Marshall Fund and from the Center for Research on Utilization of Scientific Knowledge at the University of Michigan. The writing of the final chapters was completed while I was a visiting fellow at the Battelle Seattle Research Center in 1973.

During the survey stage in 1966-67 we were fortunate to have available the advice and collaboration of several colleagues at the Institute for Social Research. We are particularly grateful to Rensis Likert, who has supported this project from beginning to end; to Donald C. Pelz, who assisted in the construction of the questionnaires and joined us in the interviewing; and to Stanley Seashore, David Bowers, Floyd Mann, and Patricia Hoobler. During the later stages I profited greatly from conversations with Irving C. Bupp, the students in my graduate seminar at Harvard University on The Public Bureaucracy, Victor Murray, and John Craig.

Several individuals helped sharpen the analysis through their comments on substantial portions of the draft manuscripts. These included William J. Crockett, Rensis Likert, George C. Homans, George Farris, and Glen Fisher. James Q. Wilson and William Bacchus were especially helpful in recommending changes in the semifinal version. Frederick C. Mosher, Donald C. Pelz, Francis Rourke, Herbert Kaufman, I. M. Destler, Charles Perrow, and Herbert Kelman also offered useful comments or encouragement on specific chapters and related articles. Ann Orlov of Harvard University Press served not only as an astute editor but as a good friend in bringing this book into publishable form. Thanks are due as well to Vivian Wheeler for her impressive work as final editor. And we are very much indebted to Enid Davis and to the staff of the Secretarial Services Division of York University for their assistance in typing several drafts of the manuscript.

In conclusion, we gratefully acknowledge the cooperation of those who have allowed us to cite material under their jurisdiction:

Basic Books, Inc., for permission to quote from John Franklin Campbell, *The Foreign Affairs Fudge Factory*, © 1971 by Basic Books, Inc., Publishers, New York.

Professor Frederick O'Riley Hayes for permission to quote from unpublished manuscript on his experiences as budget director in New York City.

The Inter-University Case Program, Inc., Syracuse University, for permission to quote from Frederick C. Mosher (editor), *Governmental Reorganizations: Cases and Commentary* (1967).

Oxford University Press for permission to quote from Harold Seidman, *Politics, Position, and Power: The Dynamics of Federal Organization* (1970).

Yale University Press for permission to quote from W. L. Warner, P. P. Van Riper, N. H. Martin, and O. F. Collins, *The American Federal Executive* (1963).

D. P. W.

# Contents

# Tables

# Figures

# Part I    Background

# 1 • Explaining Bureaucracy

Social scientists have more often deplored than explained governmental bureaucracy. Many have recognized, on the one hand, the dramatic increase during the present century in the sheer number of public agencies and in public sector employment. In the United States the percentage of the labor force employed by government agencies at all levels was 4.1 in 1900, 7.3 in 1930, 15.7 in 1960, and 16.8 in 1965 (Downs, 1967, p. 254). Other indicators of bureaucratization, such as the tallness of hierarchies within agencies and the volume of published rules and procedures, have shown comparable increases. This surge in visible public bureaucracy has been even more evident in the socialist states and in Third World nations such as Uruguay, which have become heavily dependent on public sector employment.

In the United States the modal responses to this trend are fear about the implications of bureaucracy for individual freedom and outrage at its cost. Critics claim that governmental organizations become the master rather than the servant of the people, stifle initiative, inculcate fear, multiply reporting requirements, circumscribe action, waste time, and deplete the federal treasury. And yet, for all of the concern about "big government," there has been surprisingly little research into the causes of its growth. Even now, there is not a single study that traces *and explains* the bureaucratic expansion of one major executive department or agency. Most students of government have followed the stricture of C. Northcote Parkinson (1957, p. 51) in the conclusion to his essay on bureaucracy: "It is not the business of the botanist to eradicate the weeds. Enough for him if he can tell how fast they grow."

With two case studies of reform in foreign affairs agencies as a point of departure, this book attempts to develop a theory of bureaucratic growth and persistence in the U. S. federal executive system. We try to show why bureaucracy grows, why it stays, and why it shows strong powers of regeneration when a part is removed. The focus is on the proximate roots of bureaucracy—the sources within and immediately surrounding an agency—rather than on the broader societal and historical factors leading to the emergence of this organizational form. The study actually began as an evaluation of an effort by the U. S. Department of State to reduce bureaucracy in its largest section, the Administrative Area. The sequence of events touched off by this experiment shed light on the original sources of bureaucracy, the pressures for maintenance, and the tendencies toward regeneration. The findings on the State Department and other foreign affairs agencies are used to develop a theory of bureaucratization with more general applicability to the U. S. federal executive system.

### Bureaucracy

The term *bureaucracy* has many meanings, some scientific and some derisive. Martin Albrow (1970) notes that definitions of the term fall into seven categories: (1) rational organization; (2) organizational inefficiency; (3) rule by officials; (4) public administration; (5) administration by officials, in either the public or private sector; (6) an organizational form characterized by such qualities as hierarchy and rules; and (7) an essential quality of modern society.

Our approach comes close to Albrow's sixth variant: a form of organization. For present purposes the defining characteristics of a bureaucracy are the following:
—a hierarchical structure involving the delegation of authority from the top to the bottom of an organization;
—a series of official positions or offices, each having prescribed duties and responsibilities;
—formal rules, regulations, and standards governing operations of the organization and the behavior of its members;
—technically qualified personnel employed on a career basis, with promotion based on qualifications and performance.

These, of course, are the main characteristics of the "ideal type" of bureaucracy set forth by Max Weber (1947) and elaborated by many writers since his time.

In this study two of the defining characteristics, hierarchy and rules, will be treated as variables, with the remaining two serving as constants. We shall be particularly concerned with explaining the expansion and contraction of hierarchy and rules in response to various intra- and extraorganizational conditions. We see these as the more movable elements of a bureaucratic organization in the U. S. federal system. The other qualities, such as having official positions and offices or a merit basis for employment and promotion, may vary somewhat, but not a great deal.

## Bureaucratization

In general, bureaucratization is the process of moving toward the prototypical characteristics of bureaucracy. This generic term covers three rather different kinds of research questions: the historical development of the organizational form identified as bureaucracy; the expansion of organizations built on this form; and variations in the degree of bureaucratization within a given organization. The present study, which focuses on the third problem, must be set in the context of the first two.

The pioneering work on the evolution of bureaucratic organization was carried out by Max Weber. A central concern in his research was to explain the development of rationality in Western society. For Weber the essence of rationality was the deliberate calculation of means-end connections, whether in religion, the economic sphere, or the establishment of organizations. The ideal type of bureaucracy was the supreme embodiment of rationality applied to the problem of organization. In Weber's view a structure relying on hierarchy, specialization, rules, and technically qualified career officials was a highly efficient means of harnessing individuals to organizational ends. The growth of this form, in turn, paralleled and expressed the development of "legal-rational domination"—authority based on a belief in the rightness of laws and the legitimacy of those in superior positions to issue commands. The bureaucratic model can function effectively only so long as superiors are perceived by subordinates as duly appointed or elected officials working within the context of established legal or administrative procedures.

Weber's attempts to trace the rise of rationality and legal-rational domination are well known, and thus deserve only brief comment (cf. Bendix, 1960). His point of departure was the notion of *traditional domination* based on a belief in the legitimacy of a system that has always existed. The ruler or leader is the Master, who commands authority by virtue of an inherited position. When he speaks, his subjects obey; not because he represents "the law," but because his very position demands obedience and because he is acting in accordance with custom. The clearest expression of traditional domination is seen in the patriarchal household, which takes two forms. In the *patrimonial* system officials are personally dependent on the Master for remuneration and act at all times as his agents. Because their obligations consist mainly in personal loyalty to the Master rather than adherence to a fixed set of administrative rules, this system is open to great arbitrariness and abuse. The *feudal system*, on the other hand, reduces the extent of personal dependence on the Master and replaces it with some degree of contractually fixed obligations. Officials under this system take an oath of fealty to the Master, but typically retain a sphere of independent jurisdiction. The introduction of a contractual element into the authority relationship decreases the emphasis placed on custom and sets the stage for the emergence of legal-rationality. The full flowering of rationality was to come with the rise of Calvinism and the related growth of the spirit of capitalism. The advent of economic rationality prepared the way for the rationalization of the administrative apparatus of the state.

Several writers have focused specifically on the development of the bureaucratic form in governmental administration. Bendix, in fact (1968, p. 208), limits the term *bureaucratization* to the "substitution of bureaucratic conditions of governmental administration for non-bureaucratic ones." He continues:

The term "bureaucratization" serves to designate this pattern of social change, which can be traced to the royal households of medieval Europe, to the eventual employment of university-trained jurists as administrators, to the civilian transformation of military controllers to the Continent, and to the civil service reforms in England and the United States in the nineteenth century.

Both Tout (1920-1933) and Hintze (1908) show how a relatively independent and stable public bureaucracy grew out of a system of personal retainers in the royal households of England and Western Europe. The increasing size and complexity of governmental administration, the growth of a money economy, improvements in transportation and communication, and the impossibility of maintaining a peripatetic corps of officials all led to the breakdown of the household system and the establishment of regional clusters of permanent officials. Other antecedents of contemporary governmental bureaucracy include the employment of clerics and later university-trained jurists in public service, and the transformation of military controllers in conquered provinces into civilian administrators (Bendix, 1968).

A second broad approach to bureaucratization focuses more on the size of government organizations than on their form, which is assumed to be bureaucratic. The guiding questions are, "Why has the government become so large? Why are there so many employees on the public rolls?" The following are the most common explanations.

(1) Population growth increases the normal administrative demands made on governments—for police and fire protection and record-keeping, for example. Public employment expands to meet these demands.

(2) The increasing specialization of functions and division of labor in urban-industrial societies creates a highly complex pattern of relationships among individuals. The greater the complexity, the greater the likelihood of conflicts between specialized segments of the society and actions by one part that impinge on the welfare of others. Under these conditions there is rising pressure for the government to act as the agent of public welfare and the arbiter of private conflicts.

(3) A combination of population growth, industrialization, and pressure for the concentration of corporate power generates increasingly large private organizations. Large firms not only benefit from economies of scale but, according to some critics, are in a position to

[7]

establish monopolistic control. Governmental bureaucracies arise to: (*a*) provide the political and economic stability needed to protect the investments of the corporate giants; (*b*) protect the interests of society against the corporations; (*c*) prevent political chaos by mediating between large corporations and organized labor; or (*d*) act as agents to stimulate economic activity by corporations and channel it in constructive directions.

(4) The increasing specialization of knowledge favors the rise of a new "managerial elite" in both the public and the private sectors. In *The Managerial Revolution* James Burnham (1941) argues that specialization makes it difficult for the ordinary individual, including the stockholders of corporations, to understand the intricacies of technology, finance, and administration. As a result, a new class of specialist-managers steps in to fill the information vacuum. Their presence in government swells the size of the public bureaucracy.

(5) Increased levels of abundance generate new demands for services typically provided by public organizations, including education, welfare, health, and recreation. In many cases no single arm of government is willing or able to take full responsibility for a given set of services. The action is divided among several agencies, with considerable duplication of effort and new demands for interagency coordination.

The third approach to bureaucratization, adopted here, is concerned with variations in the *degree* of bureaucracy within and between organizations. Governmental agencies of approximately the same size may show more or less hierarchy and be governed by varying amounts of formal rules. The central task of this book is to develop a theory of bureaucracy in the public organization, with specific reference to the U. S. federal executive system and the Department of State. A guiding assumption is that the levels of hierarchy and the volume of rules seen in a government agency will vary with such conditions as the agency's task and mission, its relations with the external environment, the reward system for employees, and other conditions.

A key difference between this study and much of the earlier research on bureaucratization lies in the emphasis placed on organization-environment interaction. Most studies, even of government agencies, have been essentially inner-directed, focusing on such conditions as size, functional complexity, and professionalization (cf. Terrien and Mills, 1955; Anderson and Warkov, 1961; Rushing, 1967; Blau, 1968; and Blau and Schoenherr, 1971). Here we argue that one simply cannot understand bureaucracy, or even explain much of an agency's organizational behavior, without considering such factors as congressional control, interest-group pressures, and alliances between agency officials and various external actors. Internal factors are, of course, highly important, but they must be set in the larger context of agency-environment relations.

**The Case Studies**

The U. S. Department of State provides a choice setting for the study of bureaucracy. In the postwar period State acquired the dubious distinction of being almost *the* model of bureaucratization in the U. S. federal executive system. Caught in an incredible tangle of hierarchy, rules, clearances, interdependencies, internal wars, and external constraints, the department in the 1960s was a constant target of criticism for its rigidity and inaction.

Our opportunity to study bureaucratization in vivo arose in a rather unexpected manner. In June 1965, the department launched one of the most extensive attempts ever made to *reduce* bureaucracy. Under the leadership of Deputy Under Secretary for Administration William Crockett, the department's Administrative (O) Area eliminated 125 positions from its roster, transferred 160 positions to other parts of the department, and decentralized several of its core operations. But the most striking feature of this reorganization was its frontal attack on the two variable components of bureaucracy: hierarchy and rules. Crockett removed six levels of supervision between his own office and the operating programs in O, reduced clearances, and greatly simplified the rules covering personnel and budgetary functions. Most organizations have scarcely six levels of supervision available for removal; in the O area, itself two rungs from the top, six were removed with several more remaining.

In June 1966, the department invited a team from the University of

Michigan, of which the author and his colleagues were a major part, to document and evaluate the reorganization. During the following year we interviewed all of the key participants in the reorganization, including Crockett, and administered questionnaires to several hundred managers and employees. Before we were finished, it was evident that debureaucratization was giving way to rebureaucratization. Crockett resigned in early 1967 and was replaced by a traditional administrator. Almost immediately pieces of the old bureaucracy began to reappear. First one level was restored, then another. A new deputy under secretary was appointed in 1969, and promptly replaced the highest level that had been abolished by Crockett, that of assistant secretary for administration. By 1970 the cycle was complete, with most of the pre-1965 hierarchical levels once again appearing on the organization chart for the O area. Between 1968 and 1973 the author made periodic visits to the State Department to follow these changes, and also initiated a series of interviews with Crockett about the antecedents and consequences of these and related changes. The material in the following pages is drawn from the original study carried out in 1966-67 as well as from subsequent interviews and published reports. Further details on the background and concomitants of the study are reported in the Appendix.

Also in 1965 and 1966 the State Department, in cooperation with several other agencies, attempted a total overhaul of the foreign affairs personnel systems. The vehicle through which this was to be accomplished, the Hays Bill, serves as our second major case study. The goal of this legislation was to reduce excessive bureaucracy by establishing a single personnel system that would integrate Civil Service and Foreign Service employees in the State Department and related agencies. If the O area reforms brought out the organizational dynamics leading to bureaucratization and bureaucratic regeneration, the Hays Bill debate underscored the powerful forces leading to bureaucratic persistence.

From here on we shall basically follow an inductive approach, presenting case material and then exploring the broader issues that it raises. Chapter 2 sets the stage for the following sections by presenting an overview of the structure and dynamics of the State Department.

The five chapters in Part II all deal with the questions of bureaucratic growth and regeneration. Beginning with a dissection of the O area reforms (Chapter 3), the discussion moves to the role of the external environment (Chapter 4), the internal environment (Chapter 5), motivation and reward systems (Chapter 6), and the escalation of decision-making (Chapter 7) in the development of bureaucracy. Part III, in turn, considers the pervasive forces supporting bureaucratic persistence. Chapter 8 reviews the history of the Hays Bill and lays out the sources of resistance to change that it revealed. Chapter 9 then moves to a more general consideration of the factors holding bureaucracy in place in the U. S. executive system. Finally, Part IV offers a number of conclusions drawn from this research, pertaining to both the study of organizations and bureaucracy (Chapter 10) and the prospects of governmental reform (Chapter 11).

# 2 • The Setting

The outcomes of both the O area reforms and the Hays Bill were strongly conditioned by the history and organizational structure of the State Department. The problems that these programs attempted to solve trace their origins in part to the peculiar history of the department and its allied agencies, especially in the postwar period. And the conflicts and resistance they touched off followed long-standing lines of cleavage in attitudes and organization. A brief review of State's history will show the importance of the past in shaping current possibilities for bureaucratic change.

### Early Traditions

The Department of State formally came into being after the ratification of the U. S. Constitution in 1789. Two early developments left their impress on the department's nascent image: the adoption of an essentially European model of diplomacy, and the country's mistrust of foreign relations.

By the time the United States joined the diplomatic community, the ground rules of precedent and protocol had been set by European countries. The practical meaning of representation, negotiation, and intelligence—the traditional triad of diplomacy—was defined under Secretary of State Thomas Jefferson. Following the European prototype, he prepared a set of careful instructions for the handful of diplomatic and consular representatives abroad. When the continental experience was codified at the Congress of Vienna in 1815, the U. S. Foreign Service embraced its norm as an instant role model. The result was a heightened espirit de corps for the service, but also a professional image that would later bring it into conflict with the American public. While the diplomatic corps became cosmopolitan in identification, the country remained isolationist and inward-looking. Built into the American ethos was a deep-seated conviction that republican institutions and diplomacy do not mix (Ilchman, 1961). For many the Revolution had been fought to free America from entanglements with European powers. George Washington captured the prevailing mood in his farewell address: "It is our true policy to steer clear of permanent alliance with any portion of the foreign world." Jefferson echoed the same theme: "Peace, commerce and honest friendship with all nations—entangling alliances with none."

More subtle aspects of the immigrant mentality also affected the early attitude toward diplomacy. Kenneth Thompson (1962, p. 36) writes of the settler: "Having shaken the dust of the old world from his feet, he was anxious to prove that none of its ancient failings were his failings. Their purposes, often sullied by the ambiguities and compromises bound up with national existence in the cockpit of Europe, were not his purposes." As a concrete expression of concern with European contamination, the Continental Congress ruled that diplomats could remain overseas no more than three years. Rapid corruption thereafter was feared. But one part of their European heritage that the settlers did not scuttle was a profound suspicion of diplomacy. For the majority, foreign representation carried overtones of Machiavellian intrigue and sinister politics, Italian style. Sentiment was strong to ban the pomps of *Il Principe* from the American continent. Public mistrust of diplomacy in general and of its foreign-oriented practitioners was to surface later in the McCarthy era.

One practical result of this public ambivalence was that the United States was slow to build its diplomatic service. Even in the last decades of the nineteenth century, a period of rapid economic expansion, diplomacy did not keep pace with the growth of commercial relations. In 1889 Henry Cabot Lodge (quoted in Ilchman, 1961, p. 23) remarked that foreign affairs filled "but a slight place in American politics and excite only languid interest." Ilchman's depiction (p. 18) of the Foreign Service in the late 1800s suggests that some of the current complaints about the State Department are not new:

The service was tied down by an antiquated system of appointments and menacing inflexibility. It was chronically either shorthanded or overstaffed. No adequate salary scale existed. Members were not selected for their qualifications for diplomacy, and they, in turn, entered the service for reasons quite apart from desiring to serve the nation. The service was spoils-ridden and could offer no prospect of permanent tenure or promotion by merit.

By the end of the century the demands of empire made isolationism increasingly untenable. Economic interests created a need for a sizable navy, a traveling Marine Corps, far-flung coaling stations, and an interoceanic canal to facilitate commerce. The process of securing raw materials concessions required attention not only to technical questions, but also to power structures and political sensibilities. The economic climate thus favored the emergence of a professional diplomatic service. No longer could the United States deal casually with single issues on a bilateral basis. The First World War greatly accentuated these pressures, and the Treaty of Versailles further dampened isolationist tendencies. The war itself, preparation for a peace conference, and rising overseas involvement underscored the inadequacies of a small, unorganized diplomatic corps.

The professionalization of the diplomatic service was tortuous but ultimately successful. The Rogers Act of 1924 created the Foreign Service by name and united under its wing the previously separate diplomatic and consular services. Rivalry continued between these two career lines, and it was not until 1939 that the notion of interchangeability from one to the other was completely accepted. Even today there are signs that consular officials have never been fully accepted by "mainstream" diplomats.

The separation between the Foreign Service and other parts of the State Department—a critical factor in the 1965 reorganization—was apparent even after World War I. An incident shortly after the war illustrates the gap between the traditional officer's conception of foreign affairs and alternative approaches. H. O. Yardley, a military intelligence expert whose functions had been transferred to the State Department, let it be known that he had successfully deciphered secret messages to a diplomatic mission in Washington. Secretary Henry Stimson, reflecting the prevailing attitudes in the Foreign Service, ordered an end to his activities. He added a one-line explanation: "Gentlemen do not read each other's mail."

## The Legacy of World War II

Significant, far-reaching, and irreversible changes overtook the department during the Second World War and the years immediately following. Some would argue that State collapsed during this period and has never recovered. At the very least, the department's relative position among power contenders in the foreign affairs arena weakened drastically between 1941 and 1949. Four developments were especially critical in this process: State's response to the wartime challenge; the proliferation of foreign affairs agencies during the war; postwar policy demands; and heightened dependence and competition among the foreign affairs agencies.

### The Department and the War

More than most agencies, the State Department was poorly equipped to meet the sudden demands of 1941. This inadequacy was glaringly evident in its intelligence operations. In 1945 Secretary Dean Acheson told a congressional hearing that the information-gathering techniques used in 1941 were essentially the same as those employed by John Quincy Adams in St. Petersburg and Benjamin Franklin in Paris. Similarly, the department's corps of intelligence specialists numbered four in 1909, five in 1922, and only eighteen in 1943 (Ransom, 1958, pp. 52-53).

As the war approached, President Roosevelt tried to remedy these deficiencies by creating the Office of the Coordinator of Information, later to become the Office of Strategic Services (OSS). Significantly, this unit was set up outside the State Department, organized as a semimilitary operation, and directed by a military intelligence expert. The pattern had been set. Time and again in the following years activities intimately related to foreign affairs were detailed to agencies other than the State Department. This practice undoubtedly stemmed in part from Roosevelt's policy of dispersing functions across the bureaucracy to "divide and rule." But in addition the State Department was not a hospitable environment for innovation. In 1945 the intelligence analysts of OSS were transferred to State. True to form, veteran members of the Foreign Service greeted the newcomers with hostility and were "unwilling to admit to the need for the new activity or accept the new personnel as members of the State Department team" (Ransom, 1958, pp. 121-122). This reception added impetus to the creation in 1947 of a separate unit, the Central Intelligence Agency.

## Proliferation of Agencies

The manifold strategic requirements of the war produced a host of new agencies with overseas operations. Among these were the Office of Lend Lease Administration (1941), the Board of Economic Warfare (1941), the Office of War Information (1942), the Office of Foreign Relief and Rehabilitation Operations (1942), and the Office of Foreign Economic Coordination (1943). Many operated under the aegis of the Office of Emergency Management within the Executive Office of the President. From the standpoint of the State Department a critical aspect of this pattern was that the new agencies were controlled and directed by the White House; the department's role was typically confined to "policy guidance." Other contenders could make their way directly to the President or his staff to bargain for their agency's advantage. In the resulting contest of wills and interests the State Department lost much of its policy initiative to the newcomers. Former ambassador Lincoln Gordon comments:

While the State Department sought from time to time to assert its authority to coordinate at least civilian activities, and later the major aspects of occupied area government, during most of this period it was swamped by the emergency agencies and their specialized foreign missions. Conflict between such missions and the regular diplomatic establishments became common. Ambassadors were frequently simply disregarded. The authority of the State Department as leader in foreign affairs fell precipitously (Barnett, 1965, p. 22).

Although State lost influence, it did not grow smaller. In 1913 it had twenty-three organizational subunits; by 1944 it had ninety-four. The department's growth was accelerated in 1945 after it was ordered to provide a home for many of the special war agencies. The total number of employees in that year, excluding foreign nationals, was 6,452. By 1946 the figure had jumped to 10,677 and in 1947 to 13,312. Employment leveled off at that point, with the exception of a spurt in 1951-52 and a decline the following year. Predictably, the doubling of employment in a two-year period and the addition of dozens of new and disparate functions played havoc with the department's internal organization. The present structure of regional and functional bureaus, which will be elaborated later, was in good part an attempt to impose order on the postwar organizational chaos. This point should be remembered when we discuss the attempt in 1965 to reduce hierarchy and centralization. In many ways the organizational structure of the State Department is less the result of organic growth in a single entity than a series of ad hoc grafts onto a common trunk. In some cases the branches were united to the larger system with little difficulty. Others remained organically separate, sometimes drawing nourishment from congressional committees or other outside sources, but always vigilant of their nexus to the department.

## Postwar Policy Demands

For better or for worse, U. S. foreign policy had changed drastically by the end of the war. The Marshall Plan and similar programs implied active involvement in the affairs of recipient countries. The onset of the cold war further blurred the boundaries between domestic and foreign policy. These developments and the U. S. position of dominance in world affairs placed a heavy burden on the State Department and the Foreign Service. The new demands also clashed with some of the most venerable traditions in diplomacy. One of the strictest rules in the diplomatic code, for instance, is that the diplomat is a guest who is not to interfere in the political life of his host. As James McCamy points out (1964, pp. 70-71), this norm did not mesh with the realities of postwar foreign policy:

All the new programs required interference in the affairs of other countries. No nation will give aid without placing conditions on its use. To promote trade or to distribute propaganda is to bring pressure. The polite vocation in which reporting and representation were the main purpose, and negotiation when it had to be done was stately, was invaded by ruffians who demanded changes when they waved promises of supplies, arms, and loans. As soon as the new men discovered the reluctance of the State Department to accept them and their boldness they lost respect for State.

Also under attack was the Foreign Service generalist. The Rogers Act envisaged a corps of diplomats trained to perform almost any task at any post in the world. The limits of this tradition became apparent in such fields as economic and commercial reporting. As U. S. policy came to rely heavily on economic planning and forecasting, the casual reporting techniques of the generalists proved obsolete. Similar changes were seen in representation and intelligence-gathering. The United States no longer dealt with governments alone, but with a plethora of public, semipublic, private, and often underground agents. As historical forces carved a new international role for the country, specialization became the order of the day. If the Foreign Service could not provide the necessary skills, others could—and did.

## Interagency Dependence and Competition

By 1949 a total of forty-seven departments and agencies were involved in overseas activities. The State Department lost its primacy in foreign policy and has never regained it. Increasingly, its role was that of a diplomatic specialist and supplier of support for the international activities of other agencies.

The postwar years also brought a marked rise in interagency competition for influence and resources in foreign affairs. The most notable development was the meteoric climb in U. S. military involvement. Former ambassador Ellis Briggs observed:

During World War II, the State Department and its overseas personnel were rather generally pushed aside, and the military took over diplomacy. Since the surrender of Germany and Japan brought not peace but the cold war, the military remain very much—and very willingly—in the diplomatic picture (Jackson, 1965, p. 148).

The rapid gains in military ascendancy were consolidated in 1947 with the establishment of the National Security Council. Through this mechanism the Defense Department and the Joint Chiefs of Staff gained direct access to the President, a right they did not enjoy under Roosevelt. The council itself was largely the inspiration of James Forrestal, the first Secretary of Defense, "who wanted to enhance the defense role in peacetime policy-making and especially to insure regular consultation by future Presidents with their principal civilian and military advisers. The purpose was at least as much to make the Presidency serve the needs of the departments as to make the latter serve the former" (Jackson, 1965, p. 148).

While on paper State remained *primus inter pares* in foreign affairs, its coordinative role was progressively undermined. The presidents during this period thus were faced with an insoluble dilemma. They were reluctant, on the one hand, to entrust new and vital overseas programs to a tradition-bound institution such as the State Department. On the other hand, they had the problem of managing a conglomeration of centrifugal agencies if they did not. This dilemma has persisted to the present.

## The 1950s: McCarthy and Wriston

### McCarthyism

On February 9, 1950, Senator Joseph McCarthy told an audience in West Virginia: "I have in my hand a list of 205 that were known to the Secretary of State as being members of the Communist party and who, nevertheless, are still working and shaping the policy in the State Department." This speech struck a responsive chord in West Virginia and the nation. Fueled by public opinion, McCarthy launched a full-scale attack on "disloyalty" in the Foreign Service. His most powerful artillery was saved for the "China hands," whom he held responsible for the "loss" of that country.

Within the department the most direct organizational effect of the McCarthy furor was the Bureau of Security and Consular Affairs. This unit, which also played a prominent part in the 1965 reorganization, was set up under the Immigration and Nationality Act of 1952. The director, R. W. Scott McLeod, was installed with McCarthy's full benediction. A former FBI agent and police reporter, McLeod immediately set out to fumigate Communism from every corner of the State Department. Security teams undertook a thorough "field study" of all nineteen thousand employees at home and abroad. Using interviews, records, and hearsay, they scrutinized the politics, drinking behavior, sexual habits, reading material, and other minutiae of department personnel. To become a "security risk," one needed little more than an unflattering remark by a colleague. The spirit of the

McLeod era is captured by a slogan in his bureau: "An ounce of loyalty is worth more than a pound of brains." Many activities in the department were paralyzed as officers waited for the guillotine to fall.

The effects of the siege were devastating—and related to our concern with hierarchy. Talented officers resigned or were drummed out of the service. Field reports began to be couched in bland and roundabout language. Few dared to list Communist countries as career preferences, while East Asian specialization became a wasteland. Rumors and gossip were rampant in the corridors, reinforced by the spot visits of McCarthy's assistants. The virtues inculcated were caution, conformity, discretion, and prudence.

John Paton Davies, Jr., the most famous of the Foreign Service exiles, wrote later (1963, p. 198): "The violence and subtlety of the purge and intimidation left the Foreign Service intimidated and intellectually cowed. With some doughty exceptions, it became a body of conformists." An entire generation of officers learned that innovation and departure from the normal were forms of bureaucratic suicide. Under these conditions hierarchy and rules became welcome buffers against a malevolent environment.

Why the State Department and the Foreign Service? McCarthy's choice of scapegoats revealed a shrewd insight into historical resentments and popular discontents. The events precipitating public frustration—the Communist rise to power in Eastern Europe and especially the "loss" of China—were in the international arena and vaguely associated with diplomatic blunders. It was thus easier to blame the State Department than the FBI. But more subtle factors were also at work. The State Department had long been tainted by its association with "foreigners." Playing upon rising xenophobia and isolationism, McCarthy and McLeod repeatedly linked the Foreign Service to alien influences. "U. S. diplomats," McLeod charged, "imitate the dress, accent, mannerisms and even the thinking of foreigners." Secretary of State Acheson was alternately portrayed as a lackey of British lords and an agent of Communist radicals in New York. The attackers also took aim at the eastern, upper-class, Ivy League origins of the Foreign Service. Their appeals to populist resentment had some basis in fact. In the 1950s Foreign Service Officers were heavily drawn from Ivy League universities and the most prominent diplomats were unmistakably Anglo-Saxon: John Carter Vincent, Robert Woods Bliss, G. Howland Shaw, Ellis Briggs, and Outerbridge Horsey III. Moreover, diplomacy as a profession places a premium on grace, bearing, manners, and related patrician qualities. McCarthy deftly exploited these sociological hues to create an image of the cookie-pushing, tea-sipping, morally weak, striped-pants snob whose Harvard socialization set the stage for "selling out." His artistic efforts were aided by the perennial ambiguity of diplomacy and the lingering Mephistophelian image of the diplomat.

A significant by-product of the loyalty attacks was a marked separation of the Secretary of State from his own department. In 1952 John Foster Dulles agreed to accept the position of secretary only if he did not have to be responsible for managing State and the Foreign Service. His style from the beginning involved reliance on a small coterie of associates and great independence of action. Taking office at the height of the McCarthy attacks, he had no interest in defending his subordinates against charges of disloyalty. In fact, he was reported to have given Scott McLeod free rein in his purges, and to have sought his counsel on all appointments. He thus drove a wedge between his office and the department that is still in evidence. A recent departmental self-study (U. S. Department of State, 1970) concludes: "Under the combined effects of Secretary Dulles' closed-shop modes of operation, the onslaught of McCarthy, and the confusion of Departmental expansion, the creative contribution of the Department and the Foreign Service fell to new lows." By the end of the 1950s the severance was nearly complete.

## Wristonization

The second organizational event of the 1950s was the overhaul of State's personnel system by the Wriston Committee. By mid-decade it was no secret that the department was in trouble. Public confidence had been destroyed by the McCarthy assaults and internal morale was abysmal. In 1954 a panel headed by Henry Wriston was asked to propose changes in the department and the Foreign Service. Obviously influenced by the mood of the time, the Wriston

Committee recommended "Americanization" of the service. It noted that a disproportionate number of diplomats came from Ivy League colleges and argued that it was a mistake to "keep so much of the Foreign Service orbiting overseas so long" (Secretary of State's Public Committee on Personnel, 1954, p. 11). To democratize the service, increase its contact with American reality, and improve its responsiveness to new demands, the committee proposed a massive infusion of outside talent, a recommendation that was accepted. Within two years 1525 outside employees entered the service laterally ("Wristonization"), mostly in the middle and upper ranks.

The Wriston influx had critical effects on both the lateral entrants and the existing career service. The Foreign Service Officers of the time deeply resented what they perceived as a rapid dilution of their elite corps. Many saw the newcomers as poorly trained interlopers who simply had no business being in the Foreign Service. These feelings carried over to the reforms discussed in this book and proved to be a significant obstacle to change. In the Hays Bill deliberations Senators Pell and Hickenlooper made specific reference to the Wriston reforms as a reason for opposing further changes (see Chapter 8). The Wristonees, for their part, smarted at the incessant taunts about their dubious professional origins and faced an uphill battle for equal citizenship in the service. A further effect of the reforms, to which we shall return, was overcrowding at the top of the Foreign Service personnel pyramid. The officers who entered in the middle in the 1950s today form a frustrating bulge at the top of the distribution, slowing promotions for younger aspirants. Summarizing the events of the fifties, John Franklin Campbell writes (1971, p. 125): "The combined shocks of McCarthy and Wriston seemed designed to produce a surplus of cautious organization men and a shortage of trained diplomats. Today, nearly two decades later, most senior Foreign Service officers are either the survivors or the beneficiaries of McCarthyism and Wristonization."

### The 1960s: Kennedy and the New Diplomacy

John F. Kennedy's election ushered in new efforts to bring coordination and direction to U. S. foreign policy. The first step was abolition of the Operations Coordinating Board, an interagency unit associated with the National Security Council under President Eisenhower, and assignment of its responsibilities to the State Department. Although theoretically this change provided State with a means of regaining some measure of influence, ambiguity about the authority of the secretary prevented its having any real impact (Bacchus, 1974b). In 1961 Kennedy took a further step in giving ambassadors responsibility for supervising and coordinating all agencies operating out of their posts, including the CIA. President Johnson moved even more firmly in the same direction when in 1966 he instructed the Secretary of State to assume responsibility for the overall direction, coordination, and supervision of the interdepartmental activities of the U. S. government overseas. This directive, which will be discussed in greater detail in Chapter 9, also provided, at least on paper, organizational mechanisms for achieving the necessary coordination at the cabinet, regional, and country levels.

Behind this concern with coordination was the vision of a "new diplomacy." The Herter Committee report of 1962 broadened the goals of diplomacy to include "rapid social, economic, and political progress," and urged that the new diplomat be adept in such fields as technical assistance, intelligence, military aid, counterinsurgency, and cultural exchange. The State Department, in this view, was to be the repository of formal authority for cross-agency leadership and coordination. But subsequent events showed once again that entrenched rivalries and established patterns of relationships cannot be broken by memoranda and idealized coordinating mechanisms. The roots of power in other agencies were too deep and too well nourished by outside constituencies to be extirpated by executive orders. And, when all was said but little was done, it was clear that neither the President nor the Secretary of State fully believed in or trusted the new arrangements (Bacchus, 1974b). The resulting power vacuum quickly came to be filled by a budding corps of White House advisers on foreign affairs.

The 1960s also saw several efforts to grapple with the problem of bureaucracy in the State Department and other foreign affairs agencies. The Jackson subcommittee pointed to excessive bureaucracy as a prime source of dissatisfaction with the department's output:

In a cold war, the ability to act and react quickly is one of our most powerful weapons. A prompt move can dispose of a crisis right off the bat. But if officials are occupied in following routines, respecting petty procedures, chasing around from one "concurrence" after another, and spending hours in committee meetings until every last voice is heard, then the opportunity to act in time is lost. A stale product is the natural off-spring of bureaucracy (Jackson, 1965, p. 45).

The first large-scale attempt to pare down the department's bureaucratic structure came in 1965 and is one subject of this book.

### Organization of the Department

The 1965 reorganization underscored the importance of the system within which a change takes place. Long-standing cleavages, rivalries, and tensions surfaced with speed and vigor when the reforms were announced. Moreover, at several points the reorganization had to be curtailed because of actual or imagined congressional opposition. Thus both external relations and internal structure played a key role in the change experiment.

#### External Relations: The Role of Congress

Every executive agency depends on the Congress not only for its annual budget but also for statutory authority to continue in operation. In practice its success hinges on favorable relations with the relevant legislative and appropriations committees, both of which wield enormous power and influence. Annual review meetings between agency representatives and the committees lead to an understanding about what the agency will and will not do within a twelve-month period, and what funds will be available.

By law, control over the appropriations for the State Department is the joint responsibility of the House and Senate. Over time this control has come to be exercised almost exclusively by the House. Within the House, the recommendations of the Appropriations committee are generally considered final. These come largely unchallenged from the Subcommittee on the Departments of State, Justice, Commerce, the Judiciary, and Related Agencies, under the chairmanship of Congressman John Rooney of Brooklyn; within this subcommittee Rooney's decisions are authoritative. The Rooney subcommittee is thus the most powerful external controller of the internal operations of the State Department.

The legislative bodies responsible for State are the Senate Foreign Relations Committee and the House Foreign Affairs Committee. In the mid-sixties relations with these two groups, especially the Senate committee, were clouded by the Vietnam War. Commenting in a 1970 interview on his experiences with Congress, former Deputy Under Secretary William Crockett noted:

The relationships of the Department of State with Congress are as varied and complex as are any of the other relationships which are dependent upon the whims, images, concerns, ambitions, etc. of a great many people on both sides. The relationships are never stable, never one way or another and never totally predictable. They shift with the personalities, with issues and with situations and conditions. They shift with the condition of the economy, the state (success) of the U. S. effort and image abroad, the political party in power, the "feel" of the country, etc., etc.

The 1965 reorganization showed that difficulties with congressional committees arising out of "substantive" issues can set limits on a department's freedom for administrative change.

### Internal Structure

The State Department has four major organizational components: the Office of the Secretary, the regional (geographic) bureaus, the functional bureaus, and the Administrative (Management) Area. In recent years there have been some minor changes in the organization of the department and in the designation of particular units. To avoid confusion, we shall normally use the organization chart and terminology in effect during most of the period of this study (1966-1973). The following discussion, however, reviews both the older and the more recent structure.

The *Office of the Secretary* consists in the principal officers of the department and their staffs. At the time of our study they were the Secretary of State; the Under Secretary; the Under Secretary for Political Affairs; the Deputy Under Secretary for Economic Affairs; the

Deputy Under Secretary for Administration; one or more Ambassadors at Large; and the Counselor of the Department. The organization in 1974 was as follows: Secretary, Deputy Secretary, Under Secretary for Political Affairs; Under Secretary for Economic Affairs; Under Secretary for Security Assistance; Deputy Under Secretary for Management; Ambassadors at Large; and Counselor of the Department. In 1969, 342 employees of a total of 6,874 were attached to the Office of the Secretary. Because of the secretary's heavy liaison responsibilities with the White House and with Congress (and in the case of Henry Kissinger because of extensive personal diplomacy), he spends relatively little time on internal management. Many responsibilities in this area are handled by his immediate operating staff, the Executive Secretariat.

The following five *regional bureaus* are the department's front line in foreign policy: African Affairs, European Affairs, East Asian and Pacific Affairs, Inter-American Affairs, and Near Eastern and South Asian Affairs. Apart from some internal changes, these bureaus have remained the same over the past decade. Each is headed by an Assistant Secretary of State, followed by several Deputy Assistant Secretaries. Beneath them is the operating level, made up of Country Directors and Desk Officers. The regional bureaus theoretically are responsible for the overall coordination and guidance of foreign policy in their respective areas. In practice this responsibility is greatly diluted by the diffusion of foreign affairs activities across several dozen agencies. The major operating responsibility of the bureaus is the staffing of embassies, missions, and consulates.

The *functional bureaus* deal with activities cutting across the various geographic regions. The kinds of activities are suggested by their titles: International Scientific and Technological Affairs, Intelligence and Research, Economic Affairs, Public Affairs, Educational and Cultural Affairs, and Politico-Military Affairs. The major change in recent years is that the Bureau of Security and Consular Affairs, previously under the Deputy Under Secretary for Administration, now appears on the organization chart on a par with the other functional bureaus. The Bureau of Economic Affairs has also been renamed the Bureau of Economic and Business Affairs. In 1969 the functional bureaus employed a total of 1,645 persons. Each bureau is headed by either an Assistant Secretary or a Director.

The *Administrative (Management) Area,* known as *O* at the time of this study, was the largest and least prestigious of the subunits. In 1969 it included no less than 3,307 of State's 6,874 Washington employees. In addition to handling such traditional housekeeping tasks as budget and finance, personnel, operations (space, printing, travel, and the like), *O* Area served as the principal link befwen the State Department and the Congress. It was also an umbrella for various para-administrative activities, including security, passports, visas, the Foreign Service Institute (a mini-university), and the Office of Communications, which handles messages to and from all parts of the world. Its most critical responsibilities, however, were and are budget and personnel, money and men. The head of *O* was the Deputy Under Secretary for Administration.

The administrative-management section has been the most reorganized part of the department over the past decade. In 1972, *O* area was redesignated the Office of the Deputy Under Secretary for Management (*M*). Subsequently, additional changes were made. For purposes of clarity and consistency we shall refer to this section as *O* or the Administrative Area and not deal with the most recent changes. Figure 1 shows the organization chart for the Department of State as of 1970. This was approximately the organization and terminology during most of our study.

A full accounting of the administrative component of the department would also have to include regional and functional bureau staff involved in tasks such as budgeting, personnel, and post management. Campbell (1971, p. 126) estimates that "between 20 and 25 percent of bureau staffs comprise the deputies and office help and special and technical staffs of the assistant secretaries. In all, administrative and staff overhead of each of the policy bureaus thus accounts for 30 to 40 percent of the total bureau personnel." Many of the "buried" administrators in the regional bureaus spend their time on "post management"—providing housing, schools, food, clothing, and related services to overseas personnel. Others are budget and personnel officers who work closely with their counterparts in *O.* The result is a

Figure 1. Department of State organization chart (1970)

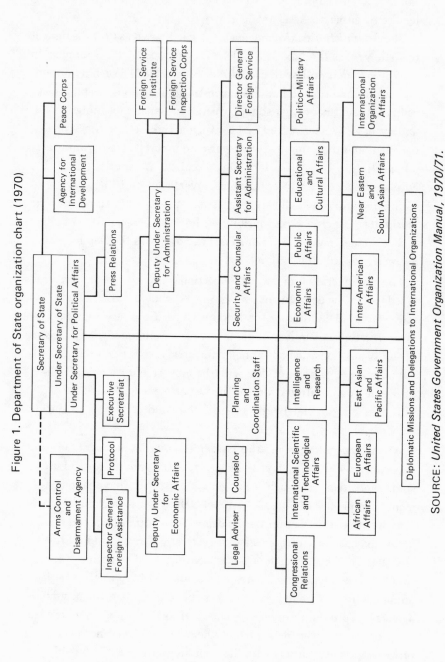

SOURCE: *United States Government Organization Manual, 1970/71.*

labyrinthine administrative system almost unrivaled in complexity. The 1965 reorganization was in part an attempt to streamline and rationalize this network.

## Organizational Cleavages

Beneath the formal allocation of authority in State is an intricate web of conflicts, rivalries, and alliances. The fissures produced by the reorganization moved along familiar lines of disparity in attitudes and organizational structure.

A prime source of cleavage is the multiplicity of personnel systems. State has no less than seven systems: the Foreign Service Officer Corps (FSO); the Foreign Service Reserve (FSR), general and limited duty; the Foreign Service Staff Corps (FSS); the Civil Service (CS); custodial and protective employees; and Wage Board employees (truck drivers and the like). The major point of division, however, is the concept of an elite Foreign Service Officer Corps (hereafter called the Foreign Service).

### The Department and the Foreign Service

The Foreign Service is unquestionably the mainstream career in the State Department. Foreign Service Officers (FSOs) hold most of the key policy-making and executive positions in Washington and serve as the chiefs, deputy chiefs, and political officers of the embassies. The present status of the Foreign Service derives from its original constitution, the Rogers Act of 1924. Congressman Rogers and his associates envisioned a career service that would be semi-independent of its parent body, the State Department, and also separate from the Civil Service system. It would be governed by an autonomous board appointed by the Secretary of State. From the outset the service placed great emphasis on "substantive" skills and held "management" in some contempt. Unlike corporate organizations, where prestige and advancement are commonly won by administrative ability, the service dispensed its rewards to those excelling in political reporting and negotiation. This tradition was consistent with the European model of diplomacy. The ideal officer was the substantive generalist.

The major organizational mechanism for producing the generalist was the rotation of assignments. Young officers aspiring to an ambassadorship were expected to have experience in many facets of foreign relations: consular work (visas, passports), political reporting, economic analysis, and perhaps cultural activities or even administration. This policy was an immediate source of tension between the service and the specialized programs. During the present study the chief of a consular division complained:

Another problem we have is that our FSOs are assigned here for three years at most and usually, at the end of one or two years, they get fed up over here . . . It takes six months for these people to acquire proficiency over here, then they leave in another few months, and you can't blame them. They know that to get anywhere career-wise, they're better off in the political or economic field than in consular work.

A budget official in one of the functional bureaus noted the same problem: "The FSOs consider a budget assignment a dead end, a limbo, and naturally they're less interested and dedicated to it." The organizational tension is clear: to become a promotable generalist the FSO must have experience in several specialized activities, but to stay in the mainstream he cannot become identified with any of the minor currents. Quite understandably, the less prestigious areas feel themselves exploited by the Foreign Service and its rotation system.

The Foreign Service has also shown signs of cultural insularity within the department (cf. Harr, 1969). The main thrust of its norms is traditional and elitist. The Foreign Service culture places great emphasis on the history of the diplomatic profession and on the intellectual and social superiority of its members. Strains of elitism are reflected in the widely shared support for rigorous selection, entry at the bottom rather than laterally, the choice of a man for a lifetime career rather than for the first job (as opposed to the Civil Service, where recruitment is for a position), rank in the person rather than in the position, belief in self-government for the Foreign Service rather than submission to "administrative bureaucrats," and commitment to a strong esprit de corps.

The service further sets a strong value on being in the mainstream of foreign policy decision-making, and on the "diplomatic approach," including subtlety, skill in negotiation, cultural sophistication, and good manners. Within this culture status differences are accentuated and the role of the ambassador is idolized. A corollary norm is that the successful diplomat must build and maintain his personal effectiveness. This is an amalgam of information, negotiating skill, style, and connections. To be effective the officer must know when and when not to fight an issue. Critics of the service have argued that the "when not" has won out over the "when" in recent years. For example, on the basis of sensitivity-training sessions with senior diplomats, Chris Argyris (1967, pp. 37-38) identified the following norms in the Foreign Service: suppression of interpersonal issues, minimal openness and trust, dependence upon the superior, minimal risk-taking and responsibility acceptance, cautious memo-writing ("don't make waves"), and so on. Apologists would counter that caution, suspended judgment, restraint, and even an air of detachment are essential qualities for successful diplomacy. Most observers seem to find a fairly distinctive Foreign Service ethos that is at least partially linked to the intrinsic tasks of diplomacy and that commands considerable prestige within the department.

An obvious problem created by the presence of an elite corps is that other groups are, by definition, nonelite. Civil Service employees in particular have complained of inferior status and neglect within the department. To test the seriousness of this problem, we asked a sample of 564 employees in the O area about the extent of conflict, tension, and friction between Civil Service and Foreign Service personnel. Almost half of the respondents (46 percent) reported "some" or "a great deal of" conflict, tension, or friction. Personal interviews with nearly all the division chiefs and program managers in O revealed the same problem. Even an FSO remarked: "If I was a civil servant I would feel that nobody was looking after me." Given the heavy concentration of Civil Service personnel in the administrative area and in the functional bureaus, this rift is reinforced by the other major cleavages in the organization.

### "Substance" vs "Administration"

Even by the standards of other federal agencies, the separation between policy formulation and administration is unusually sharp in the State Department. One informant spoke of a "perpetual warfare between these two groups," so that State became two instead of one.

Foreign Service Officers frequently complain that the department is being taken over by administrators. A comment by former ambassador Henry Villard is typical: "In the State Department, the administrators are no longer the servants of the policy makers—they are rapidly becoming the masters . . ." In some quarters O area administrators are affectionately known as "pants pressers." The implication, of course, is that Foreign Service should wear the pants, while O should provide the valets. The usual tensions between line and staff are aggravated by the lack of a clear "line," and by the range of control exercised by the O area, not only within the department but over other agencies. Ironically, the conflicts are often most sharply drawn between administrators in the regional and functional bureaus and their counterparts in O. The problems are well stated in these comments by two regional bureau managers:

O is not a service organization. It masquerades as such. They are really a control organization because they allocate money and people, assignments and promotions. They've got power! Despite the sweet talk, they are able to make a program go or not . . . Control shouldn't come from O because O can't understand the overseas efforts of State and other departments.

The conflicts betwen O and the regional bureaus are over control, in two ways: offices in O trying to infringe on the management responsibilities of the bureaus—frequently some of them handle things that are our direct responsibility. The second way is in terms of the control of overseas posts—the central offices still have some things centralized, such as motor vehicles. We don't feel they give the post enough operating authority and responsibility.

Others also reported problems, but added that they could be ironed out with frank and open discussion.

For their part, O managers resent the low status of administrative work. Given the department's prestige system, they complain, the most able Foreign Service Officers opt for other specialties or for the classic generalist pattern. Hence administrative positions must be filled either with Foreign Service leftovers or with Civil Service staff.

According to an *O* manager, "there's a big split between the FSOs and
*O*. The Foreign Service people feel 'they' (the *O* people) foul up things,
and they're impatient to get on with the substance of things." This internal stratification also leads FSOs who take assignments in *O* to fear
for their professional future. As one officer put it,

There's a problem in this type of program—it'll be hard to get another
overseas assignment. It's easy to get buried here. The bureau says,
"Who's [NAME]?" and "What's [PROGRAM]?" Ultimately, if this thing
continues I'd never get another foreign assignment—I'm too far removed. It gets you into a fringe area so that you need support from on
high. If they don't, they won't get anybody but clods.

Because of the low status of administration, it is considered good sport
and even a challenge to ignore, by-pass, subvert, or sabotage changes
proposed by *O*. FSOs often see such action as a counterstroke against
the encroaching bureaucracy.

*Regional vs Functional Bureaus*

Dealings between the regional and functional bureaus also are
marked by differential power and prestige. Because of their closer
links to foreign policy decisions and the preponderance of FSOs within their ranks, the regional bureaus carry greater weight in the department. They exert a strong influence on overseas assignments—
the prizes in the system—and it is to them that the ambassadors report. The functional bureaus regard their work as no less important,
but suffer from second-class status. Tensions are aggravated by overlapping responsibilities. The Bureau of Intelligence and Research, for
example, is organized into five geographic regions. When a question
of intelligence arises for Europe, it may not be clear if it should be
handled by the intelligence expert in the European Bureau or the European expert in the Intelligence Bureau. But the competition is most
keen in the assignment process. An administrative officer in the Bureau of Economic Affairs commented:

The functional bureaus are hassling back and forth about first-rate
people, especially economists. The functional bureaus don't have
much sex appeal for the FSOs—they're divorced from international relations. When you're trying to get officers to work on cotton textiles

you get violent reactions. Commodities is the thing that people really shy away from.

Most respondents agreed that the regional bureaus have a great advantage in bidding for talented FSOs.

Some also criticized the personnel offices of O for aggravating this situation.

O is organized principally to service the Foreign Service and the regional bureaus. It bears little relationship to the needs of the functional bureaus nor does it reflect any understanding of the role of the functional bureaus in the Department of State (executive director, functional bureau).

In dealing with O the functional bureaus feel they are the poor relations within the system. The regional bureaus get preference . . . Until recently we were not represented on the Mid Career Program and the Senior Officer Program assignment panels, but the regional bureaus were (administrative official, functional bureau).

These perceptions returned to haunt the O area in the 1965 reorganization.

The organizational life of the State Department thus reflects its unique history and position in American society. The traditional ambivalence of the U. S. public toward the department weakens its bargaining position in Congress and lends support to its detractors. The postwar chaos in the foreign affairs arena is mirrored in the current mosaic of organizational subunits and the tensions between them. The effects of the McCarthy siege and the massive influx of "Wristonees" are still evident and closely tied to the problem of hierarchy. The long-standing separation between the department and the Foreign Service underlies and reinforces the present-day cleavages between "substance" and "administration" and between regional and functional bureaus. These divisions have acquired a meaning of their own and serve as powerful obstacles to organizational change. With a combination of low prestige and high power, the O area has stood as a particular anomaly on the organizational scene. Into this setting came the changes of 1965.

# Part II  Bureaucratic Growth and Regeneration

# 3 • Bureaucratic Regeneration: The O Area Reforms

The fastest way to uncover the political structure and dynamics of an organization is to change it. Viewed in the short run, the 1965 reforms in the State Department showed that hierarchy and rules can be reduced without a loss in operating efficiency, and that many managers reared in the traditional "layered" system can respond positively and even creatively to increased autonomy. But a decade later, the most impressive features of this reorganization are its fragility and impermanence. One after another the changes introduced by Crockett were either sabotaged by his subordinates, qualified by his superiors, or dismantled by his successors. This story, which is classic in the annals of the executive bureaucracy, points up the omnipresent and multifaceted pressures for hierarchy and rules in that system. A careful examination of these reforms provides insight not only into the organizational politics of the State Department, but also into the general dynamics of bureaucracy in the U. S. federal system.

## The Changes

In July 1965 Deputy Under Secretary Crockett called a meeting of some 450 managers and employees of the O area to announce a major reorganization. Although rumors of the reforms had been circulating for some weeks, the nature and scope of the changes caught even the most reorganized veterans off guard. A year later there followed a second set of changes designed to remedy the more egregious flaws and extend the more successful features of the first.

### Stage I: 1965

The reforms in the first stage were threefold: the reduction of hierarchical layering through "Management by Programs"; increased autonomy of decision-making through "Management by Objectives"; and the decentralization of certain key functions from *O* to the regional and functional bureaus. The first two were given the summary title "Management by Objectives and Programs," with the unfortunate acronym *MOP*.[1]

The most dramatic and controversial feature of Management by Programs was the elimination of up to six levels of supervision between the deputy under secretary and the operating manager. The ax was applied to 125 positions ranging from middle-level to top management. Among the slots eliminated were the offices of the Assistant Secretary and the Deputy Assistant Secretary for Administration—the two positions immediately below Crockett. Using the former Employment Unit as an example, Figure 2 shows the drastic effects of the reorganization on the structure of *O*. In June 1965, six levels of hierarchy stood between the deputy under secretary and the director of the Employment Program; afterward, at least in theory, the manager reported directly to Crockett. In all, twenty-seven operating units were removed in this fashion from the traditional hierarchy and were placed under Management by Programs. The remaining units in *O*—still the majority—retained their former designations as offices, divisions, and branches, as well as basically the same internal structure of authority. The main effect of the reorganization was above them, with an abbreviation of the lines of reporting from the office directors to Crockett.

The second step, Management by Objectives, provided the newly designated program managers with greater autonomy in operating their units. The plan was simple enough: each program manager was to specify the objectives, target dates, and resources needed for his unit. He or she would then discuss these points with the deputy under secretary until an agreement was reached. The resulting program statement became an operating charter for the following year, and a yardstick for measuring progress. Thereafter the manager was to

---

[1] Crockett's staff quickly began to speak of programs being "Mopped" and of the general process of "Mopping." The terminology was soon picked up by the targets of the action, with predictable effects.

Figure 2. The Employment Unit in *O* before and after the 1965 reorganization

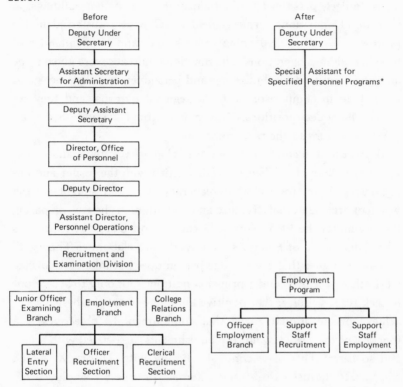

*Provides coordination

SOURCE: Adapted from *A Management Program for the Department of State,* Office of the Deputy Under Secretary for Administration, U.S. Department of State, 1966.

carry out the day-to-day operations of the program with a minimum of supervision. Subsequent events showed that the theory of Management by Objectives was more clear than the practice. Some managers were able to draft their charter and move ahead unsupervised, but others tripped on remnants of the old hierarchy.

The third component of the reforms was a large-scale decentralization of responsibilities to the regional and functional bureaus. In essence, Crockett tried to extend the notion of decentralization to the relations between *O* and the bureaus. The goal was to reduce clearances by moving responsibility to the real point of action. As a result, the regional bureaus were given new functions in three vital areas: budget, personnel, and administration of foreign buildings. A total of 113 positions formerly held by O were transferred in the process, with about 100 going to personnel and the remainder to foreign buildings operations. The functional bureaus were given some additional authority in budgeting and personnel, but their net gains were slight in comparison with the regional bureaus, and they received *no* added positions. This point strongly conditioned their overall reactions to the reorganization.

Motivating and complementing these changes was the management philosophy known as Theory Y. Dissatisfied with the torpor and unresponsiveness of the classic bureaucracy, Crockett sought a fresh vision of organizational structure and operation. As he was preparing the ground for the 1965 reforms, he came across Douglas McGregor's *The Human Side of Enterprise*, the work that elaborates Theory Y. McGregor argues that the average person does not inherently dislike work; that he learns, under proper conditions, not only to accept but to seek responsibility; that punitive authority is not the best way to achieve organizational goals; that commitment to objectives is a function of the rewards, not the punishments, associated with a job, and so forth. This view contrasts sharply with Theory X, which emphasizes the need for strong external controls on employee behavior. In Crockett's view the State Department had suffered too long under Theory X management and was now ripe for evangelization by Theory Y. While the latter was adopted as the official philosophy in the 1965 changes, it was not clear how, when, and where it was to be applied. Certainly it was not invoked in the process of introducing change, which one manager dubbed "Theory Y by Theory X methods."

## Stage II: 1966

In July 1966 three further changes were introduced to extend as well as to correct the reorganization. The greatest problem that emerged in the first year was coordination. The price of managerial autonomy and a reduction in hierarchy was fragmentation of functions and confusion of responsibilities. Also, by this time Secretary Dean Rusk and

Under Secretary George Ball were becoming increasingly skeptical of the new structure of O. To deal with the internal problems of coordination as well as with the concerns of his superiors, Crockett announced the establishment of an Executive Group for the O area. This will be discussed shortly. Second, the organizational principles of Management by Objectives and Programs (MOP) were applied to other existing units in O. For example, the section of the Office of Personnel dealing with Foreign Service Officers was divided into three semiautonomous programs: the Junior Officer Program, the Mid-career Program, and the Senior Officer Program. Third, several new programs were added to O, mostly in the management planning field. These added a further note of controversy by their association with the "whiz kid" management techniques developed in the Defense Department. The older bureaucrats had little difficulty understanding decentralization and autonomy, but found Substantive Information Systems and International Systems Research puzzling, if not somewhat frightening.

## The Limits of Change

Crockett had also hoped to extend MOP to some of the larger and more traditional sectors of O, particularly the Bureau of Security and Consular Affairs (SCA). Established at the peak of the McCarthy hearings, SCA was originally charged with handling both security and consular activities (passports and visas, for example). In 1962, the Office of Security was removed from its jurisdiction and given independent status with O. By 1965, the bureau consisted of an administrator with his staff and three operating units: the Passport Office, the Visa Office, and the Office of Special Consular Services. The director of one of these offices offered this comment on the origins and functions of SCA:

The establishment of the bureau was strictly a political gimmick in 1952 because of the security situation in the Department of State. It became a dumping ground for consular activities, and at one time all the personnel activities were dumped here. Then they took personnel out and put in the Foreign Service Inspection Corps, the refugee program, and then munitions control . . . we finally got rid of munitions control. Then we took Inspection out and then threw in the evacuation service and then took it out.

The administrator of SCA in 1965 was Abba Schwartz, a Kennedy appointee often identified as the leading liberal in the State Department. Crockett's original plan was to abolish the Office of the Administrator and to make the three subunits autonomous programs. In a memorandum to the White House dated July 2, 1965 he wrote: "I still consider the abolishment of the Office of the Administrator the appropriate course. It would eliminate a needless organizational super-structure, thereby saving several positions and some funds, and also permitting us to have a more efficient and streamlined operation." But the history of the department and of the SCA made it inevitable that considerations other than administrative efficiency would arise. Crockett's plan was immediately interpreted by congressional and other liberals as a conservative coup to oust Abba Schwartz. The issue drew coverage in the national press and stirred debate in Congress. Before the reorganization could be put into effect, Schwartz resigned. This development added fuel to the controversy, and exposed Crockett and his reorganization to attack. The lines of the ensuing debate are captured in a column from *Newsweek* (March 21, 1966, p. 27):

Last week Abba Schwartz felt forced to resign from State, Democratic liberals were up in arms, and President Johnson's left flank was under sharp attack.

On the face of it, Schwartz's resignation was brought about as a result of some administrative streamlining to improve the efficiency of the State Department's operations—the "layering" that Secretary Dean Rusk himself has often complained of. In this case, however, Washington liberals were quick to interpret the elimination of Schwartz's bureau as aimed primarily at Schwartz himself—and some promptly read into the incident a deep-dyed plot to frighten State back into the unbending anti-Communist passport policies of the McCarthy era.

Schwartz himself saw the "streamlining" as a thinly veiled plot by his enemies in State and Congress to remove him.

Crockett's story, set forth in a 1971 interview, was somewhat different:

[42]

It's pretty difficult in reality to reorganize a person with strong Congressional support (such as Abba had in some quarters) out of his job. The job had to be vacant. Once it was vacant, the President could reorganize the function and I could then have installed the MOP program as we did in other parts of the O area. These moves had been carefully discussed with the Office of the President and with the appropriate committees on the Hill. There was no real opposition in any quarter to our plan. The fact of the matter is that Abba was to have been taken care of in another important job, but actually resigned in a fit of pique before we had fully worked out the details of his new position. But his resignation was a great windfall for us, for it opened the door to the reorganization plan . . .

But due to the "Hill Furor" about Abba's departure (basically liberal, vocal and not very potent) we decided to hold up the plan until the air cleared.

Though the delay was intended to be temporary, it proved to be permanent.

### Initial Acceptance

The key to the success of the reorganization lay in its acceptance by two sets of actors: the program managers in O who were given semiautonomous status, and the clients of O in the regional and functional bureaus. At first sight the 1965 reforms might appear as organizational ambrosia to both groups. Managers were freed from the shackles of hierarchy, communication channels were opened, responsibility was shifted to the major points of action, and Theory Y had arrived. Yet many of the beneficiaries were wary, and some were visibly perturbed. Why?

The introduction of change in a federal agency is complicated by its sheer frequency. The life of the Washington bureaucrat is punctuated by a perpetual reshuffling of positions above, below, and around him. Each morning thousands of federal employees scan the Washington *Post* to see if their positions, their units, or even the entire agency will be abolished. Political appointees come and go. Though his or her term may be short, each new director tries to assert control over an agency by changing it. The new broom sweeps clean for a few months, but soon takes on the contours of the agency. Another follows who repeats the process. Consequently the word "reorganization" often connotes a personally inspired, impetuous, dubious, and probably ephemeral reform program that is best disregarded.

Despite the democratic reformist aspirations of the 1965 reorganization, its formulation and implementation followed the classic model of change from the top. The restructuring was hastily designed by Crockett and a few advisers, with no participation by those affected. Rumors circulated and fears mounted. After nearly being postponed because of disagreements between Crockett and Richard Barrett, his principal adviser on management planning, the program was announced in a large meeting and implemented by edict.

Not surprisingly, many of the liberated managers were baffled by the changes; a few were quite shaken. A budget officer commented: "The reasons for the reorganization were never really understood. It was almost designed to be under the table." Another program manager added: "I admire Crockett for the boldness of his views, but not enough thought went into this reorganization. It was brainstormed by people not close enough to see some of the problems." For those accustomed to the comforts of hierarchy, this unsought emancipation left feelings of nakedness and exposure. As one informant put it:

The initial stage of MOP posed severe human relations problems. The process of jumping six echelons down in the hierarchy and saying to a manager, "You come and talk to Crockett," and expect that manager to be levelling regarding his resources, objectives, etc., posed a severe threat to such individuals, particularly with the security of the old superstructure ripped out.

But most managers adapted to the new structure within a few months, and some of the initial holdouts even came to relish their mandatory freedom.

Resentment over a lack of participation was even stronger in the bureaus. Comments along the following lines were typical:

One of the big problems is that someone sits down, makes out a plan which looks good on paper, but isn't checked out with the operators. It's laid on—we're told, "You do it," but the bugs could have been worked out beforehand. There's no channel of appeal, either.

The reorganization was the poorest personnel fracture I've seen in 25 years. Rumors, rumors, and bang! A handful of people thought it up without consulting the people involved.

Another critical barrier to acceptance in the bureaus was their long-standing suspicion of *any* effort by O to change them or the Foreign Service. This reaction arose in part from the feeling that O was populated with civil service personnel who knew little and cared less about the "real" problems of foreign affairs. Many in the bureaus also felt that O had concocted so many reorganizations that the rest of the department no longer had any peace. One official complained:

O has changed so often that it is difficult to keep in reach of particular programs. It has made it more confusing because you get used to certain initials, certain channels. It has happened three times in four years. One routine is easier. All this management stuff doesn't fit the Foreign Service. The top changes, but we have stayed the same.

Finally, the image of the reorganization in the bureaus was badly tarnished by its association with a host of managerial experiments launched more or less simultaneously in O. MOP and decentralization were tarred with the same brush as sensitivity training, "computerized personnel systems," and the Planning-Programming-Budgeting System (PPBS). Two managers commented:

One thing I'm really a nut on. All these programs under Barrett, such as PPBS—why don't they concentrate on one program and complete it? I think we're spinning our wheels on a lot of this.

I'd also like to remark on the inadequate flow of information on the specialized elements of O. I'm thinking of ACORD [Action for Organizational Development] and the other more esoteric parts in management review and analysis. There's a lot going on there, and a lack of communication between those offices and bureaus who will eventually be the beneficiaries or victims.

The change program was thus part of a larger reform package whose contents were regarded with suspicion in the bureaus.

It is evident that the 1965 reforms had an inauspicious beginning. Both the program managers and the bureau clients resented changes made without prior consultation or participation. Some managers were initially frightened by the precipitous removal of the protective hierarchy and their consequent exposure to the top. And the effort was not helped by the resistance of the bureaus to any changes by *O*, and by the identification of Management by Objectives and Programs with sensitivity training and other "esoteric" management techniques.

The remainder of the chapter follows the 1965 reorganization over an eight-year period that included Crockett and two successors. The story suggests that the roots of hierarchy in a federal agency are strong and deep.

### The First Two Years: The Reforms under Crockett

Within the first two years a sharp distinction must be drawn between the first stage of the program, beginning in July 1965, and the second stage occurring a year later. The most striking positive effects in the first period were in the area of managerial autonomy. An intensive survey of program managers revealed a marked reduction in the number of clearances required for action, as well as in the amount of direction received from superiors. The same data showed a slight to moderate improvement in the efficiency of communication (especially upward), job motivation, and, at least in the eyes of the managers, actual performance. The following comments convey the flavor of these findings:

The big advantage is the abolition of layering. Personnel, when I arrived, was a quagmire. There were miles of people between me and Crockett. At first it was a naked but satisfying feeling.

The biggest advantage is that it tries to give each of us as much autonomy as possible, to work out our own program, give us our own facility to implement, so objectives are more easily realized.

It has cut down on a helluva lot of clearances and red tape.

Measured against its own goals, with the exceptions to be noted, the reorganization scores rather well in the areas of managerial autonomy and decision-making. Several layers of bureaucracy were removed, communications within *O* were improved, the managers seemed somewhat happier with the new system than the old, and the work of the organization progressed at least as well as before.

The impact of the changes on the clients of *O* was more mixed but, on balance, positive. The most important clients, the regional bureaus, reported greater speed and flexibility in their work as a result of the decentralization of functions. They also noted slight improvements in the quality and speed of services obtained from the restructured O units. The internal clients of O, those programs and divisions dependent on other O units for services, were even more enthusiastic in their ratings of the quality and promptness of services. The functional bureaus, as we shall see, were considerably less happy with the changes than the other clients.

A final positive effect was a spirit of experimentation that went beyond the original sites of change. "I gained personally from being part of the experiment," one supporter commented. "I borrowed some of this to apply to [UNREORGANIZED UNIT], but structured it in a different way." A division chief observed: "The last five years have been a period of great turmoil in the philosophy, organizational structure, and attitudes of O. This has been good, for there has been progress in the turmoil—a modernization." Others added that even though Crockett went too far too fast, he was to be commended for launching a frontal attack on the inveterate problems of layering and clearances.

Still, the first year was far from organizational bliss. The reforms were hobbled from the outset by the initial suspicion and resistance of those most intimately involved. The hastiness of the changes, the narrow base of participation, and poor communication about its scope and intent also generated concern and resentment in other parts of the Department. The acceptance of MOP was further stymied by the long history of reorganizations in the department, leading to the feeling that "we've seen it all before"; by its glaring departures from managerial orthodoxy; by a string of other reforms undertaken at about the same time; and by perennial bad blood between O and the bureaus, between "substance" and "administration." Some of these difficulties were surmounted during the first year; others persisted.

The most troublesome side effect of the reorganization was a drastic decline in coordination. Both managers and clients reported an excessive fragmentation of programs and functions, particularly in personnel; difficulties in finding the "right man" to answer a question; a failure to relate program objectives to the realities of scarce resources; and frequent absences by Crockett, the linking pin of the decentralized system. Even the program managers—the prime beneficiaries of autonomy—complained that O had been splintered and that "responsibilities are spread all over." Others felt that the reorganization had created an excessive span of control at the top, with forty-five independent programs reporting directly to Crockett. This feeling was reinforced by Crockett's frequent absences, usually the result of official trips outside the country. By July 1966, it was increasingly apparent that, while MOP might have been suitable for another organization, it did not fit the circumstances of the State Department. Even Secretary Rusk and Under Secretary Ball, who had originally backed the reorganization, were becoming concerned at the rampant decentralization in O.

Not far behind on the list of problems was the disruption of an already lopsided power relationship between the regional and the functional bureaus. Whether measured by prestige in the department, bidding power on assignments, or claims on budgetary resources, the regional bureaus had long held the edge. The reorganization further strengthened their hand by giving them 113 new positions as well as major responsibilities for personnel, budget, and foreign buildings decisions. The worst blow for the functional bureaus was in personnel assignments. One senior official said: "Decentralization of the personnel function has put [BUREAU NAME] at a disadvantage since they are given less consideration now than the regional bureaus. The latter know who the good people are, and these people never come up for grabs." Respondents in the regional bureaus agreed with this assessment. Thus it is not surprising that the overall reactions to the reorganization by functional bureau managers were considerably more negative than in the regional bureaus.

## Stage II

By July 1966 pressures from several sources gave rise to a second set of reforms. As noted earlier, there were essentially two changes: the spread of Management by Objectives and Programs to new areas; and the addition of an Executive Group. While the first had the advantage of extending the benefits of the reorganization to a larger group of managers, it aggravated the already serious problems of communication and coordination. Soon there were more complaints about the fragmentation and splintering of O.

The Executive Group muddied the waters even more. The core members of this body were Crockett and the five "cone coordinators" who stood between him and the operating programs. In the original conception of MOP the cone coordinator was not to be a line supervisor, but rather a kind of helper and integrator who would tie together the work of the independent programs. The ambiguity that surrounded this position was compounded when the coordinators together became the Executive Group.

The origins of the Executive Group epitomize the politics of organizational change in a federal agency. By all accounts the single most important source of pressure was the concern of Rusk and Ball with Crockett's span of control. Crockett, in a 1966 interview, was quite candid on this point:

The Executive Group was introduced to establish the window dressing for the span of control problem, because this is a persistent problem on the part of my bosses. You draw a chart with 35 to 40 boxes reporting to me, and when I talk to people about making more programs, releasing more, and when I talk to Ball and the Secretary and they say, "Let's see the organization chart"—why, they get frightened, they get concerned. The Executive Group was intended as an elongation of me so that all of the boxes don't go into Crockett . . . This is part of the pressure on people, the pressure on me, the pressure on the organization that this kind of thing brings about. Frankly, there was concern above me because there was often a question of "how can you supervise this many people."

Rusk and Ball were clearly nervous about Crockett's flagrant departures from traditional management practices. But another factor was also at work: congressional opposition to the Vietnam War. Any agency has only a limited amount of political capital available for controversy. By 1966 Secretary Rusk was forced to husband State's resources for his continuing battles with Senator Fulbright and other opponents of the Vietnam War. The department could scarcely afford new static from internal changes. Thus Crockett was free to experiment only as long as his efforts did not stir opposition or concern in the Congress and the White House. When some of his reforms, such as

Management by Programs, set off external reverberations, a red light appeared on the top floor.

By 1966 there were also urgent demands in other parts of the department for improved coordination. In O itself the most critical problem was the poor fit between program objectives and available funds. An assistant commented that Crockett "found himself having to settle disputes, budget hassles. He was caught between the program manager and the budget director, refereeing fights. This disturbed the hell out of him." It also became evident that he had seriously underestimated the external demands on his time. The work of the deputy under secretary involves frequent contacts outside the department, especially with the House appropriations subcommittee and other parts of Congress. In 1966 these normal absences were multiplied by Crockett's work as principal coordinator for President Johnson's overseas trips. The Executive Group was introduced in part to take up the slack caused by his absences.

It was never clear if this was to be a genuine decision-making body or a glorified staff meeting cosmetically improved to allay the anxieties of Rusk and Ball. Vagueness of definition and purpose carried over to its deliberations. Members complained that the group wasted an enormous amount of time and had no sense of direction, particularly when Crockett was absent. Still, some cone coordinators saw advantages, mostly for information-sharing and coordination. The main accomplishment, one observed, is "an enlarged area where policy decisions are made . . . There is a wider hearing of every policy decision by the group. They bring knowledge, experience, background."

The program managers, on the other hand, were almost uniformly negative. Though a few saw advantages for coordination, the typical reaction was the following:

According to Crockett, the reasons he gave struck me as ludicrous, a gimmick, a trick, to counter the criticism of having too wide a span of supervision. It was set up as an extension of Crockett. But the Executive Group is nothing more than a huge bottleneck of unrelated tasks. I don't think they can function. This is government by committee in the worst way. They have no common aims.

For most managers the Executive Group was the old hierarchy masquerading as Theory Y. By December 1966 even Crockett conceded in an interview that it had brought few benefits.

Well, it has problems . . . and [they] are probably the problems of the overlay from the past in each individual. The problem of relinquishing directive authority over subordinates—this is part of the problem. How and when and what to bring up to the Executive Group is a problem. My concept was that almost anything that came to this desk was something that the Executive Group might take on . . . I was willing and am willing to play the game absolutely open with the Executive Group. You give up all your downward responsibilities, and for this you take on some upward responsibilities. You take on the problems that come to this desk, because if you don't there's a double layering. Now the question is whether they believe this totality, whether they as individuals are willing to play selfless parts in this. This has to be learned, I think.

The cone coordinators obviously were unwilling to divest themselves of their line responsibilities. Was it reasonable to expect such change without further evidence that the new system would stick? The general feeling of organizational impermanence in State was heightened by persistent rumors that Crockett planned to resign in 1966 or 1967. Under these conditions it was perhaps not only an emotional attachment to the past that prevented full implementation of MOP, but a rational reluctance to embrace what could be a managerial will-o'-the-wisp. As it turned out, only seven months after the Executive Group was introduced, Crockett did leave and was succeeded by a man who saw no value whatever in the concept.

In sum, the 1965 reorganization touched off a complex series of reverberations within the O area and elsewhere in the department. Apparent benefits in one area created dislocations in others which, in turn, precipitated demands for retrenchment. This chain of effects is summarized in Figure 3.

Taken on their own terms, did the reforms succeed or fail in their first two years? It is fair to make four summary observations in this regard.

First, on the basis of reports from program managers, the bureaus, and other internal clients, the O area was at least as productive in 1967

Figure 3. Effects of the 1965 reorganization: the first two years

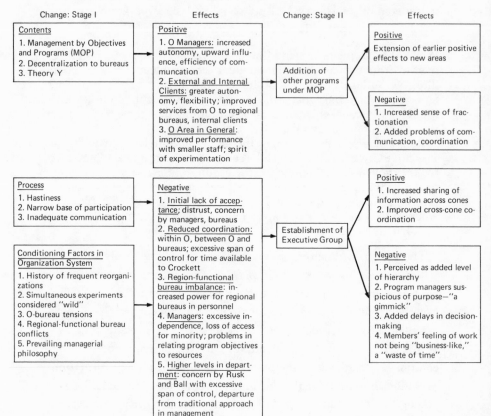

| Change: Stage I | Effects | Change: Stage II | Effects |
|---|---|---|---|
| **Contents**<br>1. Management by Objectives and Programs (MOP)<br>2. Decentralization to bureaus<br>3. Theory Y | **Positive**<br>1. O Managers: increased autonomy, upward influence, efficiency of communcation<br>2. External and Internal Clients: greater autonomy, flexibility; improved services from O to regional bureaus, internal clients<br>3. O Area in General: improved performance with smaller staff; spirit of experimentation | Addition of other programs under MOP | **Positive**<br>Extension of earlier positive effects to new areas<br><br>**Negative**<br>1. Increased sense of fractionation<br>2. Added problems of communication, coordination |
| **Process**<br>1. Hastiness<br>2. Narrow base of participation<br>3. Inadequate communication<br><br>**Conditioning Factors in Organization System**<br>1. History of frequent reorganizations<br>2. Simultaneous experiments considered "wild"<br>3. O-bureau tensions<br>4. Regional-functional bureau conflicts<br>5. Prevailing managerial philosophy | **Negative**<br>1. Initial lack of acceptance; distrust, concern by managers, bureaus<br>2. Reduced coordination: within O, between O and bureaus; excessive span of control for time available to Crockett<br>3. Region-functional bureau imbalance: increased power for regional bureaus in personnel<br>4. Managers: excessive independence, loss of access for minority; problems in relating program objectives to resources<br>5. Higher levels in department: concern by Rusk and Ball with excessive span of control, departure from traditional approach in management | Establishment of Executive Group | **Positive**<br>1. Increased sharing of information across cones<br>2. Improved cross-cone coordination<br><br>**Negative**<br>1. Perceived as added level of hierarchy<br>2. Program managers suspicious of purpose—"a gimmick"<br>3. Added delays in decision-making<br>4. Members' feeling of work not being "business-like," a "waste of time" |

as in 1965, and perhaps a bit more so. Since its work was being done with a smaller staff, per capita output seems to have increased. In this sense, Crockett's major hopes had been at least partially realized. *O* did its usual work with less hierarchy, fewer paperwork clearances, and slightly greater managerial satisfaction.

Second, the changes facilitated Crockett's own work as deputy under secretary. Because his communication with program managers was no longer filtered through a multilayered hierarchy, he found himself better informed about *O* operations and problems. Crockett also cited instances in which the added autonomy for program managers stimulated innovation and other tangible accomplishments.

Third, the reorganization created its own set of problems, particularly fractionation and a loss of coordination. These difficulties were never resolved.

Finally, the greatest drawback of all was that the changes did not take root in the department—they were never institutionalized. Neither the managers nor the bureaus nor the senior administration ever regarded the restructured system as a permanent part of the department's organizational legacy. When the bureaucratic winds shifted, most of the reforms were swept away.

## Leadership Change (1967 to 1969)

In January 1967 Crockett announced his resignation for personal and financial reasons. His successor was Idar Rimestad, a department veteran regarded as a tough old-line administrator. Rimestad made no secret of his distaste for the Crockett legacy. During an interview in October 1967, he labeled the reorganization a total failure in the personnel area. His main complaint was that there was no one to whom he could turn for a decision; responsibility was lost in a sea of minuscule programs. He also argued that he did not have the luxury of telling the Secretary of State that a given action was the responsibility of an independent program manager; he had to take responsibility himself. Complaints from managers in O and the bureaus, pressures from above and outside, and his own managerial style quickly led to retrenchment.

An added push came during the annual appropriations hearings in the spring of 1967. At issue was a report by Chris Argyris on *Some Causes of Organizational Ineffectiveness within the Department of State*. Published by the department itself shortly before Crockett's departure, the Argyris Report was presumably an objective, social scientific analysis of the Foreign Service "culture." Among the cultural norms described were minimal openness and trust; withdrawal from interpersonal difficulties and conflict; dependence upon the superior; and minimal risk-taking and acceptance of responsibility. The study became an instant issue in the State Department, and drew wide commentary in the U. S. press. It also caught the attention of Congressman John Rooney, chairman of the House appropriations subcommittee that was handling State's budget. With his usual eye for the unusual, Rooney scored the department for spending $3,000 on the research and another $1,500 for the printing. At one point he commented:

This seems to be very comprehensive. For instance, there is this passage where Foreign Service personnel were asked how they would deal with a briefing officer who goes into irrelevancies, and the majority responded, variously, "I would carefully stop him" or "I would diplomatically change the subject." Is there any way we could get that $3,000 back?

By all accounts this experience reinforced Rimestad's determination to move O back to a more traditional and accountable structure.

In May 1967 he ordered three major changes in the structure of O. The first was the restoration of line supervisors to the former cones. The concept of cone coordinator was abolished, and supervisors were given direct responsibility for the programs assigned to them. With a bow to MOP, Rimestad added: "It is definitely not my intention to increase the layering of the O area or to reduce the flexibility of the present type of organization." Second, the order abolished three of the semiautonomous programs. One of these was the Center for International Systems Research, the unit which published the Argyris Report. Another was the Foreign Affairs Program System Development. Its mission was to explore the applicability of the Planning-Programming-Budgeting System (PPBS) to foreign affairs—hardly a topic to warm the heart of the FSO. The third change involved the merger and transfer of seven other programs. The direction was unmistakable: the line of command in O was to be sharpened and its structure consolidated.

The next wave of change came in November 1967. The target in this case was the personnel system, the prime locus of discontent. Rimestad attempted to consolidate and coordinate the various personnel programs by returning them to a single Office of Personnel. The director was called the Deputy Assistant Secretary for Personnel, and he reported to the Director General of the Foreign Service. Thus came a second level of hierarchy for the personnel programs. For example, where the Employment Program previously had reported to Crockett through the director general, it would now report to the deputy assistant secretary who would report to the director general.

The new director of personnel was expected not only to provide a central point of authority, but to deal with the imbalance between the regional and functional bureaus. During an interview in 1968 he commented:

The decentralization of functions definitely strengthened the regional bureaus and weakened the functional bureaus. We had to give the Economic Bureau priority of assignment in getting economic officers. This was because of the decentralization of assignment functions. We had trouble because some of the best people were assigned before the functional bureaus knew about it.

The other changes during Rimestad's tenure were less dramatic. One worth noting is the gradual dismemberment and finally abolition of the Action for Organization Development program (ACORD). This had been the home of MOP, sensitivity training, and various other disputed innovations. One of Rimestad's associates summarized the prevailing views of ACORD:

It was a shotgun affair. There was some benefit in the African Bureau because [ASSISTANT SECRETARY] was behind it. It wasn't helped by the adverse publicity from the Argyris Report. There was a lot of criticism of the off-campus sessions of the T-groups, and the money—the trainers got $400 per day, with 30 percent overhead . . .This is the sort of experiment we can't afford . . . Barrett *et al.* wouldn't take advice, listen. They did a lot of damage, especially in the last years of the [Crockett] administration.

Hence within nine months of Crockett's departure every experimental program in the former Office of Management Planning had been eliminated, eviscerated, or totally redirected. MOP had been mopped.

### The Macomber Period (1969 to 1973)

The position of Deputy Under Secretary for Administration passed to William J. Macomber in October 1969. Shortly after taking office, Macomber restored another of the pre-1965 levels of hierarchy: the office of the Assistant Secretary for Administration. Crockett had abolished this position on the grounds that it was a needless block to communication with operating managers. Macomber, however, found the combination of internal supervision and external relations too great for one man. He restored the Assistant Secretary to handle the bulk of internal administration.

When I became Deputy Under-Secretary for Administration . . . I found that seventeen offices, employing approximately 2,700 people, reported directly to me. I thought that Bill Crockett was on the right track in trying to reduce layering. However, I found that given the fact that my job was so "outward oriented," in the sense that a great deal of time is taken up in dealing with the Secretary, the Congress, the Office of Management and Budget, other agencies and with many special problems of the Assistant Secretaries, it was necessary to have an overall deputy at the Assistant Secretary level. The latter would be more "inward oriented" . . . In addition, as you know, the job of dealing with the Appropriations committee of Congress is of critical importance. It is also very time-consuming. While the Deputy Under-Secretary must retain ultimate responsibility for this function, I felt it extremely important to have a senior deputy who had the confidence of the appropriations sub-committee with whom I could share this work—thus freeing me for other matters to a degree not otherwise possible (Personal communication, September 1970).

This was the only change since 1969 bearing directly on the 1965 re-organization. Most of the others involved either the addition of new programs or the realignment of existing units. The decline and growth of hierarchy from 1965 to 1970 is summarized in Figure 4.

### The Elements That Survived

Did anything remain of the reorganization? As Figure 4 suggests, the survival ratio was not great, but several elements weathered two changes at the top of O. First, there was still less hierarchy in 1973 than in 1965. The position of Assistant Secretary was revived and the cone coordinators again became line supervisors. However, the position of Deputy Assistant Secretary for Administration was not reestablished, and the direct line responsibilities of the present assistant secretary are more narrow than previously. Several offices that once reported through the assistant and deputy assistant secretary now have direct access to the deputy under secretary. Second, the amount of layering in the Office of Personnel is less than before. The various deputies had not been replaced as of 1973, and the entire personnel operation showed considerable streamlining. Other parts of

Figure 4. The decline and growth of hierarchy in the *O* area: the Employment Division from 1965 to 1970

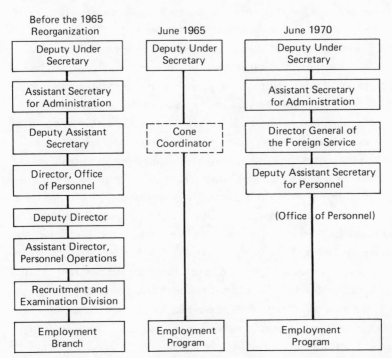

*O* also learned to live without deputy division chiefs. Finally, an important residue of Crockett's experimentation was his example to others—both good and bad. On the negative side, the reorganization showed once again that major organizational change cannot be accomplished by edict, especially if it is to last. Positively, the State Department, the Agency for International Development, and perhaps other agencies profited from Crockett's mishaps in their subsequent efforts at reform. Deputy Under Secretary Macomber, for example, made extensive use of internal task forces in attempting to implement the reform program set forth in *Diplomacy for the 70's* (U. S. Department of State, 1970). Such employee participation seemed to overcome some of the problems of internal legitimacy touched off by the 1965 changes (Bacchus, 1974a; Marrow, 1974), although it is questionable whether the reforms themselves were any more successful than their predecessors.

## Looking Ahead

This study of the MOP reorganization raises two fundamental questions about governmental bureaucracy. First, what are the origins of the tall hierarchy and the proliferating rules in the State Department (the problems attacked by MOP)? The longitudinal research suggests that these bureaucratic accretions are traceable to numerous sources, including realistic work pressures in a complex environment as well as personality factors in the bureaucrat. Second, why does bureaucracy grow back after it has been pruned? What are the sources of organizational regeneration? The next four chapters will address both of these questions, attempting to sort out the system-wide as well as agency-specific sources of bureaucratic growth and regeneration.

A third question, really inseparable from the two mentioned, concerns bureaucratic persistence. What are the forces that support and maintain hierarchy and rules once they take root in the federal system? With another case study of reform in foreign affairs agencies as its departure point, Part III will explore the hypothesis that, beyond a certain threshold of institutionalization, bureaucracy acquires a kind of functional autonomy. The sheer fact that a structure, such as a personnel system or a set of rules, has been in place "for a long time" becomes a sufficient reason to fight to preserve it. Beyond elementary organizational inertia, such forces as interest group pressures, congressional styles, and leadership rotation in the federal system join forces to strengthen bureaucratic persistence.

# 4 • The External Environment

Some of the strongest pressures for the growth and maintenance of public bureaucracy lie in the external environment of the federal agency. The reasons can be traced to the agency's very origins. Unlike the private firm, which is typically established by a single entrepreneur or a small group of business associates, the governmental organization is always created by some higher controlling body. The dependency begun at birth continues throughout the life of the agency. It must normally seek the approval of external overseers for operating authority, appropriations, or major changes in structure and emphasis. At times these higher authorities, such as congressional committees, may intervene directly to change organizational structures and operating procedures. The federal executive system, moreover, is marked by a fractionation of political power and a multitude of checks and balances, even within the same branch of government. In this milieu survival and effectiveness depend on clearances, collaboration, and alliances involving individuals and organizations within the executive and legislative branches.

## An Approach to Organizations

In considering the role of the external environment in bureaucratization, it will be helpful to draw on a fairly simple conceptual framework of the public organization. Without some basic organizing concepts this study will remain, like so much of the writing on public organizations, descriptive and anecdotal. The following view of organizations, which places strong emphasis on the interactions between an agency and its environment, is designed to take account of the salient features of the State Department and the federal executive system more generally. It is summarized in Figure 5.

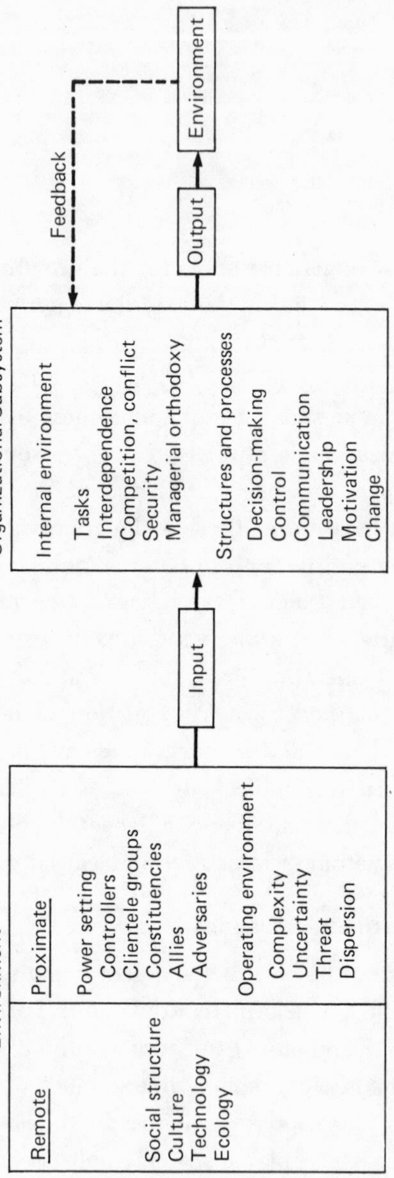

Figure 5. The organizational system of the federal executive agency

An organization can be defined as a set of explicitly coordinated and interdependent activities designed to achieve certain goals. Organizations are viewed as open systems in constant interaction with their environments, receiving inputs and feedback and affecting the environment with their outputs (Katz and Kahn, 1966). The core concepts in this scheme are the environment, inputs, organizational subsystem, and outputs.

## The Environment

An organization's environment has both remote and proximate elements. The remote environment consists of those sociocultural, ecological, and technological conditions with indirect effects on internal structures and processes. Among these are cultural norms, patterns of social stratification, and international monetary relations (all of which may become proximate elements for some organizations). Such factors are not of explicit concern here. The proximate environment has two interlocking subparts: the power setting and the operating environment.

The *power setting* (cf. Gross, 1964, vol. 1; and Downs, 1967) consists in those actors who exert or can exert an immediate influence on the organization. The following are the main actors in the case of the U. S. federal agency.

(1) Controllers: those who hold formal authority to regulate the resources or activities of an agency. There are two major subtypes:

(*a*) Higher authorities: those holding direct responsibility for one or more aspects of the organization's resources or activities. For most federal agencies the higher authorities are the White House, the relevant appropriations and legislative committees and subcommittees of Congress, and the Office of Management and the Budget, which is technically part of the White House.

(*b*) Monitors: controlling bodies whose authority is limited mainly to inspecting, auditing, evaluating, or reporting on an agency's performance and expenditures. The most powerful monitor in the U. S. government is the General Accounting Office (GAO), an arm of Congress.

(2) Clientele groups: those who receive or benefit from the goods or

services of an organization, including suppliers who stand to gain by furnishing raw materials and other resources.

(3) Constituencies: individuals or groups outside an organization with an interest in but no formal power over its activities. The most common variety is the interest group.

(4) Allies: individuals or organizations willing to support the agency in some specific debate, conflict, or campaign.

(5) Adversaries: individuals or groups impeding the organization's ability to pursue its goals, including rivals, opponents, or enemies.

The present chapter will deal with the power setting as a source of bureaucracy.

The *operating environment* is the set of conditions immediately impinging upon the organization's accomplishment of its day-to-day work.[1] Four such conditions, which will be examined in Chapter 7, are particularly significant for the federal agency: (1) complexity, or the number of elements comprising the work environment and the intricacy of their connections; (2) uncertainty, or the degree of unpredictability in the environment; (3) threat, or the extent to which the environment is a potential source of harms, losses, or other serious forms of deprivation; and (4) dispersion, the geographic scope of an organization's activities and structures.

*Inputs*

The most general input from the environment to the organization is information. Both the quantity of information entering the system and the form of its expression (for example, written vs oral) are critical to an understanding of bureaucratization. The theory developed in this and the following chapters emphasizes the role of a heavy message volume and centralization of message-handling in the development of hierarchy and rules.

---

[1] This concept bears some resemblance to the notion of "task environment" used by Dill (1958) and Thompson (1967). An important difference is that both those authors include within the task environment such actors as competitors and regulatory groups. Our concept refers primarily to impersonal *conditions,* such as complexity, rather than to individual or organizational *actors.*

## The Organizational Subsystem

The organizational subsystem is what is commonly referred to as an "organization" or "agency"—that is, the administrative body considered as separate from its environment. Within this subsystem the *internal environment* (see Chapter 5) includes the distinctive tasks, atmosphere, traditions, and options giving the organization its unique character. The more salient of these conditions for understanding bureaucracy are the clarity or ambiguity of goals and tasks, the degree of internal specialization and interdependence as well as competition and conflict, and the emphasis placed on internal security. *Organizational structures and processes* are the patterned means by which inputs are converted into outputs. These include decision-making, control and coordination, communication, leadership, motivation, and change.

## Outputs

Organizational outputs fall roughly into two classes: goods and services. Goods are commodities or items subject to fairly precise quantitative measurement, such as automobiles or bushels of wheat. Services are activities satisfying the needs, requests, or expectations of the organization's clients. A major problem for many public agencies dealing with services is that their outputs are elusive, difficult to measure, and open to evaluation by widely differing criteria. We argue later that this condition is indirectly related to the growth of hierarchy and rules.

## The Power Setting

The power setting of the federal agency is highly complex, involving actors from the executive and legislative branches as well as clientele groups, constituencies, and vocal members of the public at large. The most significant actors in the political environment of the State Department are the other executive agencies involved in foreign affairs, the Congress, the White House, and various negative constituencies.

## The Executive Branch

Every federal agency is part of a larger organizational system within the executive branch itself. For some purposes the State Department can be treated as a single organization, but it is also part of the intricate bureaucratic maze forming the federal executive system. A striking characteristic of this system is the plethora of interdependencies involved. Executives moving from private business to public agencies have been astounded at the elaborate network of clearances in Washington (cf. Bernstein, 1958). Men accustomed to giving an order and having it executed find themselves waiting days, weeks, or months for interagency concurrences on seemingly routine matters. Sometimes this is a paperwork operation—circulating memoranda for information, clearance, and/or approval. But often it means protracted face-to-face negotiations among individual representatives of the agencies involved, or even the establishment of interagency committees to meet on a regular basis.

Why is there such fractionation of power in the executive system? One reason is the piecemeal growth of governmental activities in recent decades. A rapidly changing world environment coupled with accelerated technological development spurred dozens of new demands for public services. Many were so complex that they could not be made the exclusive concern of a single bureau. Responsibility was parcelled out to many agencies, with the actions of one having important ramifications for those of another. The most obvious example is the case of foreign affairs in the postwar period (see Chapter 2). Because of new demands that could not be met by any single agency, almost every major executive unit entered the foreign affairs arena to claim a piece of the action.

Today about a third of the departments, agencies, and other units of the executive branch are deeply involved in foreign affairs. Even the Library of Congress maintains an overseas staff of some sixteen employees. In 1968 fifty-six separate agencies maintained representatives at one or more U. S. embassies. In addition to the State Department, these included the Agency for International Development, the Peace Corps, the U. S. Information Agency, the Arms Control and

Disarmament Agency, the Department of Defense, the Central Intelligence Agency, the Treasury Department, and the Departments of Agriculture, Labor, and Commerce. Scarcely a major operating agency in the U. S. Government does not have an international division or some international responsibilities.

The complexity of interagency relations in foreign affairs is further illustrated by the distribution of American personnel overseas. Table 1 shows the paid civilian employment of the U. S. government in foreign countries as of June 30, 1968. At that time 38,029 U. S. citizens

Table 1. Paid civilian employment of the United States government in foreign countries, by agency and citizenship, June 30, 1968. (The Central Intelligence Agency is not fully reflected, however.)

| Agency | U.S. citizens | Non-citizens | Total |
|---|---|---|---|
| Department of State | 7,148 | 12,218 | 19,366 |
| Agency for International Development | 4,865 | 9,277 | 14,142 |
| Peace Corps | 445 | 176 | 621 |
| U. S. Information Agency | 1,463 | 6,502 | 7,965 |
| Army | 11,247 | 69,941 | 81,188 |
| Navy | 3,490 | 31,983 | 35,473 |
| Air Force | 6,136 | 32,929 | 39,065 |
| Other Department of Defense | 375 | 446 | 821 |
| Treasury Department | 263 | 38 | 301 |
| Justice Department | 194 | 33 | 227 |
| Interior Department | 463 | 18 | 481 |
| Commerce Department | 201 | 132 | 333 |
| Department of Health, Education, and Welfare | 362 | 83 | 445 |
| Department of Transportation | 376 | 32 | 408 |
| American Battle Monuments Commission | 39 | 391 | 430 |
| Atomic Energy Commission | 24 | — | 24 |
| National Aeronautics and Space Administration | 23 | 1 | 24 |
| Library of Congress | 16 | — | 16 |

SOURCE: *Report on Statistics on Employment by Agency and Citizenship in Foreign Countries, June, 1968,* Manpower Statistics Division, Bureau of Manpower Information Systems, U.S. Civil Service Commission.

and 164,917 noncitizens were employed by overseas agencies. Of these only 7,148 of the citizens (19 percent) and 12,218 of the noncitizens (8 percent) worked for the State Department. The Department of Defense and its dependencies accounted for 56 percent of the U. S. citizens and 81 percent of the noncitizens, in addition to military personnel and their families stationed overseas. The table does not fully cover the Central Intelligence Agency, which also maintains a sizable body of citizens and noncitizens in foreign countries. Each of these agencies is jealous of its rights, prerogatives, and "territory," and is chary of being coordinated by the State Department, the nominal *primus inter pares*.

It is also a fact of life that most of the funds and personnel for operational programs in foreign affairs are allocated to agencies other than State. In practice the department's role is twofold. First, it is charged with being the principal locus of coordination for U. S. overseas activities. For various reasons, including its weak numerical position, it does not effectively discharge this responsibility. Second, it is the major source of backstopping and support services for the overseas agencies. As much as 50 percent of the department's manpower is engaged directly in such activities, and a significant part of its budget comes as reimbursement from these agencies for services rendered.

The multiple interdependencies among foreign affairs agencies may contribute to hierarchy and rules in the State Department in several ways:

(1) Interagency communication creates pressures for centralization in each of the agencies involved. When a message goes from one part of the State Department to another, it is usually not necessary to have it routed through the Office of the Secretary or some other top-level official. When a similar message goes from the State Department to another agency, it comes from the "State Department" rather than the initiating office and must thus have high-level approval. The same is true of a reply from the receiving department or agency. Hence interagency communication makes extensive use of the hierarchical ladder on both the sending and the receiving end. In bureaucratese, more

messages are "bucked up" when they deal with other agencies than with the internal business of a single agency.

(2) The resulting flow of messages to the top creates communication overload for senior officials. Two solutions to this problem are common, both involving increased hierarchy. The first is to work out a division of labor whereby the top official, such as the Secretary of State, takes primary responsibility for interagency relations, leaving internal administration to others. This approach typically requires a senior line administrator, such as an under secretary or assistant secretary, to handle the local responsibilities. Deputy Under Secretary of State William Macomber adopted precisely this solution to deal with his overload in the *O* area. The second alternative is to appoint a senior assistant to be in charge of the agency's external relations so that the ranking official will be able to manage its internal affairs. To be effective, this official must hold a recognized line position rather than an appointment as a special assistant or some other staff position. Either solution entails an added level of hierarchy between the top level and the operating managers.

(3) The greater the involvement of other agencies in the foreign affairs arena, the greater the demands for interagency liaison, and the greater the pressures for coordination by the State Department. The added pressures for coordination will increase the demands for centralization, and reinforce the felt need for hierarchy. Similarly, the larger the number of diverse actors in the arena, the greater the pressure to develop explicit rules governing their actions, especially overseas. In the State Department these rules often appear as Manual Orders or Foreign Affairs Manual Circulars sent to all foreign affairs agencies with personnel overseas. They may cover such diverse matters as a new coordinating committee or regulations covering the sale of automobiles in foreign countries. The addition of officials creates a demand for supervisors to ensure that *they* are enforcing the rules comparably and equitably.

(4) Within a given embassy, hierarchy is generated by the desire of attachés and other agency representatives to increase their presence. A former ambassador (Villard, 1965, pp. 27-28) describes this process very well:

Not only do other agencies feel free to establish branches in our diplomatic missions, but one attaché usually leads to another. With a foot in the door, he must have an assistant; the assistant, too, must be assisted, until there is a vested interest and an ever growing staff in the office.

The cycle continues as the presence of more staff in the embassy requires a larger staff in the regional bureau to provide interagency liaison and coordination. A mathematically inclined observer could probably work out a latter-day Parkinson's Law indicating the number of Washington staff added for each $x$ embassy attachés. And, of course, the larger the Washington staff, the greater the need for supervisors to provide internal coordination.

*Political headships.* Another significant feature of the federal executive system is the overlay of political heads at the top of each bureau. The use of political appointees rather than career officials has several implications for the growth and survival of bureaucracy. For one, the political head's job is generally seen as temporary. Secretaries, under secretaries, assistant secretaries, and administrators come and go while the career services stay on. As a result, the political head may find it hard to gain control of his own organization. Career officials can fight an unpopular order or change with the oldest and most lethal weapon in the arsenal of the public bureaucracy: delay. The agency head can respond to resistance by increased bureaucratization— greater formalization and impersonalization, more rules, and an increased insistence on adherence to formal channels of communication. He may also add a new assistant director to serve as enforcement agent and expediter. Gouldner (1954) has documented the chain of reactions set off by an attempt to "tighten up" an industrial organization through increased bureaucratization. In the federal agency the added rules may produce short-term compliance, but long-term organizational sclerosis through increased formality and hierarchy.

Career officials may also find advantages in rules, regulations, and formal procedures. Bureaucracy can be a bulwark against the shifting tides above. Political heads come and go, but the permanent employees continue to be responsible for the smooth operation of the agency and for its day-to-day work. Rules and hierarchy can help buffer the initiatives of an impetuous agency director and can also serve as an effective means of sabotaging change. While both the top and the bottom of an agency can engage in bureaucratic warfare, the bottom often has an edge because of its intimate familiarity with the battlefield.

The MOP reorganization also showed that the constant rotation of agency heads hinders acceptance of an effort to reduce bureaucracy. Many in the O area were doubtful that Crockett's reforms would last beyond his departure. By Washington standards Crockett was a relative veteran with six years as assistant secretary and deputy under secretary for administration. Nevertheless, the career bureaucrats knew that he would not continue indefinitely, and they acted accordingly. The implications of this point are pursued further in Chapter 9.

*Managerial orthodoxy.* A further prop for bureaucracy lies in the managerial philosophy pervading the federal executive system and for the most part shared by Congress. The basic tenet of this orthodoxy is that efficiency requires a clean line of authority from top to bottom in an organization. The central responsibility of the superior is the faithful implementation of policy directives sent from above and accountability to his own superiors; the key responsibility of the subordinate is obedience. Dwight Waldo (1952) summarized this view with his phrase: "Autocracy during office hours is the price of democracy after hours."

The administrative orthodoxy guiding the U. S. government is found in pristine form in the reports of the first Hoover Commission:

The organizational commandments laid down by the first Hoover Commission constitute the hard core of the fundamentalist dogma. The devils to be exorcised are overlapping and duplication, and confused or broken lines of authority and responsibility. Entry into the Nirvana of Economy and Efficiency can be obtained only by strict adherence to sound principles of executive branch organization. Of these the most essential are the grouping of executive branch agencies as nearly as possible by major purposes so that "by placing related functions cheek-by-jowl the overlaps can be eliminated, and of even greater importance coordinated policies can be developed"; and the establishment of a clear line of command and supervision from the President down through his department heads to every employee with no subordinate possessing authority independent from that of his superior (Seidman, 1970, p. 4).

The following excerpt from the Hoover Commission reports conveys the flavor of its assumptions about authority and accountability:

*The President, and under him his chief lieutenants, the department heads, must be held responsible and accountable to the people and the Congress for the conduct of the executive branch.*
Responsibility and accountability are impossible without authority—the power to direct. The exercise of authority is impossible without a clear line of command from the top to the bottom, and a return line of responsibility from the bottom to the top (1949, p. 3).

The commission postulates that the only way to have accountability and responsibility is the classic structure of hierarchical authority.

As is true of many social theories, the deep penetration of administrative orthodoxy into the collective consciousness of government creates a tendency toward self-perpetuation. Specifically, there are at least three ways in which it works to increase and reinforce hierarchy and rules.

First, in establishing or reorganizing an agency, Congress will often take pains to spell out not only the general lines of authority but also the specific boxes on the organizational chart. While this step is often a political move designed to prevent the administration from changing an agency in undesired directions, it may also flow from deeply held assumptions about the proper structure of executive organizations. We shall see later that the legislative specification of administrative structures can become a formidable obstacle to change.

Second, orthodox theory provides a helpful working model for a manager or even a President confronted with an organizational problem. For many agency heads or division chiefs it is the *only* operating model of organizations to which they have been exposed, and one with which they have lived. When it is necessary to expand or reorganize their own agencies, they will invoke the orthodox model almost reflexively. As Harold Seidman notes,

Flawed and imperfect as they may be, the orthodox "principles" remain the only simple, readily understood, and comprehensive set of guidelines available to the President and Congress for resolving problems of executive branch structure. . . They have the virtue of clarity, a virtue often scorned by the newer orthodoxies, especially the behavioralists and social psychologists, who tend to write for each other in an arcane language which is unintelligible to the lay public (1970, p. 8).

Third, the prevailing norms of proper management can act as a brake on organizational innovation and change. In the MOP reorganization Crockett's superiors were concerned about his departures from the traditional span of control. The precept that one man should not supervise more than seven to ten others became a yardstick for judging the acceptability of change in O. They also seemed to fear that violations of this norm by the State Department would draw negative comments from a Congress that held to the same philosophy. Managerial ideologies may thus be both a positive force for bureaucratization and a constraint on attempts at debureaucratization. Either way, their influence is very strong.

*The White House.* The success of a federal agency is closely tied to its relations with the White House. A bureau with strong White House support can afford to be bold with policy initiatives, innovative in organizational design, and confident in its dealings with Congress. An agency without such support may be condemned to the bureaucratic backwaters.

The relations between the State Department and the White House since World War II have been difficult and complex. As noted in Chapter 2, State rapidly lost ground to other power contenders in the postwar expansion of foreign affairs activities. In 1961 President Kennedy took various steps to restore its role as principal coordinator of foreign policy. Kennedy wanted State to take charge, to "end the faceless system of indecision and inaction which diffused foreign policy among the three great bureaucracies of State, Defense, and the CIA" (Schlesinger, 1965, p. 426). However, his romance with the department was short-lived. Impatient for action and pithy policy suggestions, he had little use for the long, roundabout position papers churned out by State. He and his advisers also could not accept the elaborate system of concurrences "which required every proposal to run a hopelessly intricate obstacle course before it could become policy" (ibid., p. 410). By the end of 1961 Kennedy was convinced that the department could not be trusted with a major leadership role. Thereafter he largely disregarded it, turning increasingly to his own staff for advice and policy alternatives.

The process continued under President Johnson and was seen at least until 1973 under President Nixon. By 1970 the shift in policy initiative had become so complete that Washington watchers spoke of two State Departments: the legally constituted unit in "Foggy Bottom," and the real department directed by Henry Kissinger from the White House basement. With Kissinger's appointment as Secretary of State in 1973, the balance began to shift back to the department in some areas. However, his heavy reliance on personal diplomacy coupled with continuing internal difficulties in the department make it difficult to predict the long-term implications of Kissinger's tenure for the balance of influence among foreign affairs agencies.

The declining influence of the State Department in the 1960s left it with a largely negative role, which increased its propensity to hierarchy and rules. In this period the White House staff prepared proposals and sent them to State to determine their loopholes and flaws. The department became the lawyer and the critic rather than the initiator of foreign policy. It was well-prepared for this role. With its ingrained emphasis on precedent and tradition, it possessed an excellent organizational memory—a capacity not associated with the White House staff. And the system of concurrences was a superb mechanism for detecting loopholes in proposals initiated by others. But the cost was an accentuation of the very tendencies that originally forced State into a negative role: slowness, hierarchy, clearances, and caution. The Foreign Service Officer came to be known as "a man for whom the risks always outweighed the opportunities" (ibid., p. 414).

*Congress*

The legal authority granted to Congress provides a powerful means of controlling and cajoling executive agencies. Every agency depends on the Congress for two vital assets: money and statutory authority to act. The legislative branch may also intervene directly in the affairs of an agency by passing a law to change its structure or by using the budget as an instrument of policy. Congressman Frank T. Bow, formerly a member of the Rooney appropriations subcommittee, summarized the power of the House as follows:

The House is at liberty to insert provisos or instructions in appropriations bills. We have the effect of determining or modifying policy. Congress may withhold funds altogether and thus completely cancel an executive policy. To the extent that funds are withheld, or terms and conditions set for the expenditure of Treasury money, Congress may prescribe its own policy. But this is as it should be (Quoted in Leacacos, 1968, p. 202).

The most powerful external controller of the internal operations of the State Department is the House appropriations subcommittee chaired by Congressman Rooney. During his tenure Rooney has become the scourge and the Scrooge of the State Department. Former ambassador Henry Villard writes:

Outside Washington and the Foreign Service, the name of John J. Rooney is not well known; he is not a national figure, like some congressmen who spring into print at the drop of a controversy. But as *Time* magazine reported: "In 300 U. S. embassies, legations, consulates, and special missions throughout the world, nothing is more likely to cause hot blood and cold sweats than the mention of [Rooney's] name." The Rooney rulings on how the State Department spends its money—and how much it gets—are absolute. None of his colleagues cares to cross him; there is no appeal from his decisions; and no one actively connected with the Foreign Service would dare to offend him for fear that the State Department's budgetary requests might be adversely affected (1965, pp. 107-108).

Similar comments were heard during our interviews. Whether this is an accurate depiction of Rooney's influence is irrelevant; the perception itself has significant effects on the department's organizational life.

An important pressure for bureaucracy emanating from the Rooney subcommittee is intimidation. Department officials are acutely aware that they may be called to account for their actions and expenditures at the next round of budget hearings. The flavor of the performance is conveyed by an excerpt from the hearings for the 1970 appropriations, held in March 1969.[2] The discussion focuses on the department's cultural exchange program. Mr. Canter is the main spokesman for the exchange programs, while Mr. Bator is an officer with the U. S. Information Agency.

Do we have that gentleman here who reviews the cultural presentations which go abroad, Mr. Bator?

MR. CANTER. He reviewed this specific project, Mr. Chairman.

## Background of Reviewing Officer

MR. ROONEY. Mr. Bator, how long have you been with the Department or Foreign Service?

MR. BATOR. Twelve years, sir.

MR. ROONEY. What is your background?

MR. BATOR. I am with the USIA actually. I started out 12 years ago in Helsinki, went to Florence, Italy, Belgrade, Yugoslavia, to Naples, and to Washington.

MR. ROONEY. Have you had much background in the theatrical world?

MR. BATOR. No sir.

MR. ROONEY. Do you make a hobby of going to musicals and plays?

MR. BATOR. Yes, sir; whenever I can . . .

## Review of the Presentation

MR. ROONEY. I understand you went out to Kansas to view a presentation of a set of plays called the Kaleidoscope of the American Dream which were being considered for export this year to some Iron Curtain countries. Is that correct?

MR. BATOR. Yes, sir; I did . . .

MR. ROONEY. We note that after the intermission they presented a short play called "Chicago" by Sam Shepard. Did you see and hear that?

MR. BATOR. Yes sir.

MR. ROONEY. What did you think of it?

MR. BATOR. I thought it was quite amusing, sir.

---

[2] The full reference is Hearings before a Subcommittee on Appropriations, House of Representatives, Ninety-First Congress, 1, pt. 2, Department of State, pp. 992-994 (Washington, D.C.: U.S. Government Printing Office, 1969).

MR. ROONEY. Amusing?

MR. BATOR. Amusing, yes. It was a comedy, or meant to be a comedy. I viewed it as such. I think from the reaction of the audience the audience viewed it as such.

MR. ROONEY. Did you hear the sentence "They'll all be —— for the young virgins that walk the beaches in their two-piece flimsy things"?

MR. BATOR. Yes; I did, sir.

MR. ROONEY. What did you think of that?

MR. BATOR. I think in context it did not affect me negatively.

MR. ROONEY. What do you mean by that?

MR. BATOR. I mean that the person who said it was, I believe, soliloquizing at the time. He was acting out a fantasy, and this is the way I viewed it, as a fantasy.

MR. ROONEY. And the following sentence, "Then they"ll come onto the land and start —— everything in sight." You thought that was fantasy, too?

MR. BATOR. Sir, taken out of context like that I object to those phrases—.

MR. ROONEY. I am not taking it out of context. That was the next sentence.

MR. BATOR. I don't mean you, sir. If one takes a phrase like that out of context I find it very objectionable as a phrase. I find the words objectionable . . .

MR. ROONEY. Are you a married man?

MR. BATOR. Yes, I am.

MR. ROONEY. Family?

MR. BATOR. Yes, sir.

MR. ROONEY. How many children?

MR. BATOR. Two children, ages 15 and 12.

MR. ROONEY. Sex?

MR. BATOR. Girl and boy; the girl is 15.

MR. ROONEY. Would you want your 15-year-old daughter to listen to this sort of thing?

The discussion continues in this vein for several more pages.

Incidents of this sort create demands for bureaucracy from two directions. The first is from the bottom up. The message to Mr. Bator's counterparts elsewhere in the department is clear: if you engage in any experimentation or do anything out of the ordinary, you may be called before Rooney to explain yourself. Given this possibility it may be very rational for the lower-level employee in State to press for rules to guide his work and for specific authorization from a superior to protect himself. He might also hope that it would be the superior, rather than himself, who would have to appear before the Rooney subcommittee. Bureaucracy may thus emerge as a defense against hostile forces in Congress. The second demand is from the top down. If the subordinate wants some defense against attack, the superior wants to prevent the attacks from taking place at all. If he is to be accountable for the actions of those below him, he must be informed about what they are doing and exercise restraint on controversial innovations. If, at the same time, he is suffering from communication overload internally or is heavily involved in external relations, it is quite rational for him to add one or more assistants to maintain accountability. A clear illustration of the top-down pressure for hierarchy was seen when Idar Rimestad succeeded William Crockett as deputy under secretary for administration. Soon after taking office, Rimestad was called to account for the Argyris Report. This experience apparently reinforced his conviction that the O area had to retreat to a more traditional and accountable hierarchical system. The central argument of this book is that bureaucratization in federal agencies results in good measure from the confluence of top-down and bottom-up pressures for hierarchy and rules.

## Constituencies

The congressional grip on the State Department is fortified by the department's constituency relations. It is often said that State has no domestic constituency. The reasons cited are its small budget—which offers few possibilities for building a clientele—and its output—which is intangible, ambiguous, and oriented to other countries. This view must be qualified in two ways. There are interest groups, such as the fishing lobbies, that do have a direct stake in some aspects of State's "output." And over the years the department has built up a kind of negative constituency. While its roots go deep into American history, the most vociferous contingent since 1945 has been the anti-Communist groups. These range from veterans' organizations still embracing McCarthyism to Cuban and East European refugee groups. The negative side is bolstered by the patrician image of the Foreign Service and lingering public suspicion of the entire State Department.

The absence of a positive constituency coupled with a moderately vocal negative constituency allows the Rooney subcommittee fairly free rein in its dealings with State. In its hearings Rooney plays on several time-honored populist themes—the Ivy League background and elitism of the Foreign Service, its image as "cookie pushers" and "striped pants boys," and the department's general isolation from the American public (seen, for example, in its choice of plays for export). Unless he has a strong base of external support, anyone who dares to innovate must be prepared to defend himself in the next set of hearings.

One unit that did have such support in the sixties was the Passport Office. Under the direction of Frances Knight it developed a reputation as the most efficient operation in the State Department and one of the best in the federal government. Its cause was not harmed by annually returning money to the Treasury from passport fees—a rare feat in Washington. Over the years Mrs. Knight won the support of outside constituencies, including the travel industry, and powerful members of both House and Senate. Significantly, though her personal relations with Rooney were strained, he consistently exempted the Passport Office from the customary budget cuts and interrogation. In fact, for several years Mrs. Knight simply refused to appear before the appropriations subcommittee. Rooney's potential for intimidation seemed to be inversely correlated with the strength of an official's power base. The difference between Mrs. Knight and Mr. Bator in this respect is striking.

*Alliances*

It would be misleading to create the impression that the power relations between Congress and executive agencies are unidirectional. Closer analysis reveals a complex lattice of alliances and working relationships involving career officials, members of Congress, and sometimes outside constituencies. The political vulnerability of the career official provides strong motivation to form such alliances. Earlier we argued that political appointees are less powerful than they might seem in their own units because of their actual or perceived transience. The same holds true in their dealings with congressional committees. The chairman and ranking members may give due recognition to the agency head, but their most enduring ties are with high-ranking career executives. As Gawthrop (1969, p. 77) puts it, "Every legislative sub-unit has a tie-in with some executive sub-unit; this alliance is continuous, it is operationally meaningful, and, if the career employee is at all astute, it should be mutually beneficial." It is also an indirect contributor to the top-down demand for hierarchy and rules.

Why should members of Congress, who hold the formal strings of power, enter into bargaining alliances with career officials in "their" agencies? In general, three underlying motives are at work: (1) the legislator's desire for information about the specifics of governmental administration; (2) his need for services for his constituents or political support for his own work in Congress; and (3) a desire to control those aspects of agency operations that impinge on his work. The common idea that agencies consult with Congress on policy and then implement it on their own terms is almost the reverse of the actual situation.

Congressmen have an apparently incurable tendency to concern themselves with the details of administration, particularly when those details directly affect a legislator's home district—e.g., the establishment of a new federal installation in a congressman's constituency, or perhaps its liquidation. Of course, it is very often by intervention in the details of administration that a legislator is able to make his most effective contribution to the policy process (Rourke, 1965, p. xiv).

Thus congressmen trade off jurisdictional authority, money, and political support for the right to intervene in the operational decisions of federal agencies.

For the permanent official, such as the Civil Service office director, ties with congressional committees provide significant rewards. One of his (or her) major frustrations is the succession of political appointees above him. Beyond their sheer impermanence, which injects enormous uncertainty into the life of the agency, these heads cannot be counted on for support in times of crisis. They often do not have great power to begin with, and their long-range interests usually lie outside the agency. Hence it may not be worth the political costs for them to defend a lower-level employee against attack from Congress or the press. The employee is left to fend for himself if called before

Rooney or his counterparts. The career official knows this and seeks support elsewhere, especially in the subcommittees with which he has regular dealings. Having the backing of a powerful committee chairman and several senior members is a crucial asset in the unending bureaucratic struggles that face the public employee. The classic case in the present study is that of Frances Knight, already mentioned as director of the Passport Office. Because of her ties with a powerful congressional subcommittee it would have been extremely difficult for Crockett to apply Management by Objectives and Programs to the Passport Office. (This case will be explored in Chapter 9.) In their study of the federal executive system Warner and his colleagues (1963, pp. 245-246) aptly summarize the situation we are describing:

The world of government, our interviews show, is a highly personal one, interlaced with ties and involvements. The career executive counts as major assets the transient people he knows on the Hill and in the White House, or the other permanent people in the agencies and departments and in the offices of unions, business, and education located in Washington. The relationships are reciprocal. The congressman who can pick up the phone and call a friend in one of the departments or agencies may be able to call into play unexpectedly powerful support for one or another piece of business he has on hand. Opportunities for better jobs, the facility to slip around a roadblock, and the ability to take care of protégés are only a few of the indications of the functioning of the network of interpersonal relationships in the city of government. Through the years one's ties with this network come to have close personal and emotional meanings. Violations of the feelings of trust, loyalty, and moral obligation which are implied by these relationships can have serious psychological implications for these people.

These external alliances contribute to the growth of hierarchy and rules. Their immediate effect is to weaken the internal control system of the agency. In the State Department it was no secret that Abba Schwartz, administrator of the Bureau of Security and Consular Affairs, had less political muscle than Frances Knight, his subordinate. Schwartz was a political appointee, Knight a civil servant. In hydraulic terms the bureaucratic system suffers from power leaks. A high official applies pressure and nothing happens. With a strong external power base a senior career manager such as Knight can ignore, bypass, or contravene directives from above, especially when such action is taken quietly. If a conflict develops with the political head, there are numerous appeal routes. The career official may find a senator or congressman who would take particular delight in calling a hearing to embarrass the agency director. Most political appointees have enemies in Congress; Abba Schwartz was no exception.

To fight back, the political appointee can resort to the most potent weapon at his disposal: an increase in hierarchy, rules, and clearances. He may appoint an assistant director to "ride herd" on the civil servants, or he may demand that more decisions be sent directly to his level for clearance. Our interviews suggested that the latter tactic may have been adopted by the Bureau of Security and Consular Affairs under Schwartz. The office directors and division chiefs under him expressed considerable dissatisfaction with the number of clearances and regulations imposed from above. Three managers commented:

They [SCA] don't help me at all. I deal with them directly on restricted areas. There is a mass of transmittal of mail up and down. If we followed their directions we'd be in a mess.

There are so many delaying factors. You have to go through SCA and H [Congressional Relations] before things can be signed. We have a three-day rule for congressional letters, and frequently changes are made and sometimes these are not accurate. We have so many people in between—it's a delaying factor.

I must say that in my experience I would have flunked them all [SCA administrators], but the last [Schwartz] was the worst of all. He was a political appointee, and if he doesn't know the substantive or administrative area, you're cut off.

Other evidence points to increased bureaucratic warfare between the SCA superstructure and its operating offices during the tenure of Abba Schwartz, and a decrease later. The apparent rise in clearances under Schwartz may have been prompted by a desire to obtain more firm control of his own agency in the face of opposition from powerful subordinates. This example illustrates how a combination of external alliances and internal struggles becomes an incubator of bureaucracy.

## Monitors

Federal agencies are subject to government-wide standards on purchasing, contracting, budgeting, expenditure, accounting, job classification, recruitment, dismissal of employees, pay scales, and other matters. Both the executive branch and the Congress use various monitors to enforce these standards. As we have said, the most powerful and most feared is the General Accounting Office (GAO), the watchdog agency of Congress. Others include the Office of Management and the Budget, the Army Inspectorate General, various specialized auditing programs, and, on certain personnel matters, the Civil Service Commission.

The presence of monitors has two direct effects on the federal agency. First, it further increases the accountability of the agency director and other superiors, both ex ante and ex post facto. He is subject to before-the-fact controls in the form of standards and regulations prescribed by agencies such as the Office of Management and the Budget and the Civil Service Commission. In addition, the General Accounting Office holds the potential for a wide range of after-the-fact scrutiny. It may audit not only the legality but the efficiency, propriety, and wisdom of an official's actions. Many superiors thus feel compelled to hold a fairly tight rein on the activities of subordinates for which they may be called to account. Second, the monitors increase the amount of record-keeping and reporting required in the agency.

Once a separate monitoring organization has grown large enough to become a bureau in itself, it exhibits typical bureaucratic behavior. Its officials become advocates of greater control over the operating bureaus they monitor, both because they wish to perform their function better and because this increases their significance. As a result, the officials in separate monitoring bureaus tend to agitate for ever more detailed reports from operating bureaus, and ever greater limitations on the discretion of those bureaus (Downs, 1967, pp. 149-150).

The combination of heightened accountability and expanded reporting contributes to the bureaucratization of the agency in several ways:[3]

(1) The agency may have to take on additional staff to meet the demands of the monitors. More staff means more supervisors to coor-

[3] This discussion borrows from the superb analysis of the monitoring process by Anthony Downs (1967).

dinate their work, especially in the most sensitive areas of the agency's operations. Over time the supervisor may need an assistant to help with his overloading, and so on in an expansion of the hierarchical ladder.

(2) Pressures will be great to prepare lengthy reports to impress the monitors, particularly on controversial decisions. The longer the reports the more time required to read them. Depending on the subject matter, which could be most damaging to the agency's interests, supervisors up the line will want to clear the memoranda. However, the sheer flow of paper will make it difficult for the agency director personally to digest and approve each report. The monitoring process · may thus provide one more reason for him to add a trusted assistant whose judgment he respects and accepts on such matters. In a large agency the same top-down reproduction may take place at lower levels, so that two or more rungs are added to the ladder.

(3) The presence of monitors gives the lower-level employee further reason to restrict his discretion and seek clearances from his superiors. To quote Downs (1967, p. 150):

Operating bureaus monitored by separate agencies exhibit certain defensive reactions. They behave in closer conformity to the orders of their superiors than they would if not monitored . . . They try to create an appearance of following the orders of their superiors more closely than they really do. This involves generating a great deal of information and analysis justifying whatever behavior they have actually carried out, and concealing other acts through secrecy or false reports.

The limitation of discretion creates a bottom-up pressure for hierarchy and rules by passing more responsibility to higher levels in the organization. The possibility of concealment or secrecy at lower levels augments the top-down demand for scrutiny and accountability, both of which require hierarchical authority.

### Summary

The power setting of the federal agency includes several major actors: other executive agencies working in the same area; the White House; the legislative and appropriations committees of Congress; external constituencies; alliances between career officials and members of Congress; and monitors such as the General Accounting Office and the Bureau of the Budget. This chapter argues that the power setting creates both top-down and bottom-up pressures for hierarchy and rules. At the lower levels the ubiquity of monitors and the possibility of congressional investigation serve to limit the discretion of agency officials. This means that even minor decisions are sent to higher levels for clearance and concurrence. The result is an increase in the flow of communications within the organization and a greater need for supervisory personnel. Furthermore, lower-level career officials may find hierarchy and rules a helpful insulation against the vagaries of political appointees above them.

The top-down pressures arise from essentially three problems: communication, accountability, and control. The combination of intra-agency clearances, interagency concurrences, and the reporting requirements of monitors and Congress places a severe strain on the information-handling capacity of senior officials. One solution involves an expansion of the hierarchical ladder and a corresponding increase in rules. The demand of accountability on the part of top officials is also great. Congress, the White House, monitoring agencies, and the press all contribute to "life in the goldfish bowl." If the official is to be accountable to his controllers, monitors, and perhaps constituencies, he must be able to monitor and control his own agency. The traditional means for effecting internal accountability are once again hierarchical authority and explicit rules. Finally, alliances between career officials and outside groups make it difficult for some political appointees to maintain control of their organizations. Increased bureaucratization may be introduced to plug the resulting power leaks.

Our discussion considers also the influence of elements somewhat unique to the power setting of the State Department. Among these are the extraordinary complexity and confusion of interagency relations in foreign affairs, the declining influence of the department on the White House, the unusually strong grip held on the department by Congressman John Rooney, a weak positive and a moderately strong negative constituency, and the peculiar status of the Bureau of Security and Consular Affairs and the Passport Office.

# 5 • The Internal Environment

Hierarchy and rules draw nourishment from certain internal conditions in the governmental agency. Some are structural, others perceptual, but all lend impetus to bureaucratization. This chapter examines the internal sources of bureaucracy common to many agencies and others more or less unique to the State Department.

## Goals and Tasks

The goals of most federal agencies are vague, intangible, and not readily subject to quantification. At the beginning the agency's broad purpose and initial operating goals are set forth in a mandate created by executive order or legislation. Over time the organization develops a variety of purposes and activities reflecting the interests and perspectives of its successive administrators, outside pressures, internal politics, and often the effects of age. At any given time it is almost impossible to isolate *the* purpose or *the* operational objectives of an executive organization. As Gawthrop notes (1969, p. 55), it is "geared to provide numerous services, to meet basic needs, to satisfy various desires, to assume certain responsibilities, to apply certain regulations, and to maintain various standards—all with little regard being directed to the question of the financial solvency of the organization, i.e., the federal government." The resulting vagueness of goals means that administrators and employees have few direct, measurable indicators of how well they are doing. The Bureau of the Budget (1966, p. 3) observes:

In private enterprise, the guidance on what to produce and the incentive to produce it with maximum obtainable efficiency are provided by the workings of the profit motive in a market system. Moreover, business organizations can gauge their success from the financial statements. But in government the system of goals and incentives is different and, with very few exceptions, the managers of government agencies have no general indicator of the effectiveness of their choices or the efficiency of their performance comparable to the profit and loss statement.

Goal ambiguity and the absence of firm performance criteria favor the development of rules and fixed operating procedures. Rules and standards have the advantage of being means-oriented, if not ends-oriented, guides to success. The official may not be sure of what he has produced or how well he has produced it, but he can be sure that he did it in the right way. This is not to say that bureaucrats lack other means of gauging their performance. Feedback from White House assistants, criticism or praise during congressional hearings, increases or decreases in appropriations, standing in the national and Washington press—all are indirect but significant measures of success. Nevertheless, for thousands of officials who are not tuned in to these networks, compliance with rules remains the most direct and reassuring sign of a job well done.

Measured by its formal goals, the State Department's most significant product is an elusive compound called "foreign policy." State is also responsible for a variety of additional outputs, including support services for other agencies, passports, visas, educational exchange programs, and miscellaneous services to U. S. travelers. But in the local ethos, policy towers above all else. The problem is that it is not clear just what policy is, or who makes it. It may consist in formal decisions and explicit plans of action or it may be a vaguely formulated set of attitudes toward another country or even an implicit decision to ignore a certain issue. Moreover, in State as elsewhere, policy is made at all levels of the organization, not only at the top. A consular official's decision to refuse a visa to a student activist in Latin America is as much an expression of U. S. foreign policy as formal proclamations opposing student radicalism. William Crockett, in a 1970 interview, offered this description of State's policy-setting process:

But the product of State is not action but reaction. It is not something that comes out of production lines nor out of kitchens. It comes out of and results from all the levels and sophistication of the human communication process—all man's relationships to and evaluation of another. It is not made with machines nor with hands, but it is a product of minds, intuition, and subtle judgments.

Policy comes from a melding process. It takes a great many intangible gut feelings, mixes them with a host of assumptions, and plugs in a few facts to come out with a goal, a plan, and an action program.

Boiled down to specific tasks, the most direct expression of policy is a written report. Words and paper take on enormous importance in the life of the State Department. Following the classic model of the gentleman generalist, the Foreign Service exalts graceful prose and the well-turned phrase—both of which augment the production of words. A recent self-study by the department had this to say about the paper problem:

The Task Force found widespread agreement that the paper flow in the Department and the Foreign Service is an impediment to creativity. This is because so much time is spent by most of us in drafting and reading what our colleagues have drafted that there is insufficient leisure for the quiet reflection which is an indispensable element in creative thinking. Writing has become an occupational disease of our service. The Service has prized drafting ability above almost all other skills. We emphasize this skill in recruitment and reward it generously in our promotion system. The prize jobs in the service are the reporting jobs. Foreign Service Inspectors habitually examine reporting officers "chron" files to determine whether there has been an adequate volume of production. Little wonder that our ablest and most energetic officers literally seek out opportunities to report, whether the need is urgent or not (U. S. Department of State, 1970, pp. 313-314).

Chapter 7 will show how the volume of words, interacting with several other internal and external conditions, contributes to hierarchy by straining the information-handling capacities of senior executives.

### Specialization and Interdependence

Another source of hierarchy lies in the peculiar combination of functional specialization and interdependence of activities in the State Department. In part this grows out of the organizational chaos in foreign affairs since 1945. We saw earlier how responsibility for foreign policy came to be dispersed across several dozen agencies. The resulting changes played havoc with the internal structure of the State Department.

Basically there are three overriding differences between the structure of State and that of other agencies: (1) separation of policy formulation (substance) from management (administration); (2) separation of operations (implementation) from both policy formulation and administration; and (3) use of the administrative sector of one department to provide major backstopping for the operational activities of another. The first refers to the unusually sharp cleavage in State between substance and administration (see Chapter 2). The second is a by-product of the suspicions generated during the McCarthy period. Lacking confidence in his own department, Secretary Dulles allowed most of the operational programs of State, such as foreign assistance, to be handed over to other agencies. Shorn of its policy "implements," the department was left with a vacuous and unenforceable coordinating role. The third difference is that, despite its declining operational and policy role, State actually expanded its administrative work by controlling policies and procedures for other overseas agencies. This development sharpened the split between substance and administration within the department and increased the demands for hierarchical coordination between the bureaus and the O area. The effects were clearly reflected in reactions to the MOP reorganization.

The changes and tensions in interagency relations were also seen in microcosm within the department. The broad sweep of foreign affairs in both places was toward greater functional specialization. Even the Foreign Service generalist was expected to have a specialty such as economic reporting, commerce, agriculture, or administration. In addition, the department took on or trained large numbers of specialists with no pretenses at being diplomatic generalists. As State moved toward functional specialization, it ran up against the classic problem of integration—how to tie together the many specialties. Specialization tends to breed narrowly defined interests, an indigenous vocabulary, and pressures for autonomy from the rest of the system. The combination of distinctive language, interests, and procedures coupled with frequent interaction gradually led to greater physical and psychological separation among the subunits. The agriculture specialists found it increasingly easy to talk with one another but not to the political officers, and so on in a spiral of organizational tribalism. Even within a small embassy, segmentation by functional specialties may inhibit communication and coordination. The department's Task Force on Creativity commented that "one of the deterrents to creativity in the mission is the impairment of internal communications resulting from the over-rigid division of the Embassy into political, economic, information, administrative, military, and other sections" (U. S. Department of State, 1970, p. 334).

Basically three factors interact to increase internal demands for hierarchical coordination: the vagueness of foreign policy, overlapping of functions, and specialization. Because no one is quite sure what policy is or where it is made, everyone potentially involved wishes to be consulted. Unlike many organizations, there is no recognizable distinction between line and staff in the State Department. In the 1970 interview cited previously Mr. Crockett observed:

It is true that the functional bureaus supposedly are staff and the regional bureaus are line. But this is a blurred distinction. Of even greater import is the fact that they are headquarters-based, and this tends to mute the clarity of issues, diffuse the ownership of responses (solution, point of view, etc.) and therefore blunts the ability to pinpoint responsibility for recommendations and decisions. Therefore, there is an air of "ambiguous anonymity" about everything decided at State. Who? Everyone! No one!

Even on a relatively minor issue, as many as fifteen different subunits may have to be consulted just within the State Department. Specialization increases the perceived need for intra-agency concurrences by providing easily identifiable checkpoints. Moreover, when asked to comment in the capacity of a specialist, the individual will often express opinions that maximize the interests or mission of his own section. The result is a  profusion of diverse viewpoints requiring hours to classify and even more time to translate into policy recommendations.

One reason for the elaborate hierarchy in the State Department, therefore, is the need to sift and sort different interpretations of problems and alternative policy recommendations. The greater the number of units to be consulted and the greater the quantity and diversity of views expressed, the greater the need for hierarchical co-ordination. This basic mechanism of hierarchical differentiation has been well stated by Anthony Downs (1967, p. 52) in a discussion of dispute settlement:

Let us visualize an organization that is small enough to have one coor-dinator who has authority over all workers. If the organization increases in size, he soon becomes overloaded settling conflicts arising from the interdependence of the workers' activities. A second conflict settler is appointed to handle the inconsistencies that arise in a certain part of the organization. However, there is bound to be some inter-dependence among activities that are under the separate jurisdictions of the two conflict settlers. Therefore, they must themselves agree on coordinating such activities. If the organization continues to grow, the number of conflict settlers multiplies. There inevitably comes a time when they must resort to differential authority to resolve conflicts among themselves, just as the first-level officials eventually created a second level of conflict settlers.

Generalizing this discussion, Downs proposes a Law of Hierarchy: *Coordination of large-scale activities without markets requires a hierarchical authority structure.* We would qualify the emphasis placed on organizational size. It is not only size, which is obviously important, but the extent and nature of participation in decisions. Even with size remaining constant, as it has in the State Department for almost twenty years, the demands for hierarchy will increase with rising participation (as illustrated in concurrences) and diversity of viewpoints.

### Competition and Conflict

Related pressures for hierarchy arise from competition or conflicts between organizational subunits or categories of individuals. A common source of conflicts is the presence of two or more career systems within the same organization. The most frequent duality is between political appointees and career officials. Tensions are added when employees are appointed to other categories as well. The State Department has several personnel systems: Foreign Service Officer

Corps, Foreign Service Reserve, Foreign Service Staff, Civil Service, and others. The strains will be most serious when, as is true in the State Department, one category is an elite corps standing above the others in prestige, influence, and perhaps salary level. "Tensions between corps of this kind," Mosher writes (1967, p. 491), "become most virulent when there is overlapping in function, where two or more categories of personnel work together on the same things with comparable responsibilities and yet there is a difference in the way one category is treated in comparison with the other." The most serious conflicts in State are between the Foreign Service Officer Corps and the Civil Service employees. As early as 1949 a task force report prepared for the Hoover Commission mentioned a "cancerous cleavage" between these two groups. Our study produced evidence that the tensions and frictions were still very much alive in the mid-1960s.

Other tensions grow out of bureaucratic struggles between competing organizational subunits. In the State Department we found these contests to be numerous: regional vs functional bureaus; both sets of bureaus vs the O area; consular offices vs the O area. The issues at stake may be money, talented personnel, status within the organization (a problem for consular officials), or clearances. Whatever the issue, the effect of competition and conflicts is the same: an increased demand for organizational umpires. The greater the number of competing or conflicting subunits and the greater the diversity of issues at stake, the greater the number of umpires needed. The more numerous the umpires, the greater the likelihood that they themselves will need referees with authority to resolve their differences.

The MOP reorganization illustrates the relation between hierarchy and organizational tensions. One of its elements was a large-scale decentralization of personnel decisions to the regional bureaus, and a much smaller decentralization to the functional bureaus. The result was that the regional bureaus solidified their already strong position on assignments, while the functional bureaus lost further ground. After Crockett resigned, his successor added a level of hierarchy to the personnel system partly to remedy this imbalance. The director of the new Office of Personnel explicitly cited the need for greater hierarchical coordination of assignments as one reason for the change. By implication, he argued that hierarchy was needed to protect the weaker units against the encroachment of their more powerful brethren and to ensure an equitable distribution of scarce talent across the organization. These seem to be common reasons for expanding hierarchy in government agencies.

## Status Equalization

In a rank-conscious organization such as the State Department, serious problems are created when officials with equal responsibilities and frequent bargaining relationships differ significantly in grade level. An example was seen during the MOP reorganization. The new charter called for all aspects of program administration, including relations with other units, to be handled by the program manager. Under the old system difficult negotiations were usually carried out by officers at about the same grade level. After the reorganization there were greater disparities in rank. One of the program managers found disadvantages in the decentralized system:

The program manager here in this spot is at a disadvantage because of grade level. I am FSO-3. Crockett naturally turns to an ambassador and FSO-1s for information even when they aren't nearly as familiar with the situation. . . The Executive Group will also listen more attentively to an FSO-1 than an FSO-3. In fact, I have recommended that this program be headed by a [FSO-] 1 or 2.

Hierarchy may thus emerge as a status equalization mechanism. When operating programs are directed by managers ranging from top to middle grades, there may be pressures to appoint senior coordinators to even out the status discrepancies. The last quotation suggests that these pressures may come from the middle as well as the top of the organization.

## Security

A heavy emphasis on internal security procedures generates additional rules and regulations. These will typically cover recruitment (security clearance), entry to and exit from buildings, the proper behavior of employees in sensitive situations, and above all the reception, distribution, storage, and retrieval of classified information. Demands for security arise from two related sources: the nature of the agency's work and regulations imposed by external controllers. Agencies dealing with life-and-death matters, such as the State Department, Defense Department, Central Intelligence Agency, Secret Service, and Federal Bureau of Investigation, typically enforce strict standards of security. Those whose work is less controversial and involves little secrecy can afford to be more relaxed. In addition to procedures developed internally, the organization may be forced by law or extreme political pressure to multiply its security measures. The State Department is the prime example of an agency subjected to external controls exceeding internal demands. In 1952, under the Immigration and Nationality Act, Congress established the Bureau of Security and Consular Affairs within the department. The bureau was literally imposed in response to the McCarthy loyalty attacks. Its result was not only a new set of rules, but an administrative hierarchy embedded in federal statutes.

While the State Department's security consciousness subsided considerably between the 1950s and the 1960s, it remained relatively high at the time of this study. Even the casual observer could note many signs of vigilance on a tour through the main State Department building. To gain entrance the visitor had to have an appointment with someone in the building, and the appointment had to be verified by the receptionist. Envelopes on the mail carts were clearly marked according to their level of sensitivity and carefully watched along the delivery routes. Even the burning of waste paper was stratified by security level. (We did not check the disposal of the ashes.) Offices throughout the building prominently displayed posters worded more or less as follows: TIRED? NEED A VACATION? WANT TO GET AWAY FROM IT ALL? LEAVE YOUR SAFE UNLOCKED TONIGHT! Drawers left open on classified file cabinets carried large red markers to reduce oversights. Safes were omnipresent, as were RESTRICTED ENTRY signs in the Office of Communications. Inspectors appeared unannounced to maintain a high level of compliance. Employees who violated security regulations were given a formal reprimand. Under these conditions even secretarial and clerical employees favored precise rules on message-handling to protect themselves.

Additional rules and regulations have been instituted to cover the security of overseas personnel and embassies. Each embassy has one or more security officers responsible for wide-ranging surveillance of both staff and physical facilities. (In smaller missions this may be a collateral duty for officers assigned to other areas, and the procedures may be more informal.) Many embassies also have CIA representatives, often listed under other titles (for example, agricultural attaché), who have similar responsibilities. Conference rooms and offices are constantly checked to prevent or uncover bugging devices; these have been found even in the "friendly" countries of Western Europe. The department also maintains a close watch on the personal habits of its overseas employees, especially on homosexuality and other behavior that could be used for blackmail. Foreign Service Officers who chat for more than a few minutes with Russian diplomats are expected to file a Memorandum of Conversation. Such elaborate procedures increase the volume of rules in the department and the need for supervisors to enforce them.

### Distance from Center to Periphery

The operating environment of the State Department requires the maintenance of diplomatic missions in over 150 countries throughout the world. The result is maximum separation of the center and the periphery of the organization. The internal environment of the department thus takes on special characteristics related to hierarchy and rules. For one, detailed regulations must be developed to cover the varying contingencies arising in the farflung field outposts. To cite an example: In the 1960s a minor political crisis was provoked in Chile when an embassy official sold a late-model Buick for approximately double its original purchase price. At that time there was such a scarcity in Chile of large, late-model automobiles that any well-kept American car brought a good price, while a special premium was placed on luxury models. If the Buick had been purchased on the local market at prevailing prices there would have been no problem. However, in Chile, as in most countries, diplomats are able to import at least one car duty-free, and sell it a year or two later with little or no duty. When the U. S. official pocketed an instant capital gain of about $5,000, the Chilean press protested that such transactions used diplomatic privileges to exploit the national market. The State Department then was under strong pressure to develop and enforce rules to prevent similar embarrassing incidents. To be effective, such rules had to take account of the peculiar conditions of automobile markets (and black markets) in Santiago, Rome, Lima, Bamako, Port Louis, Ouagadougou, and dozens of other cities. The official who developed the rules told us that they had to be so comprehensive that no one could "beat the system" by arguing ambiguity. The result was not only a sheaf of highly detailed regulations from Washington, but supplementary guidelines prepared at each mission to cover local customs agreements and other unique conditions. For the ordinary employee the new controls meant more time devoted to learning the rules and filling out the required forms. For the department they meant an increased demand for superiors to explain the technicalities of the rules and to enforce them. In many cases enforcement involved negotiations not only with the employee about to sell a car, but with local customs officials who had to approve the sale.

The distance between the center and the periphery also increases the volume of formal communications. In agencies working primarily in Washington or some other single location, a high proportion of official business can be accomplished through informal communication such as telephone calls or staff meetings. Similarly, many problems can be forestalled when officials of interdependent units are in regular contact in the same office, corridors, and cafeterias. In the State Department such informal or semiformal procedures are ruled out by the geographic dispersion of overseas missions and the interagency structure of foreign affairs. Personal contacts between Washington and the field are rare, and telephone calls expensive. Moreover, because almost any piece of department business may touch the interests of other agencies, the simplest course is often to "put it in writing"—with copies to all concerned. The resulting increase in word production further clogs the formal channels of communication and strains the information-handling capacity of officials both in the missions and in Washington. We shall return to this point in Chapter 7.

### Overstaffing and Job Dilution

In 1961 the Senate Subcommittee on National Policy Machinery concluded:

There is a serious over-staffing in the national security departments and agencies . . . The size of the national security departments and agencies has swelled out of proportion even to the increased number and complexity of our problems . . . Unnecessary people make for unnecessary layering, unnecessary clearances and concurrences, and unnecessary intrusions on the time of officials working on problems of real importance (Jackson, 1965, p. 67).

The State Department has often been criticized for overstaffing and job dilution. Comments to this effect came up during our interviews:

I think there are too many people, organizations, too many offices that have no perceivable function—they are just people with a tendency to get underfoot. I sympathize with the secretary and the under secretary's views that if we could find the right way to do it, we could reduce the personnel in this building by 25 percent and be better off.

I think O has become the dumping ground of the whole administrative side of the department. They didn't want to fire anybody so they had to put them someplace.

We have an upside-down Christmas tree—more [FSO-] 1s and 2s than we have jobs to challenge them.

We have legal advisers coming out of our ears—they get into everything that there is.

Many felt that the problem of overstaffing was particularly acute at the upper levels of the Foreign Service:

The system is top-heavy with FSR and FSO-1s, and this makes it difficult to place them. Many of the senior officers are in programs in universities, or at the military colleges. These people are sometimes placed there, that is, on university assignments, because there isn't anything for them to do.

The Senior Officer Program is different again. They're very pragmatic. They have more officers than positions, and they're tough about forcing officers into any job to get them out of circulation.

Problems of overcrowding were aggravated in 1967-68 by a staff-cutting exercise called BALPA (Balance of Payments). To reduce the U. S. balance of payments deficit, President Johnson ordered a 10-percent cut in overseas civilian employment. Through BALPA, 452 State Department employees were brought back from the field to Washington. A similar exercise (OPRED—Operations Reduction) was carried out under the Nixon administration. Both programs produced an influx of senior officers into an already top-heavy bureaucracy.

Overstaffing at the top spawns hierarchy in at least two ways. The first is by vertical differentiation—adding new supervisory positions to accommodate high-ranking officials. To bring an FSO-1 to Washington and assign him to a middle-level position in one of the bureaus would produce intolerable levels of status incongruence. To preserve the balance between rank and position it is much easier to create a new position and title appropriate to the officer's rank, or to elevate an old one. One of the most common forms of vertical differentiation is deputizing. If new positions are needed, they are created by adding the world "Deputy" to an existing slot (for example, Deputy Assistant Director of Special Operations). Interestingly, over the past fifteen years State Department and embassy jobs have been reclassified upward by an average of two grades.[1] The result has been "more positions for chiefs but fewer and fewer responsible posts for Indians" (Campbell, 1971, p. 123). If the new position adds another rung to the hierarchical ladder, the incumbent becomes a regular filtering point for messages moving up and down.

The second response involves horizontal rather than vertical differentiation. The senior official is given his due by dividing a position previously held by a single individual. This technique works more easily with staff than with line positions. Problems of line authority are created when two men are appointed Deputy Assistant Director of Special Operations. These difficulties are greatly reduced when the candidate is named Special Assistant to the Director, or Legal Adviser, or is placed in some other senior staff capacity. The result can be

[1] At the time of writing there is a move afoot to reduce the grade levels of all jobs in the department except those at the very top. The American Foreign Service Association (AFSA) is strongly opposed to this step, mainly because it would result in slower promotions.

summarized as the Law of Overstaffing: *Positions expand to accommodate the officials available.* To prove that he is alive and active, the new appointee will contribute his share of reports and attend his complement of committee meetings. The other incumbent or superior will continue to do likewise. The net effect will be an increase in the total volume of paper, with the overloading effects already noted.

## Summary

Pressures for hierarchy and rules arise from the goals, culture, and internal structure of the government agency. When agency goals are ambiguous and officials have no direct indicators of performance effectiveness, adherence to rules may emerge as the most useful operational guide to success. The organizational goal of "policy" in the case of the State Department leads to a heavy emphasis on written reports and thereby to increased message volume in the system. A heavy message volume, in interaction with other conditions, strains the information-handling capacity of senior officials and creates the conditions for added hierarchy. A second source of pressure for hierarchy and rules is a combination of functional specialization and interdependence of activities. In the State Department the vagueness of "foreign policy" coupled with the dispersion of responsibility in the foreign affairs arena means that many different agencies and many different subunits within the department participate or concur in a given decision. This situation creates a demand for hierarchical authority as a means of reconciling diverse views and arriving at an ordering of policy alternatives. Similar demands for hierarchy arise from competition or conflict between organizational subunits such as the regional and functional bureaus, or personnel systems such as the Foreign Service Officer Corps and the Civil Service. Hierarchy may also be added to equalize status relationships in a rank-conscious public organization.

In the State Department a major source of rules and regulations as well as demands for hierarchy is the unusually heavy emphasis placed on internal security. This emphasis stems in part from the McCarthy loyalty attacks of the 1950s and in part from the sensitive nature of diplomacy and foreign affairs. Special problems are also created by the great distance between the center and the periphery of the State Department's organizational network. The separation between Washington and the field and the great variation in conditions from one field post to another increase the volume of formal communications and the need for rules and regulations to cover the shifting contingencies. Finally, one of the most direct sources of increased hierarchy is overstaffing, especially at the senior levels of an agency. An excess of officials at the top is typically accommodated in two ways: vertical differentiation, or the adding of one senior position beneath another, and horizontal differentiation, or the splitting of one position into two or more at approximately the same level.

# 6 • Abdication at the Bottom

Bureaucracy seems to flourish in public agencies with high accountability at the top and low risk-taking at the bottom. Dean Rusk once remarked: "There are those who think that the heart of bureaucracy is a struggle for power. This is not the case at all. The heart of the bureaucratic problem is the inclination to avoid responsibility." While Rusk missed the connection between power struggles and the avoidance of responsibility, there is much truth to his observation. If operating officials refer even minor decisions to their superiors, hierarchy will expand to fill the responsibility gap. If the buck-passing continues through higher levels, the hierarchy will be further elongated. Hierarchy thus comes to serve as an organizational extension ladder. As decisions are passed upward, the ladder stretches to cover the distance between the point of origin and the point of action.

It is too easy, however, to attribute low risk-taking to an "inclination to avoid responsibility." This statement implies a character deficiency in the bureaucrat that has nothing to do with his organizational experience. In effect it says that he, rather than the system, is to blame for the growth of bureaucracy. Such a view has obvious ideological appeal for a man sitting at the top of an organization and receiving reams of paper from below, but it is misleading. More to the point is an approach that considers two interacting conditions: the personality characteristics of the official entering the organization and his learning experience in that milieu.

### Initial Tendencies

The public employee is often stereotyped as a semi-incompetent whose passion for security outweighs his drive to innovate. He is someone who takes refuge in the bureaucratic cocoon because he can't make it in business, industry, or elsewhere. Avoidance of responsibility thus is a natural outgrowth of his basic personality. Is there any evidence to support this view? Does the public servant really show a distinctive character structure?

Warner and his colleagues (1963) explored this problem in their massive study of U. S. federal executives. The results suggest that, as adults, these officials are unusually dependent on the external world. This mode of adaptation, they contend, was learned early in life and brought to the job. "It is a mode that requires adapting oneself to other people, to handling situations within a framework of cooperation and interdependence, of holding in check one's own piercing desires and aspirations until the moment is judged propitious" (p. 248). Supporting data are drawn from a projective device known as the Thematic Apperception Test (TAT).

The authors argue (pp. 241-242) that the environment of the public organization arouses considerable fear and anxiety in the dependency-prone executive.

For a person functioning within such a system, there is an Indian behind every tree. The executive cannot, however, in a fit of aggressive action simply go out and scalp the Indian. The system, with its carefully balanced set of structures, obligations, and rewards, demands above all both correctness and a show of deference.

The solution lies in a trade-off between spontaneity and security. To reduce his own ambivalence about aggression and to meet the demands of the system, the official falls back on the more safe and predictable elements of the environment—rules, regulations, and precedent. The federal system and the specific agency environment become sources of security and emotional support. If one complies with their demands they can be reasonable and nurturant masters. But to retain the nurturant and to restrain the noxious, the executive must act with caution. He cannot call too much attention to himself, "make waves," or provoke hostility from others (ibid., p. 247).

While this argument has an appealing simplicity, the supporting ev-

idence is far from convincing. Even if we accept the data showing relatively high dependence among federal executives, it does not follow
that such dependence is a basic personality trait antedating employment. Caution and low risk-taking may also arise as direct responses
to experience in the federal executive system. This interpretation
would square with evidence suggesting marked differences in aggres-
siveness and risk-taking among federal agencies, even in the field of
foreign affairs. During our study a senior official at State commented:
"I could not conceive of groups that did not wish to expand upon
their areas of authority . . . It was so contrary, such a dramatic contrast, with the aggressive thrust of the Commerce Department, for example, in their efforts to take over the overseas commercial functions." We thus return to a primordial question in the social sciences:
is it official nature or organizational nurture that leads to low risk-
taking? The findings of the Warner group do not supply an answer to
this question.

### Bureaucratic Socialization

A more direct damper on organizational risk-taking is the reward
system of the public agency. Three critical questions can be raised
about any reward system: (1) what behaviors and attitudes does it encourage and discourage; (2) what are the motives to which it appeals;
and (3) what is the range of rewards and punishments available to
produce conformity. The more an employee identifies with the organization, and the greater the range of its potential control over his life,
the greater the likelihood of producing conformity. The root question
is one of socialization: to what extent is an organization able to mold
an individual to fit its own behavioral expectations?

A pivotal hypothesis is that appeals to different motives, when
backed by appropriate sanctions, lead to different patterns of organizational behavior. A firm that relies exclusively on appeals to fear ("if
you're five minutes late you'll be fired") can expect, at best, high predictability and low innovation. A research and development organization that appeals *only* to the ego satisfactions of its scientists may be
marked by high innovation but low predictability. Table 2 shows

some common motivational appeals in organizations, together with their likely consequences for organizational behavior.[1]

The motivational mix in federal agencies varies, but in most cases includes heavy emphasis on security. The rewards are job tenure, regular promotions, adequate salaries, a clean work place, and better-than-average retirement benefits. Many positions, particularly at higher levels, involve inherently interesting work and offer the employee ample opportunities to express his talents. But in most established agencies there is little call for entrepreneurship, creativity, innovation, and risk-taking. These qualities are neither solicited nor rewarded, and may be punished. As Gawthrop puts it (1969, p. 213):

One of the basic problems facing executive branch personnel officials in all departments and agencies is that only limited rewards are available to career bureaucrats who demonstrate a capacity and a willingness for innovative behavior. On the other hand, substantial rewards are generally available to the executive administrator who chooses to respond faithfully to the expressed needs of his clientele and congressional groups.

If fear is not the dominant motivational appeal, it usually lurks in the background. The bureaucrat quickly learns that he may be subject to attack from many fronts: head-hunting columnists, headline-hunting congressmen, irate constituency groups, opportunistic White House assistants, rivals in other agencies, a fickle agency director, or consumers' groups. Widespread public suspicion of bureaucrats and bureaucracy reinforces an atmosphere of muted (and sometimes not-so-muted) fear.

Swift to censure and slow to praise, the public exerts its pressures upon the federal executive in no uncertain terms. The public image of the bureaucrat may be just or unjust; it may be highly rational and hysterical; criticism may be directed at one man or one action; it may

[1] See Katz and Kahn (1966) for a similar typology. They propose four major motive patterns: legal compliance, instrumental satisfaction, self-expression, and internalization (the incorporation of organizational goals or subgoals into one's value system and self-concept). Their schema seems better suited to the private corporation than to the public agency. It makes no reference, for example, to the power motivation seen in many public organizations, nor to the motivation for group loyalty seen in such groups as the Foreign Service.

Table 2. Motivational appeals and organizational behavior

| Primary motivational appeal | Dominant organizational behavior |
| --- | --- |
| 1. *Fear:* punishments for failure to meet expected standards. | 1. Minimal compliance with performance standards; no risk-taking; strong pressure for additional rules to cover ambiguous situations. High turnover. |
| 2. *Security:* adequate salary, fringe benefits; job tenure, stability of employment; semiautomatic advancement. | 2. Dependability; occasional risk-taking in response to extraordinary circumstances; moderate pressure for rules to reduce ambiguity, increase dependability; performance sometimes beyond minimal standards. |
| 3. *Group identification:* esprit de corps, loyalty to traditions of elite cadre in larger organization (such as FBI, Foreign Service, Marine Corps, Communist Party in Russia). | 3. Conformity to traditions of group, maintenance of ties with it; risk-taking if rewarded by group; if part of a larger organization, pressure to advance interests of elite at expense of nonelite; strong competition for advancement within group; inter-unit conflicts. |
| 4. *Power:* individual advancement; increased influence over policy decisions in agency; greater access to and influence in other centers of power (for example, the White House); broader jurisdictional or other "territorial" rights for self or agency. | 4. Intense competition; high risk-taking if associated with advancement; development of external alliances to enhance internal influence; low dependability, high individualism. |
| 5. *Pride in work:* satisfaction in a job well done, whether measured by one's own standards or those of a craft or profession; intrinsic gratification with tasks performed. | 5. Organizational behavior dependent on other conditions, such as performance goals, expectations of colleagues, and nature of work. Low predictability, problems of coordination in a "loose" system. |
| 6. *Internalization:* incorporation of organizational goals into one's value system and self-concept (Katz and Kahn, 1966). | 6. High risk-taking and innovation if called for by organizational goals; low emphasis on rules, external means of compliance; low demand for hierarchical supervision; moderate to high competition between individuals and units. |

be a shotgun attack on a whole agency, a whole program, or a whole administration. It does not matter. The civilian executive suddenly finds himself in the position of a meek subordinate answering to an overbearing master (ibid., p. 241).

This combination of fear and security creates a strong pull toward the tried and true. "Wild ideas" are suspect from birth. They may bring harm not only to their creator, but to his unit or even the entire agency. Commenting on the MOP reorganization, a division chief in the O area expressed an attitude widely shared in the federal government:

My personal reaction was that government structures are built up by trial and error and working up structures that fulfill a task. Getting rid of this layering broke down all the filters that are safeguards in the system to see that ideas are soundly staffed. There is too much emphasis on the judgment and authority of one man. It is so drastic that it has not become an effective mechanism.

Significantly, the main emphasis is not on whether the MOP system did work, but rather on the certainty that it *could not* work because of its drastic departure from precedent. While bureaucratic entrepreneurship is certainly permitted and often practiced, it must be done quietly and without arousing attention or perceptions of "unsoundness." Within such a motivational framework, the rewards for risk-taking are few and the hazards many. Limited discretion, adherence to rules, and checking with one's superiors are the most direct and sensible ways of minimizing fear and maximizing security.

### The Foreign Service

The most striking feature of the reward system in the Foreign Service from 1966 to 1970 was the strength of its de facto appeals to fear. Since that time several efforts have been made to change this system, but they have not removed the underlying causes of fear.

In 1969 the State Department's Task Force on the Stimulation of Creativity sampled a wide range of opinion within the Foreign Service on the general question of organizational rewards. It concluded:

Conformity is prized in the Foreign Service above all other qualities . . . The pressures to avoid rocking the boat, to avoid dress and behavior which depart from the norms of the group, to avoid expression of controversial views are of the subtle, unspoken kind which are hard to document. But we have the testimony of a broad cross section of the officers whose views we sought that they are a powerful, all-pervasive influence. Such pressures, of course, are the death of the creative impulse (U. S. Department of State, 1970, p. 310).

On the basis of the typology proposed in Table 2, one might also expect to find heavy emphasis on group loyalty to an elite corps. There was, indeed, such an emphasis. The same Task Force commented (p. 311): "The Foreign Service has traditionally prided itself on being a kind of elite corps." However, given the peculiar conditions of the post-McCarthy environment, identification with this elite indirectly raised the salience of fear. The dilemma is acute: the greater the eliteness or prestige of an organization, the more the member will identify with it; the greater the identification, the greater the desire to stay in it; the greater the desire to stay in, the greater the fear of being thrown out; the greater the perceived probability of being thrown out, the greater the anxiety about staying in; the greater the anxiety about staying in, the more effective are appeals to fear and pressures for conformity within the system. Such was the motivational plight of the Foreign Service Officer during the period in question.

*Selection-Out and the Age Lump*

In the late 1960s there were two immediate and related sources of anxiety for the Foreign Service Officer: the provision for selection-out, and an unfortunate "age lump" in the hierarchy.

Under 1968 regulations an FSO ranked in the lowest 10 percent of his class for more than a year became a candidate for selection-out. The normal anxieties of professional advancement were aggravated in the Foreign Service by the age lump at the top of the career ladder. Largely as a result of Wristonization, the service had a heavier concentration of staff in the upper and upper-middle levels (FSO-1 to 4) than in its lower ranks. The seven to eight hundred remaining Wristonees were clustered around FSO-2, 3, and 4. Table 3 shows the distribution of FSOs by rank in 1969. Interestingly, there were over a hundred more officers in the top two of the regular ranks (FSO-1 and 2) than in the bottom three (FSO-6 to 8).

Table 3. Foreign Service Officer personnel by rank, July 1, 1969

| Grade | Number of personnel |
|---|---|
| Career ambassador | 3 |
| Career minister | 55 |
| FSO-1 | 324 |
| FSO-2 | 425 |
| FSO-3 | 661 |
| FSO-4 | 645 |
| FSO-5 | 547 |
| FSO-6 | 421 |
| FSO-7 | 167 |
| FSO-8 | 26 |
| Total FSOs | 3,274 |

SOURCE: Personnel Chart, Department of State, July 1969.

From a motivational standpoint, the tightest squeeze was in the middle. With the upper reaches crowded, the FSO-4s and 5s faced intense competition to be promoted before reaching the maximum time-in-grade of eight to ten years. For men in their thirties, with few job prospects elsewhere, this situation produced evident anxiety. Tensions were heightened by the odium attached to selection-out. One officer commented:[2]

The worst cases involve FSO-4s who may have twenty or more years of service but who have not reached age fifty. Unlike the military services where retirement after twenty years is considered both honorable and pensionable, such is not the case in the Foreign Service. These men, normally with children still going through the educational process, are thus forced on the job market without the cushion provided by even a small pension. Worse yet, by now in their forties, they have little in the way of marketable skills. (What business wants to hire a broken-down political officer?)

[2] The author served as a consultant to the State Department's Task Force on Performance Appraisal and Promotions and had access to the background material collected for its report. The above statement was made in a letter to this task force.

Figures on dismissal showed an objective basis of concern for the FSO-4. Between 1967 and 1970, ninety Class 4 officers were selected-out, compared with fourteen Class 5, twenty-six Class 6, and nine Class 7 officers. In the same period, 35 percent of the officers selected-out were between the ages of forty-three and forty-seven—occupationally obsolescent but ineligible for retirement.

Although the greatest pinch was felt by midcareer officers, the specter of dismissal instilled fear in all except the very top levels of the service. During our study an officer observed:

There is something wrong with our entire personnel system. It doesn't encourage a very creative, lively atmosphere. Maybe we need a substitute for the present efficiency reports, selection-out, and promotion. I don't have the answer, but there's a tremendous stigma to selection-out. There should be a system to permit a person to bow out with grace and without such shame.

Another man wrote to the Task Force on Performance Appraisal and Promotions: "The up-or-out promotion system has an all-pervasive effect in State; it keeps people anxious and unsmiling . . . it penalizes coaching, it creates hostility and apathy toward the service."

## The Performance Appraisal System

The appraisal system in the Foreign Service was and is a prime source of uncertainty and anxiety about promotions. It calls for an officer to be reviewed each year by specially appointed selection boards. The critical materials for the review are the efficiency reports prepared by his superior during the preceding year, as well as earlier performance ratings. At the time of this study, the performance evaluation form contained two parts: an efficiency report completed by the superior and shown to the rated officer; and a Development Appraisal Report, which remained secret unless the officer was a candidate for selection-out.[3] The latter contained ratings of such personal characteristics as the officer's appearance, bearing, range of interests, family (for example, his wife's representational ability, attitude toward the

---

[3] The secret report has subsequently been dropped. Many feel that this change has solved nothing, since it increases the likelihood of bland reports allowing for little discrimination among candidates.

host country, participation in local community organizations, involvement in U. S. functions), as well as limiting factors such as leadership and executive ability, growth capacity, and advancement potential. The concrete task for the selection boards was to rank-order all candidates within a given grade level. Because the board was not familiar with all of the candidates, and because the number was typically large, the written reports played an extremely important part in the appraisal.

Three aspects of the rating process deserve close scrutiny because of their impact on anxiety and risk-taking: the rating dimensions; factors influencing the rater's judgment; and the inability of the selection boards to make adequate discriminations among the efficiency reports.

*Rating dimensions.* The criteria suggested in the 1968 instructions to rating officers placed great emphasis on caution, judgment, and deference (cf. Warwick, 1970). The "Precepts for the 1968 Selection Boards" further suggested that the department was much more sensitive to past failures than present successes. Consider this instruction:

Single unfavorable episodes from the past should be appraised as to lasting importance, and failings which have been overcome should be discounted. To give undue weight to past reports of defects which have already been corrected would be patently unfair to the officer concerned.

Despite the disavowal at the end, the message to the boards was clear: watch out for the troublemaker and look for the problems that *may* recur. The instructions also emphasized "good judgment," "service discipline," and "discretion," with no mention of originality, initiative, innovation, and results. The tone of the document was captured by this sentence: "Initiative should be judged not only on results but also on demonstrated soundness of reasoning and judgment." If an officer wished to innovate, he ran the risk not only of failing in the experiment itself, which would almost certainly be held against him, but also of being accused of poor judgment even if the effort was successful. As the Task Force on Creativity notes: "Under circumstances in which the quality of service is high and panels are under pressure to find failings, the best way to insure a high probability of being right is simply to minimize risks, the antithesis of creativity" (U. S. Department of State, 1970, p. 311).

[*108*]

*Supervisor-subordinate relations.* The relations between supervisors and subordinates in the State Department's hierarchy also colored the rating process. The department's managerial philosophy is much the same as that pervading the federal executive structure—a top-down, chain-of-command approach exalting the authority of the superior and above all the ambassador. Crisis orientation and security consciousness reinforce such attitudes. In this milieu the line between risk-taking and insubordination is blurred. A member of the selection boards observed:

Advocacy of innovation can all too easily become identified as indiscipline. Indeed, the more earnestly that some officer presses his case, the more likely it is that his harried superiors will take offense and remember the matter at the time for writing efficiency reports. Yet, if the advocate merely offers his new idea in a genteel fashion which hurts no one's feelings, it is very improbable that the idea will get anywhere in the bureaucratic maze . . . case histories can be cited of even moderately crusading officers whose careers have been adversely affected in consequence of their policy enthusiasms (ibid., p. 312).

The generality and ambiguity of the rating dimensions meant that interpersonal frictions could be translated into unfavorable efficiency reports. If a superior disliked a subordinate but could not fault him on performance, he could shift his ire to amorphous dimensions such as integrity and courage, adaptability, versatility, motivation, and, of course, tact. It is obviously damning to have one's integrity impugned on an efficiency report. A low rating, offered with little or no explanation, could be used by promotion panels as a justification for holding the officer back for another year. Personality-oriented evaluations, such as those used in 1968, were also potentially greater sources of anxiety than a results-oriented rating scheme. It may not be gratifying but it is at least tolerable to learn that one's written reports suffer by comparison with other officers'; it is a much more severe blow to learn that one is deficient in intellectual caliber, discretion, ambition, or integrity—all dimensions appearing on the 1968 forms.

*Ranking in a vacuum.* Despite the previous comments, the greatest problem with Foreign Service efficiency reports was their blandness. Ratings were heavily skewed toward the favorable end of the scales, allowing little discrimination among officers. This tendency toward "soft" ratings is common in many fields, ranging from graduate schools to the military services. In the Foreign Service it was accentuated by the provision for selection-out. Raters knew perfectly well that a single negative rating might hold up a subordinate for years, and perhaps even bring him to the point of dismissal. The practical consequences were twofold: (1) large numbers of officers were virtually indistinguishable on the basis of the current year's efficiency reports; and (2) given the widespread inflationary tendency, negative or even indifferent ratings became highly damaging on a relative scale.

The problem for the selection boards was to find some reasonable way of differentiating among officers in this rating vacuum. In any given year a few candidates would stand out as being exceptionally promising. These were set aside and given the top ranks. A few were so obviously poor that they were relegated to the bottom. The rest might very well look alike in their recent ratings—all good to excellent. In this circumstance it was tempting to look for "burrs" in a candidate's folder. The evaluation process shifted from promoting to *not* promoting an officer. Those whose folders were relatively clean were placed in the upper ranks, the rest in the lower. As one officer put it:

Performance reports for a large number of our better officers tend to be so concentrated on the higher end of the scale that it is difficult to discriminate among the officers. Differentiation comes very quickly, however, if an officer at some time in his career gets a substandard performance report, even if it may be primarily because he and his supervisor have a personality difference.

Even a single skeleton could rattle in the officer's personnel closet for eight or ten years. Hence the strong pressures to avoid "incidents."

*The effects: caution and conformity.* The performance appraisal and promotion system in the Foreign Service removed most incentives for initiative and risk-taking. The Task Force on Creativity reported

a widespread belief among Foreign Service Officers that the promotion system tends to stifle creativity, discourage risk-taking, and reward conformity. The effect appears to be due in large part to the interaction of two factors. The first is the fiercely competitive nature of the Service resulting from the selection-out principle. The second is the exceptional importance of the efficiency report in determining the rate of an officer's advancement. The knowledge that the good opinion of his supervisor is crucial in determining whether he advances at a normal rate or falls behind and is eventually selected out can act as a powerful deterrent to a forthright expression by an officer of views on policy matters which may be at variance with the views of his supervisor (ibid., p. 312).

Another officer expressed similar conclusions:[4]

Our present performance appraisal and promotion policies are eliminating the very bad *and the very good officers* and pushing along the careful, the cautious, the "cooperative," and the conservative. In my last four years in the Service, I have seen one very fine officer forced out because of the jealousies of a politically-appointed ambassador, and several others stalled in their careers—not because they were lacking, but because they were too good and too honest . . . The point is that you cannot have it both ways. We cannot have an appraisal system which rewards conformity by calling it "cooperation," is suspicious of boldness—calling it "combativeness"—and discourages initiative because it is "reckless," and expect that system to produce brave, innovative, creative officers . . .

The problem, as I see it, is that every pressure in the system operates downward from superior to subordinate—generating forces for conformity, caution, and non-creativity, which are almost overwhelming.

A senior official with experience in the Central Intelligence Agency and the Federal Bureau of Investigation contrasted their internal climate with that of State. Both the FBI and the CIA, he said, maintain tight control over their employees. "However, these are nothing like State, where everyone runs scared so far as levelling with their officers [superiors] is concerned." He attributed this behavior to the promotion system. "No one wants to jab someone for fear that it will get in their file and contribute to that person being selected-out. There is much concern with the possibility of ruining someone's career and the fact that once something gets into a file, it can dog that person forever." In such an atmosphere avoidance of risk-taking and narrowing of discretion were rational courses of action. The result, however, was an increased demand for hierarchy to provide the necessary supervision, and greater pressure for rules to signal correct behavior.

[4] From a 1969 letter to the State Department Task Force on Performance Appraisal and Promotions.

*Recent Developments*

Since about 1970 the performance appraisal and promotion system has been marked by considerable turbulence and fluidity, although to date it has not changed drastically. The relevant task force report in *Diplomacy for the 70's* (U. S. Department of State, 1970) recommended a major overhaul of the rating system, as well as other changes. A key point in the suggested reforms was a shift away from personality-oriented evaluations to a more results-oriented approach in which an officer's performance would be related to a unit's goals. The merits and demerits of this method have been subject to considerable debate, but no basic change has resulted.

An event that precipitated intensive scrutiny of the promotion system both inside and outside the department was the suicide of FSO Charles Thomas upon news that he had been selected-out. The Thomas case stirred such an uproar that selection-out was suspended for about two years and, at the initiative of the American Foreign Service Association, subjected to court challenge. In December 1973 the practice of selection-out without a prior hearing was ruled unconstitutional by a federal judge in Washington.

Despite the earlier observations on caution and conformity, it is only fair to note a heightened Foreign Service militancy in the past five years, particularly among younger officers. If one could hazard a guess about the future, it would be that the present generation of officers in grades 5 to 8 will be less passive than their elders in the face of a threatening reward system. The caution and deference reported by many observers, including the rated officers themselves, may have been a unique response to the devastating events of the 1950s, including the age lump created by the Wriston program. As the American Foreign Service Association becomes a more active bargaining agent, we may expect further changes to lessen the fear-provoking aspects of life in the Foreign Service.

**Summary**

Low risk-taking in public organizations favors the emergence of tall hierarchies. While many have argued that public employees tend to restrict discretion and avoid responsibility, the explanations of this behavior have been unsatisfactory. One line of thought is that employees enter public organizations with strong dependency needs and satisfy these needs by abdicating responsibility. The evidence to support this view is fragmentary. The line of explanation favored here emphasizes the employee's experience with the reward system of the organization. Even federal agencies differ greatly in the appeals made to such motives as fear, security, power, and group loyalty. The central hypothesis of the discussion is that the dominant motives tapped by the reward system will have far-reaching effects on employee behavior, and thus indirectly on demands for hierarchy and rules. In most federal agencies the overriding motivational appeal is to security, with a lesser emphasis on fear. As a result there is little incentive for risk-taking and innovation, while predictability and faithful response to outside demands are rewarded.

In the Foreign Service in the late 1960s a variety of historical and organizational circumstances raised the salience of fear above security. The two major sources of fear were the provision for selection-out and restricted promotion possibilities. The relatively high occupational prestige of the service stigmatized officers who were selected-out. Yet overcrowding at the top meant limited possibilities for promotion. This situation generated intense competition within the Foreign Service. The performance appraisal system also contributed to heightened anxiety about retention and promotion and fostered an attitude of caution, limited discretion, and low risk-taking. Several recent events, including increased Foreign Service militancy and a court decision against selection-out, may have lessened the pressures for conformity.

# 7 • Escalation to the Top

Pressures for hierarchy and rules arise at the top as well as at the bottom of a public organization. If the hierarchical ladder is pushed upward by the tendency of lower-level officials to seek clearances, it is also pulled upward when high-level administrators insist on clearing, approving, authorizing, and deciding routine matters. In general, the greater the volume of communications and the greater the demand for centralization of decision-making, the greater the pressure for added levels of supervision to serve as intermediate filters. And the larger the number of hierarchical levels, the greater the demand for explicit rules to cover the reception, distribution, storage, and retrieval of information entering the organization. This, in essence, is the story of bureaucratic growth in many agencies.

The State Department provides a prime example of the elongation of hierarchy through the combined forces of heavy communications volume and tight centralization of decision-making. Many observers have been amazed at the flow of paper to the Office of the Secretary. Some descriptions suggest a gargantuan vacuum cleaner drawing thousands of the most routine messages from Washington and the field to the seventh floor of Foggy Bottom. In the course of a 1966 interview William Crockett described the resulting bottleneck in rather blunt terms:

The more we go this way [decentralization] the better the State Department is going to operate—the less burdened they are going to be with stacks and stacks of papers, things that are called up to them. I don't think that in today's world the State Department can be centralized and the people on top do their jobs properly, because they're going to be swamped with crud. This is what they're swamped with down there, and this is what they complain about; they're collection points of crud now. They won't let anyone use their head and take on responsibility. If you don't do that you can't really complain about all the stuff coming up.

While part of the reason for this overload is the reluctance of the Foreign Service to make decisions, it is also clear that the upper echelons of State insist on being the final clearance point for a high proportion of the department's actions. Two elements play a critical role in defining this pattern of reporting and decision-making: the overall volume of communications entering the Department of State, and strong demands for centralization. To understand these elements we must examine the total organizational system of the department, including its operating environment, power setting, leadership patterns, tasks, and other internal characteristics.

## The Operating Environment

An agency's operating environment is the setting within which it carries out its day-to-day activities. As noted in Chapter 4, four characteristics of this environment are particularly significant for governmental organizations: complexity, uncertainty, threat, and dispersion.

The operating environment of the State Department is the international system. Specifically, it is the set of nations with which the United States maintains diplomatic relations or in which it has a political interest. The department's specific mission is to represent the United States in a variety of areas, gather information on the political, social, cultural, and economic conditions in a country or region, and practice other aspects of diplomacy. Given the scope of international relations, the values at stake, and the intricacies of the events involved, State's operating environment is marked by a high degree of complexity, uncertainty, threat, and dispersion. These conditions call for extensive data-gathering and reporting to and from field posts.

The inherent uncertainty of international politics means that large amounts of information must be gathered "just in case." A political officer assigned to a remote African nation may spend weeks on end clipping articles from local newspapers, attending diplomatic receptions, entertaining local officials, and manning such other listening posts as are available. His output may consist mainly of weekly or fortnightly reports summarizing his observations of politics, intrigues, and power contenders in a seemingly insignificant nation. His associate in the economic section may also spend hours compiling statistics on the country's imports and exports, major commodities, fiscal and monetary policy, and economic plans. Suddenly a traditional oligarchy is replaced with a left-leaning, modernizing military junta. The new chief of state, a colonel, immediately threatens to expropriate foreign holdings in the country, expel thousands of East Asian and British merchants, and develop close relations with Communist China. As the wire services crackle, the somnolent African republic moves to the front stage of international politics. The ambassador, the country director, the Assistant Secretary of State for African Affairs, the Under Secretary, the Secretary, and the White House demand an instant background report on the crisis. All available data from State, CIA, Defense, and other agencies are combed for diagnostic information. When a crisis erupts, woe to the FSO caught with his intelligence down. The penalties for overreporting are negligible; those for oversight are severe.

Because of the complexity of the events covered, reports from the field usually must be expressed in qualitative terms. A full and nuanced account typically requires a lengthy prose narrative rather than a brief set of statistical tables. The latter are useful for summarizing balance of payments deficits and monetary fluctuations, but they can scarcely encapsulate multifaceted political intrigue, complex personalities, and intricate alliances. But qualitative expression requires more words and thus a heavier flow of communications into the State Department. The word count is often inflated by the traditional emphasis of the Foreign Service on faultless prose and the well-turned phrase.

State's operating environment also contains a strong element of threat. The values at stake in its daily work run the gamut from life and death to minor assaults on the prestige of the United States. However, even a seemingly trivial issue can sometimes escalate to crisis proportions within a matter of hours. Hence not only crisis, but the possibility of crisis, places a premium on extensive reporting. Since the officer in the field can never be sure which set of events may prove critical, his safest course is to provide more rather than less coverage.

Finally, the dispersion of the State Department—the distance from center to periphery—increases the volume of written communications. The distance between Washington and the field precludes informal communication such as corridor conversations. Moreover, because of the interagency setting of foreign affairs, almost any message transmitted from the field may have implications for units other than State. The standard procedure, therefore, is to send airgrams, cables, or other written messages with copies to all interested agencies and parties.

The convergence of these four conditions produces an extremely large message volume to and from the State Department. At the time of our study the telegraph branch handled about 4,000 separate messages a day for a total of 15,000,000 words a month. Over half of this cable traffic was classified, which meant special handling. In January 1967 the department sent and received almost 45,000 cables. On the receiving end copies were sent to some sixty departments and agencies, most often the CIA, the Department of Defense, the White House, and the Departments of Commerce, Treasury, and Agriculture. In the same period there were over 300 international telephone calls per day, while the department leased about 100 overseas teletype lines (Leacacos, 1968, pp. 42-43). State also handles about 20,000,000 pieces of mail each year, and maintains a staff of diplomatic couriers who log over 130,000 travel miles per annum. On a typical day a large embassy may receive 400,000 words of incoming messages, the equivalent of an 850-page book (Attwood, 1967). The message flow between the department, the field, and other agencies thus reaches astronomical proportions.

### The Power Setting

The power setting of the State Department contributes to its overall message volume as well as to the centralization of decision-making. Interagency competition for influence accentuates an already strong tendency toward voluminous preventive reporting. In foreign affairs, as in journalism, exclusive information is a prized commodity. An agency with a "scoop" is more likely to be an active participant in policy decisions than one without. The competition in the data-gathering field is stiff, and the State Department is often at a disadvantage in contests with the CIA and the military services. The very nature of the diplomat's work makes it difficult to move behind the scenes with the same facility as a CIA operative. While the latter is sitting in a café with a paid informant, the political officer may have to rest content clipping articles from the morning's paper. Under these conditions embassy reports may try to make up in quantity what they lack in exclusiveness.

The threat of congressional hearings and public criticism increases the premium on reports from the field. The political officer who fails to identify a successful revolutionary movement is liable not only to censure within the department but to public castigation from Congress and the press. An example is the scapegoating following Fidel Castro's turn to the Soviet bloc in 1960. The anti-Communist elements in the press and Congress immediately began to ask, "Why didn't the people in the Cuban embassy know Castro was a Communist?" Ironically, several prominent Foreign Service Officers were drummed out of the department for their *accurate* intelligence on the downfall of the Chiang regime in China. More recently, however, the general presumption has been in favor of knowledge.

The large element of risk in diplomacy and foreign affairs predisposes the State Department to a centralized system of communications and decision-making. This normal tendency is magnified by several elements in the department's power setting. One considered earlier is the system of multiple interdependencies among foreign affairs agencies. The resulting communications system tends to draw messages to the top of each agency for clearances, concurrences, comments, or approval. Also discussed in Chapter 4 was the demand for accountability placed on senior officials in the State Department. To cover themselves, these officials insist on a high degree of control over the actions of their subordinates. Such control usually entails a high degree of centralization. Another factor in the 1960s was the tendency of Presidents and their senior staff to break through State's hierarchy for direct access to sources of information. Commenting on this point in an interview in 1970, William Crockett observed:

The behavior of President Kennedy (and that of his brother, the Attorney General) and President Johnson (and their top staff aides) had a profound effect upon the State Department.

They frequently would call people within State directly to inquire about some crisis, issue or problem which somehow would come to their attention. This very act of direct confrontation caused most of the responsible officers of State to require a self-imposed instant, minute, and up-to-the-minute knowledge of all problems, issues, and situations in their area of responsibility, just in order to be (appear to be) knowledgeable if and when the President should call. This resulted in mad scrambles and unnecessary sucking upward of information and action and placing all delegated responsibilities into complete turmoil.

Adding impetus to centralization was the increasing tendency for foreign policy decisions to be made outside the State Department. As one officer put it, "The State Department has been reduced largely to a think tank preparing options for Kissinger to submit to the President. It has no real powers of decision left" (New York *Times*, December 9, 1970). Following President Kennedy's disaffection with State in the early 1960s, more and more decisions passed to the White House and the National Security Council. Senior officials in the department were often called in as advisers or temporary crisis managers. To perform these roles they required full information about current trouble spots, so that intelligence was again called to the top of the system. With Henry Kissinger's move from the White House to the State Department, this pattern of escalation seems to have been halted. Whether his tenure as secretary will result in a permanent reversal of the pattern of the sixties is hard to know.

### Leadership

*From Marshall to Rusk*

The senior leadership of the State Department from World War II until the Nixon administration accelerated the centralization of decision-making. According to a 1970 self-study by State, the last secretary to work effectively with the department was George C. Marshall (1947-1949). "More important than simply using his staff resources well, he carried out the recommendations of his subordinates. Instead of relying on the clearance system . . . Marshall would assign primary responsibility to one office for a given issue, instructing it to consult with all interested parties, clearly setting out policies and options" (U. S. Department of State, 1970, p. 307). He also relied heavily on the Policy Planning Staff, which became a major locus of innovation during his term.

These close working relationships began to be undermined under Secretary Dean Acheson (1949-1953). "A lawyer by training, Acheson was more used to dealing with issues and individuals than with organizations. The Policy Planning Staff also played a vigorous role under him, but more because he had complete confidence in its director, Paul Nitze, than because he respected it as an institution" (ibid.). The first step toward bureaucratization came when Acheson shifted operational responsibilities downward to the assistant secretaries. While this might seem reasonable for a busy man, its principal effect was to increase the number of clearances required before action.

The gap between the secretary and the department became a chasm under John Foster Dulles (1953-1959).

Highly qualified in international affairs and enjoying the fullest confidence of President Eisenhower, Dulles scarcely used the Department at all. He reportedly told the President he would only accept the position of Secretary if he did not have to be responsible for the management of the Department and the Foreign Service. The position of Under Secretary for Administration was created early in his period of office to relieve him of management responsibilities (ibid., p. 308).

Dulles relied heavily on a small coterie of trusted associates, "leaving the vast majority of the Department out in the cold" (ibid.). The report concludes: "Under the combined effects of Secretary Dulles' closed-shop modes of operation, the onslaught of McCarthy, and the confusion of Departmental expansion, the creative contribution of the Department and the Foreign Service fell to new lows" (ibid.).[1]

In the 1960s Secretary Dean Rusk (1961-1969) made various efforts to integrate and rejuvenate the department. Some of these were discussed in Chapter 2. Almost all ran aground on the shoals of bureaucratic conservatism, inept leadership, and especially the Vietnam

[1] For a thorough treatment of Dulles' role as secretary, see Hoopes (1973).

War. In characteristically diplomatic language the Task Force on Creativity notes three main reasons for Rusk's lack of success:

First, the limit of Rusk's time and the makeup of his personality prevented him from actually encouraging creative controversy, taking firm stands, and then arguing them through in the highest councils. Second, the top leadership of the Department during this time failed to include others down the line in the creative process . . . Third, the Vietnam crisis preoccupied Rusk and the Department during the last three years of his tenure. The Secretary did not welcome dissent on the Vietnam issue and had little time to encourage dissent in other areas (ibid., p. 309).

In effect, though his style was very different, Rusk continued the tradition by cutting himself off from his own department. Nevertheless, centralization and escalation of decision-making continued apace. While Rusk himself spent great amounts of time outside the department, his office remained the principal collection point for thousands of cables, airgrams, and other communications.

## The Downward Winds of Change

As the secretaries became more remote, much of the initiative for departmental leadership passed to two officials: the under secretary and the deputy under secretary for administration. During the 1960s the two positions were often used as a base for top-down innovation. This approach was especially apparent during the tenure of Chester Bowles as under secretary. William Crockett recalls his experience with Bowles:[2]

On numerous occasions he tried by suggestions, questions and example to infuse "the system" with enthusiasm for new approaches, new policies, new faces, and new doctrine. His trips to Africa and the Near East in the early months of 1961 were in reality part of this effort to give the Department and the Foreign Service new insight and produce new directions in the whole range of Foreign Policy (administration to substance). He encouraged all of us to take a fresh look at every activity and policy that had been around long enough to be taken for granted.

[2] From a memorandum submitted by Crockett to the Task Force on Creativity, 1969, quoted here with his permission.

He, himself, was a factory of ideas for change. He made many suggestions for reviewing the system and suggested people who, if infused
into the system, would be stimulating and synergistic.

But—the methods he used probably produced so much animosity,
fear and resentment that they had the ultimate effect of being more
hurtful than helpful to innovation and creativity.

Perhaps one of the reasons for this was the fact that he was so enthusiastically creative himself, that those of us who had the problem of
"playing catch" to his suggestions were both overwhelmed and defensive.

Interestingly, Crockett now admits that he followed essentially the
same approach in his efforts to increase the effectiveness of the O area
and the Foreign Service. He concludes:

There was such a surge of action, examination, ideas, suggestions,
critique, review, inquiry and change coming from the top of the establishment (the President's office and the Department), especially during
the Kennedy years, that there was little room left for people down the
line to feel that their creativity was wanted or needed. The climate was
pretty general at the top . . . "We know the problems and we know the
answers. We'll tell you what to do and we'll expect you to *do it.*" The
new leadership was pretty cynical about the ability of the establishment to come up with anything new and this was no doubt felt.

The net effect of this centralized creativity was to dampen initiative in
other parts of the department and to reinforce already strong tendencies to hierarchical dependence.

   Initiative at the bottom is further sapped by the restriction of critical
information to senior officials. This policy has the effect of rendering
the judgments of junior officers either irrelevant or out of date.

Senior officers aware of this tend to play down those Juniors' judgments where information has not been disseminated. In the process an
important input can be lost. Although "exclusive" and "no" distribution (EXDIS and NODIS) traffic eventually is disseminated in one form or
another, such dissemination may occur after the fact. The result is that
senior policymakers are often overworked with simply keeping
abreast of the day's developments, and have little time to seek information and judgments outside the system (U. S. Department of State,
1970, p. 384).

Junior officers may feel that it is a losing battle to try to influence policy and thus confine their attention to more routine matters. And, of

course, their nonparticipation confirms the impression above that they really have nothing of value to contribute. The vicious circle of escalation is thus complete.

### The Effects: Hierarchy and Rules

The combination of a heavy message volume, a high degree of centralization, and tight security procedures (see Chapter 5) sets the stage for the elongation of hierarchy and the proliferation of rules. Pressures for added levels of supervision build up on both the sending and the receiving ends. The complexity, uncertainty, threat, and dispersion of the international environment, interagency competition and concurrence, the threat of public criticism, and the avoidance of risk-taking at the bottom contribute to the volume of words moving through the system. Security requirements dictate that messages follow formally designated transmission channels, ultimately moving to the top. The result is a massive clogging at the upper levels. Overloading is severe on the sending end also. Cables from the department to overseas missions must be signed by the secretary, under secretary, or other ranking official. Even at the embassy, cables must be "signed off" by the ambassador or the deputy chief of mission (DCM). The pressures for centralization in receiving are strengthened by the demands placed on high officials to be instant fonts of information on crisis areas. Similarly, the dispersion of responsibility for foreign policy, the high stakes involved in international affairs, and the high accountability of senior officers argue for strict control over messages sent from the department. Because it is impossible for a handful of top officials to cope with the resulting inflow and outflow of messages, the department suffers from information overload.

In theory several options are available for dealing with overload. One is simply to reduce the volume of messages entering the system. An order could be sent out imposing a page limit on all airgrams sent to Washington from the field. Former ambassador William Attwood (1967) has also proposed that State follow the system used by the wire services and by correspondents for major daily papers: prepare special reports only when the need arises. His suggestion overlooks not only the difficulty of defining "need" in an uncertain environment, but the high cost—personally and politically—of oversight. Many officers would argue that the present volume of reporting is fully justified on the basis of need. The imposition of page limits could also backfire in a very complex political situation involving many actors and multiple scenes.

The second broad possibility is to have better filtering of information in the field. The ambassador, the DCM, or the section heads might be asked to serve as de facto editors of information transmitted from their posts. But this suggestion also is impractical for several reasons: (1) the heavy demands already placed on an embassy's senior staff; (2) the difficulty of establishing criteria for editing; (3) the possibility of damage to one's career if he happens to edit out an important passage; and (4) damage to the morale of the original drafters. The last consideration can be extremely important in overseas posts characterized by frequent interactions during and after hours. In many embassies and USAID missions, job attitudes are strongly conditioned not only by relationships among the employees themselves, but among their wives and even children (for instance, in the American school). Under these conditions the ambassadors and DCMs may feel that it is not worth the costs to local morale to engage in extensive editing of field reports.

A third alternative is to decentralize screening, the more routine decision-making, and message-sending to the office or desk most concerned such as the country director in a regional bureau. This solution encounters the same obstacles seen earlier: the difficulty in defining what is "routine," the high cost of error, the accountability of the topmost officials, and the dispersion of responsibility for most matters across several bureaus or agencies.

Given the environmental pressures, the reward structure in the Foreign Service, and the managerial orthodoxy in the State Department, the only "realistic" solution is to add more levels of control at the top. If the Assistant Secretary for African Affairs becomes overloaded, he appoints a trusted deputy to screen the "really important" messages going to and from his bureau. If the trusted deputy cannot handle the message flow, he may add a layer beneath him (which may be obscured by the designation of "Special Assistant"). The same process occurs in the Office of the Secretary and the Office of the Under Secretary. The essential quality of this solution is that it involves vertical differentiation at the very top of a system, whether this be a regional bureau or the entire department. Overload is not handled by delegating additional responsibility to the operating managers, such as the country directors, but by creating new levels of clearance between them and the top. In the State Department this process of top-level fission has the added advantage of creating suitable positions for the surplus of high-ranking Foreign Service Officers who would otherwise be unemployed or underemployed.

The new screening layers typically increase the total volume of communications in the system. The official originally appointed to be a consumer of paper rapidly becomes a producer. He may digest and discard some of the messages sent from the lower rungs, but he will also want to provide unmistakable evidence to his superiors and subordinates that he is alive and well. The easiest way is to add editorial comments on cables, memoranda, and other messages passing his way. As a message moves up and down the hierarchical ladder, it thus may be subject to five, six, or more sets of marginal notations or supplementary memoranda commenting on the substance of the proposal or explaining what the author "really means." The more controversial the ideas involved, the greater the likelihood of such comments. William Attwood observes: "The layers of fat in State's midsection also hold up action on all kinds of requests from the field. Clearances often take time because officers initialing a paper feel obliged to suggest some changes just to show that they have read it" (1967, p. 48). In this way the gains achieved through filtering may be cancelled by the comments picked up along the transmission route.

The combination of high message volume and strict security procedures generates pressure for rules and regulations to cover message reception, distribution, storage, retrieval, and disposal. Upon reception an incoming cable or airgram must first be classified by its security category. Distribution is determined in part by this first sorting, but also by the salience of its content to the work of a departmental subunit or some other agency. The transmission of messages from one agency to another while maintaining tight security requires another set of rules, as does information storage, particularly of "live" messages. The department maintains its own Office of Security to develop and enforce rules on information handling, to protect against "bulging," and to watch over employee behavior that might jeopardize security (Chapter 9).

Voluminous rules and elaborate security procedures have several direct and indirect effects on the structure and organizational behavior of the State Department. First, they reinforce the already strong tendency to rely on formal channels of communication. While the objective security risks may not be great in a telephone conversation, the mere existence of wiretapping as a possibility leads the department to discourage such communication on secret matters. Reliance on formal channels, in turn, increases the overall message volume and the strain placed on nodal points in the hierarchy and thereby generates pressure for added layers. A second effect is an increase in personnel. Employees must be added to draft, disseminate, and enforce security regulations. These employees not only become new producers of paper, but create more reporting requirements for others. Third, there is a heightened attitude of caution in the department as a whole. A pervasive fear of security leaks and the concomitant penalties further reduce an already scant willingness to take risks. Fourth, the introduction of strict security rules may lead employees to request elaboration and specification for their own protection. Clerical employees may want to know, for example, precisely when classified files may and may not be open, how they are to be marked when open, exactly who may and may not see messages classified at different levels, what may be kept on top of their desks and what may not, and so on. The resulting additions to the manuals of rules and approved procedures further encumber an already slow transmission system.

These, then, are the principal roots of bureaucracy in the State Department. The most direct source of hierarchy and rules is communications overload at various points in the system. This stems in part from the overall message volume in the department and in part from an authority structure calling a high proportion of messages to the top. The reasons for a heavy message volume lie in the operating environment and power setting of the department, the nature of its work, the motivation of the Foreign Service, and other factors reviewed earlier. Pressures for centralization emanate from some of the same sources. All of these forces lead to the extension of hierarchy and the addition of rules, conditions which reinforce each other. The chain of influence producing bureaucracy in the State Department is summarized in Figure 6.

Figure 6. The bureaucratization process in the State Department

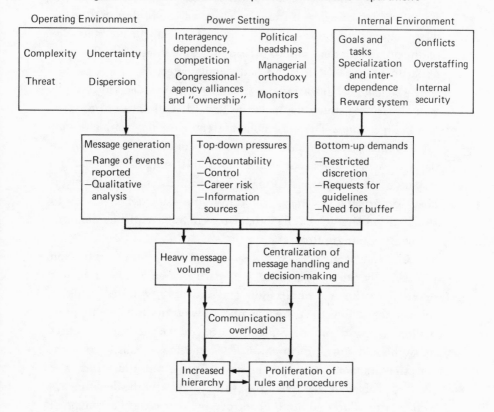

## Summary

Bureaucratic growth is stimulated by a combination of heavy communications volume and centralized information handling. The structure and operation of the U. S. Department of State show the influence of both elements. Four characteristics of the department's operating environment contribute to a heavy volume of reporting: the uncertainty of international politics, the complexity of the events covered, the values at stake, and the geographic dispersion of the organization. The convergence of these four conditions produces a heavy message volume to and from the department, and contributes to the pressures for centralized information handling and decision-making. The competitive and interdependent power setting in foreign affairs as well as the specter of congressional hearings and public criticism reinforce the same tendencies. An added source of centralization in the 1960s was the tendency of Presidents Kennedy and Johnson to make direct requests for information to midlevel officials in the State Department. The gradual shift of decision-making power from the State Department to the White House had a similar effect.

The behavior of the secretaries and other senior leaders since World War II has accelerated the tendency toward centralization in direct and indirect ways. The most notable trend, reaching its high point under John Foster Dulles, was the separation of the secretary from the department. As the senior leadership moved out, decision-making responsibilities became increasingly concentrated at the levels immediately beneath the secretary. Ironically, efforts by senior leaders to stimulate creativity from the top down seem to have further dampened initiative at the bottom.

The chapter concludes with a summary of the bureaucratization process in the State Department, with particular emphasis on the role of message volume, centralization, and security procedures. While in other organizations there are a number of ways of dealing with information overload, in the State Department various circumstances make the addition of hierarchical levels the most realistic solution. This step gradually augments the flow of paper and thus aggravates the very problem it was designed to solve. Similarly, the department's security procedures add to bureaucracy by increasing the volume of rules in the system, creating the need for additional staff to enforce them, and reinforcing the sense of caution.

# Part III    Bureaucratic Persistence

# 8 • Resistance to Change: The Hays Bill

The *O* area reforms of 1965-66 revealed potent internal pressures for bureaucratization and rebureaucratization within the State Department. Some of these, such as the perceived need for a deputy at the top of *O*, arose in response to a heavy volume of communications and demands for accountability to external controllers. Others, including the insecurities emanating from the performance evaluation system and a related fear of exposure to senior officials, were more distinctively domestic in character. But, in the definitive autopsy of MOP, it was primarily internal rather than external actions and decisions that led to restoration of the original hierarchy and rules. The next case we shall discuss, which took place at the same time and involved the same lead actor, calls attention to the hardy and pervasive extra-agency sources of resistance to change in the public bureaucracy.

The case consists of a widely debated legislative package introduced in the House of Representatives in 1965 and considered in the Senate in 1966. It had two components: (1) a bill (HR 6277) to establish a single personnel system integrating Civil Service and Foreign Service employees in the Department of State, the Agency for International Development (AID), and the U. S. Information Agency (USIA); and (2) a proposal for the lateral entry transfer of 723 USIA officers into the Foreign Service Officer Corps. The first item, known as the Hays Bill, was introduced into the House by Congressman Wayne Hays, passed on a fairly close vote, and sent to the Senate for consideration in 1966. The proposal for the USIA integration, on the other hand, was subject to action only by the Senate. It had been approved by the Senate Committee on Foreign Relations in 1965, but was defeated on the Senate floor later in the year. Because both proposals raised issues about the most suitable personnel system(s) for foreign affairs agencies, the Foreign Relations committee decided to consider them together. After public hearings in April 1966 and further deliberations continuing into September, the package died in committee. The following account, based on transcripts of the hearings as well as other sources, reconstructs the forces at work in this exercise.[1]

## Background

Unlike the MOP reforms, which by all accounts were hastily conceived, the Hays Bill grew out of the recommendations of four blue-ribbon committees spanning sixteen years and involved extensive participation by agencies and Congress. If MOP could be dismissed by some as the illegitimate offspring of a hurried affair between William Crockett and Theory Y, the Hays Bill was blessed by multiple legislative paternity.

The notion of a single personnel structure in foreign affairs agencies traces its remote origins to the first Hoover Commission of 1949. This panel recommended that "the personnel in the permanent State Department establishment in Washington and the personnel of the Foreign Service above certain levels should be amalgamated over a short period of years into a single foreign affairs service obligated to serve at home or overseas and constituting a safeguarded career group administered separately from the general Civil Service."[2] In 1950 the Secretary's Advisory Committee on Personnel (the Rowe Committee) of-

---

[1] The sources include a 326-page printed transcript and report prepared by the Senate Committee on Foreign Relations; a lengthy written interview on the Hays Bill prepared for this study by former Deputy Under Secretary of State William Crockett; interviews with several individuals directly involved in the legislative debates, including a senior staff member of the Foreign Relations committee and a former member of the Board of Trustees of the American Foreign Service Association; interviews with State Department employees, especially in the Civil Service, who would have been affected by the changes; and a variety of memoranda, clippings, letters, and so forth contained in the Senate file on HR 6277 now stored in the National Archives. For convenience, the two proposals will sometimes be referred to simply as the Hays Bill. Unless indicated otherwise, all page references in this chapter are to the Senate document.

[2] This material is summarized and excerpted in the report of the Senate Committee on Foreign Relations, p. 71.

fered a similar proposal: "There should be a single personnel system applicable to all people under the direct administrative control of the Department of State." The Wriston Committee of 1954 followed with a recommendation that there be an integrated personnel system which would put an end to "the institutional separateness of these main functioning arms of United States diplomacy"—the Foreign Service and the Civil Service.

The most thorough analysis ever made of the problems posed by multiple personnel systems came from the Committee on Foreign Affairs Personnel of 1962, the Herter Committee. Set up by the Carnegie Foundation for International Peace at the request of Secretary of State Dean Rusk, and chaired by former Secretary of State Christian Herter, this nongovernmental body probed nearly all aspects of foreign affairs management. The committee's comments on the difficulties of the existing personnel structure in foreign affairs anticipated subsequent testimony on the Hays Bill:

*The problems of continuity and specialization.* A high degree of specialized knowledge is required in staffing many departmental positions. Civil Service employees tend to remain in a particular specialty for some years and thereby develop background knowledge that is not easily replaced. Rotational assignment of Foreign Service Officers to headquarters positions results in some loss of continuity under the best of circumstances (p. 113).

*The problem of replenishment.* It is difficult to attract qualified people through the Civil Service for professional careers in a number of important areas of the Department's work. Professional positions in such fields as economic affairs . . . are staffed heavily by Foreign Service Officers and Reserve Officers . . . In effect, "If you want a career in State you had better go into the Foreign Service" (ibid.).

*The problem of equity.* While Civil Service officers recognize the need for and desirability of rotational assignment of Foreign Service Officers to departmental positions, their morale and, hence, effectiveness is adversely affected when Foreign Service Officers receive what appears to them to be the lion's share of training assignments, the preferred jobs, and promotions. They resent the fact that Foreign Service Officers frequently receive higher salaries than they do for work of equal responsibility (p. 114).

*The problem of inflexibility.* In comparison with many features of the Foreign Service system, the Civil Service system is quite inflexible. This is most apparent in the linkage of an employee's salary to the classification grade of the position he occupies . . . This inflexibility is compounded by the Veterans Preference Act and regulations described thereunder for administering reductions in force (p. 115).

*The problem of dual administration.* The necessity of operating a large and complex organization under different laws, regulations, and standards unnecessarily complicates day-to-day personnel management of the State Department (ibid.).

A good part of the problem discussed here is obviously over-bureaucratization, particularly in the form of multiple sets of personnel rules.

The solution proposed in the Herter Committee's recommendation 8 contained the essential provisions of the Hays Bill:

*The personnel of foreign affairs agencies in the United States who are now in the Civil Service system should be redesignated as foreign affairs officers and employees and should be brought within the structure of the foreign affairs services. These employees should not be obligated to serve abroad as a consequence of this redesignation. Future recruitment should, however, stress availability for overseas service, and the long-range goal should be to increase the proportion of personnel available for service at home and abroad (p. 111).*

Though ultimately introduced by Congressman Hays, HR 6277 was the product of an interagency committee set up to implement the Herter recommendations. The principal organizer was the same William Crockett, then Deputy Under Secretary of State, who represented his department and the Johnson administration more generally. Also involved were the Civil Service Commission, the Bureau of the Budget, the Agency for International Development (AID), and the U.S. Information Agency (USIA). Critics later pointed out that the drafting was done quietly and did not involve meaningful participation by the major employee groups in the several agencies, particularly the American Foreign Service Association (AFSA) and the American Federation of Government Employees (AFGE). As with MOP, this rather elitist approach came back to haunt the Hays Bill during the public hearings. Crockett was, nonetheless, technically correct when he testified that "these were interagency deliberations, and the final bill was an interagency bill" (p. 205).

## Contents

The Hays Bill had essentially two parts: legislation to create an integrated personnel system for the Department of State, the USIA, and AID; and various improvements in the working conditions and benefits of foreign affairs employees, such as additional pay differentials for personnel serving in Vietnam and other combat areas. As there was little disagreement about the second set of items, this discussion will focus only on the first. The key provisions of the new personnel system were the following:

(1) The establishment of a new career category called Foreign Affairs Officers (FAO). The purpose was to integrate the existing Civil Service officers working in foreign affairs into a personnel system comparable to the Foreign Service Officer Corps. The Foreign Affairs Officers would work primarily in U.S.-based operations, although the legislation also permitted them to serve one or more tours overseas. The FAO category would include eight classes paralleling the eight numbered classes of Foreign Service Officers and Reserve Officers. And, a point that proved to be the most controversial, all officers, whether FSO, FSR, or FAO would be subject to selection-out.

(2) No Civil Service employee in the existing system would be forced into the new Foreign Affairs system. Transfers would be completely voluntary, requiring the written consent of the employee. Employees remaining under Civil Service would continue to receive all of the normal benefits, including the protections of the Veterans Preference Act.

(3) In the case of Civil Service employees who requested transfer, further written consent would be necessary before they could be sent overseas.

(4) The protections of the Veterans Preference Act would not apply to the category of Foreign Affairs Officers, just as they did not apply to other parts of the Foreign Service. This stipulation also proved to be a fatal weakness of the Hays Bill.

(5) The FSO category as such would not be directly affected by the legislation. "It would continue to serve as the principal career professional instrument of the Foreign Service of the United States, as en-

visaged by the Foreign Service Act of 1946" (p. 73). However, as it quickly became apparent, the FSO corps looked beyond the legalities to more subtle questions such as their own prestige and career prospects.

The proposal granting lateral entry into the Foreign Service Officer Corps to several hundred USIA officers was part of the same overall effort to develop a unified and flexible career foreign service. As Crockett testified in the public hearings, "the [Hays] bill and the nominations are separate proposals which fit together in the President's plan to strengthen the administration of personnel employed in the agencies whose business is foreign affairs' " (p. 8). The integration measure was also intended to remedy the feelings of second-class citizenship and the dubious career status of the USIA officers. The principal career problem was that after ten years of service as FSRs, the tenure of USIA employees depended on an annual rider to the appropriations bill for the USIA providing authority for them to continue. Leonard Marks, director of USIA in 1966, commented as follows on the status problem:

When we interview people for employment in our Agency, the first question they ask after they have surveyed the possiblilities [is], "What about the future? Where do I stand?" And I have to tell them with all honesty they have no career status, they are second-class citizens in the eyes of the Congress, because they are not given recognition as Foreign Service officers (p. 31).

Senator Albert Gore stated the problem of USIA officers more succinctly: "You mean they are like the mule, no pride in ancestry or hope in posterity?" The proposed integration was straightforward and uncomplicated as an action step, but encountered many of the same resistances as the Hays Bill.

The crucial legislative body in the life of both proposals was the Subcommittee on Foreign Service of the Senate Committee on Foreign Relations. In 1966 its members were Albert Gore, chairman; Frank Lausche; Claiborne Pell; Bourke Hickenlooper; Eugene McCarthy; and Frank Carlson. The subcommittee hearings and related deliberations provided the stage for the supporters and opponents to make their public representations, and was the focal point of backstage lobbying.

**Supporters**

The Hays Bill drew an impressive roster of supporters, ranging from President Johnson and the Secretary, Under Secretary, and Deputy Under Secretary of State to a variety of former government officials and advisers located in foundations and universities. The list that follows is ordered by the vigor with which a supporter backed the bill, both formally and informally, rather than by the potential influence deriving from position.

*Deputy Under Secretary William Crockett*

Crockett was not only the foremost promoter of the Hays Bill in interagency negotiations but the principal spokesman for the Johnson administration during the subcommittee hearings. Compared with most of his predecessors in the position of deputy under secretary or its equivalent, Crockett reputedly ranked at or near the top in the effectiveness of his relations with Congress. However, his sheer enthusiasm for the Hays Bill package, coupled with the series of other reforms launched more or less simultaneously, touched off suspicion in some quarters of Congress about his motives. It would not be unfair to say that his friends saw him as the first real reformer of the foreign affairs establishment since the Wriston Committee and perhaps even since 1946, while his enemies regarded his unbounded activism as a power grab thinly veiled in euphoria. These bifurcated perceptions haunted both the O area reforms and the Hays Bill.

Crockett left few doors unknocked in mobilizing the support of the Johnson officialdom. He did his homework with the President, the Secretary of State, the Bureau of the Budget, the Civil Service Commission, the USIA, AID, and various outside constituents of foreign affairs reform, including Henry Wriston. The three exceptions, which proved to be crucial, were the FSO corps, the Civil Service unions, and veterans' organizations.

The transcripts of the public hearings show that Crockett and his staff were well prepared for the questions (and assaults) that came up. His own testimony was comprehensive and vigorous. Indeed, given the limited interest of several of the subcommittee members in personnel matters, it may have been *too* comprehensive and detailed. One had the sense from the transcripts that some of the well-honed defenses of the bill's fine points sailed over the heads of Senators Lausche and Carlson, and perhaps Gore and McCarthy. It was not that these men could not understand the intricacies of foreign affairs legislation if they wanted to, but that the reshuffling of personnel systems was not a subject that struck many chords in their politically tuned hearts. It was significant that the subjects that generated the most debate, veterans' preference and selection-out of former civil servants, did so because of the insistent presence of key interest groups.

The thrust of Crockett's testimony is seen in these excerpts:

The [Hays Bill] legislation has one overriding purpose. That purpose is to enable the Department of State, USIA, and AID to carry out their foreign affairs responsibilities with increased effectiveness. That purpose is to increase efficiency and management flexibility in a world of crises and a world of change. Our foreign affairs agencies must keep pace with changing needs and circumstances. . . Our task is to make the best possible use of the best possible personnel system that can be devised (pp. 69-70).

Just think of the civil service system as a great system that many agencies use. The civil service system is a concept of employment with a central body of laws and regulations, and agencies employ people who are under that stystem.

Now we are trying to constitute the same concept for agencies in the foreign affairs field, so that there would be a broad personnel system called the foreign affairs personnel system, and agencies in the foreign affairs field . . . would employ people whose basic tenure and whose basic character of employment would fall under the foreign affairs personnel system. It would have the aspect of the civil service system used in domestic agencies (pp. 184-185).

Crockett's major emphasis throughout was on such values as efficiency, flexibility, and modern management—virtues with doubtful appeal to most senators.

## Civil Service Commission

The most critical provision of the Hays Bill was the wholesale transfer of Civil Service employees to a new foreign affairs system. Without the support of the Civil Service Commission such a bill would have been doomed from the outset. As it happened, John Macy, Jr., then chairman of the commission, became one of the most forceful and articulate defenders of the reforms. And, unlike several other powerful figures who lent their name to the bill but did not turn on any legislative "heat," Macy appeared to testify and took other steps to promote the cause. By his own testimony, Macy and the commission did not support the bill until they had studied it from all angles and were convinced that it would do no harm to their major constituents, the Civil Service employees. His chief argument in its favor was the possibility of increased flexibility of assignments in the revamped Foreign Service.

In the Department of State, AID, and USIA there are currently operating, back to back, two essentially disparate personnel systems. Most headquarters jobs in these agencies are staffed by civil service employees under the general personnel system applicable to most departments and agencies. The overseas missions of these agencies are staffed by employees under the Foreign Service system. The civil service employees are under a "job" or "position" oriented system.

Foreign Service employees are under a "person" or "rank-in-the-man" oriented system. There are significant differences between the two systems in how employees are selected, assigned, and promoted. . .

Good administration requires a constant movement of oversea [*sic*] personnel back to headquarters assignments and vice versa, just as there is a steady flow between headquarters and field in all widespread organizations, whether governmental or private. Having two divergent personnel systems applicable to Foreign Service and home-based employees of the same agency hampers the free movement that should take place and unduly complicates administration (p. 48).

In the language of this book the dual personnel systems were a prime source of the proliferation of rules covering such questions as selection and promotion. Macy testified that the Hays Bill was the right solution to the problem and that it could be implemented without hurting anyone. The Civil Service unions, sad to say, did not share in this assessment.

## USIA and AID

Both the USIA and AID employed large numbers of Foreign Service Reserve Officers with the status and career problems noted earlier. Not surprisingly, Leonard Marks, director of USIA, and William Gaud, deputy administrator of AID, were strong supporters of the Hays Bill. Marks was also a leading witness for the USIA integration. The arguments of both men centered on the urgent need for equal citizenship and benefits in the Foreign Service and for permanent career prospects.

### Bureau of the Budget (BOB)

The staff of BOB participated in the drafting of the Hays Bill and carried out a thorough review of the implications of each provision. Elmer Staats, then deputy director, submitted a letter to Senator Fulbright recommending passage of the legislation in 1966. At the public hearings, Roger W. Jones, special assistant to the director, offered both informal testimony and a prepared statement supporting the bill. In the latter he cited several advantages of the revised system:

— better retention of qualified people in foreign affairs agencies;
— greater flexibility in assignment and reassignment;
— facilitation of an interchange of personnel between domestic and foreign affairs agencies;
— eliminating the "makeshift personnel provisions which USIA has been forced to use for 13 years for its career personnel";
— laying the groundwork for a nucleus of career personnel "with the status and tenure needed to man the vital posts in the foreign assistance program";
— eliminating the "unsatisfactory and illogical dual personal system"; and
— providing the President with a broader range of career talents in filling top executive posts at home and abroad (p. 252).

As a former chairman of the Civil Service Commission and former Deputy Under Secretary of State for Administration, Jones entered the hearings with impressive credentials. How much these credentials influenced the legislation is another question.

### President Johnson

In principle, Lyndon Johnson was in favor of the Hays Bill as well as the USIA integration; he submitted a strong statement to the Senate on their behalf. In a letter to Dean Rusk he wrote: "It is important in the management of foreign affairs that you and I have the improved legal framework for foreign affairs personnel that the [Hays Bill] will provide. I fully support the objectives of the proposed foreign affairs personnel program and would appreciate it if you would assume responsibility for its full development and implementation" (p. 286).

But paper is one matter and politics another. Though ostensibly a committed promoter of the legislation, Johnson did not follow through with White House "muscle" signaling seriousness of intent. By the time the Hays Bill reached the Senate, the President was so heavily involved in warding off Vietnam critics that his musclepower had to be saved for other areas, including a different wing of the Foreign Relations committee.

### Secretary Rusk and Under Secretary Ball

Secretary Dean Rusk was also a strong paper supporter of the Hays Bill but not an all-out advocate. In a letter to Senator Fulbright in 1966 listing numerous justifications for the bill, he concluded: "I am convinced that passage of a bill along the lines of HR 6277 will greatly improve the personnel administration of the three foreign affairs agencies. We believe that the bill worked out in the House of Representatives is an excellent one" (p. 262). But, like President Johnson, Rusk and Under Secretary George Ball were facing larger legislative imbroglios arising from Vietnam. In 1971 Crockett commented in an interview:

There was not much interest in the proposal by either Mr. Rusk or Mr. Ball. They saw the whole issue as another tiresome squabble with the Senate at a time when State (and Rusk) could ill afford to proliferate their problems.

Thus, their support was tacit rather than active and aggressive. But this attitude on their part may have been one of the crucial factors in causing the effort to fail, i.e., there was always the feeling on the Hill that "if they aren't interested enough to come up and support the bill, then why should we take it so seriously?" A good question!

Hence it is not only the presence or absence of support that makes a difference in administrative reform, but its intensity. Unless backing from key actors reaches a certain threshold, overt gestures of support will be interpreted as pro forma indifference or even covert opposition.

### Legislative Staff

Two individuals, one connected with the Senate and the other with the State Department, played key supporting roles in their liaison work with the Hays Bill. Carl Marcy, chief of staff of the Senate Foreign Relations Committee, was an early architect of the plan and worked behind the scenes with Congressman Hays to bring about co-operation between the relevant Senate and House committees. Despite this early support, it is not clear if he backed the measure when it finally reached the Senate. In a 1971 interview, William Crockett hypothesized that Marcy's enthusiasm may have cooled when the legislation was caught in the crossfire between the State Department and Senator Fulbright over Vietnam. When asked in 1973 about his role in the Hays Bill, Marcy said that he simply could not remember.

The second legislative actor, who also worked behind the scenes, was ambassador Douglas MacArthur, Jr., Assistant Secretary of State for Congressional Relations. He had considerable influence with several key Republican senators, and worked closely with Crockett to enlist support for the bill.

*Prominent Citizens*

The Hays Bill effort was bolstered by testimony and letters of support from over a dozen prominent citizens, typically individuals who had served on the Herter or Wriston committees or who had been involved in foreign affairs administration. Public testimony was given by Joseph E. Johnson, president of the Carnegie Endowment for International Peace, the organization that had established the Herter Committee. Johnson himself was an active member of the committee and a signatory of its report. The thrust of his remarks was to reaffirm the validity of the Herter recommendations. Four other members of the Herter Committee sent supporting letters: Don K. Price, dean of the Graduate School of Public Administration at Harvard; Milton Katz, professor of law at Harvard; Kenneth B. Clark of the Social Dynamics Research Institute in New York; and Arthur K. Watson. Favorable letters came as well from Henry Wriston and two other members of the Wriston Committee; Carlisle Humelsine and Loy Henderson, both of whom had served as Deputy Under Secretary of State for Administration; J. Edward Day, president of the National Civil Service League; Preston J. Moore, former chairman of the American Legion Special Liaison Committee to the State Department; Edward Gullion, dean of the Fletcher School of Law and Diplomacy and a retired ambassador; and a variety of officials in the State Department. But here, too, however sincere and well-intentioned they might be, letters unaccompanied by physical presence and informal lobbying were little more than handy frosting for an uncertain cake.

## Opponents and Saboteurs

As often happens, the defeat of the Hays Bill was as much the result of backstage sabotage and inaction by key officials as of outright opposition. The key opponents were the Civil Service unions, which were mainly concerned about selection-out; the Foreign Service Officer corps, which feared the dilution of its elite status; veterans groups, which were exercised about the elimination of veterans preference in the Hays Bill; Senator Pell, who identified with the concerns of the FSOs; and Senator Hickenlooper, who seemed worried about the potential concentration of power in the State Department. They were joined by a large supporting cast echoing the same themes. In this case it is difficult to rank the strength of the negative forces, although Senator Hickenlooper's personal concerns seemed the least powerful barrier and Senator Pell's links to the Foreign Service one of the most crucial.

### Civil Service Unions

The heaviest barrage of objections came from the national office and local branches of the American Federation of Government Employees (AFL-CIO). In 1966 the AFGE, which represents Civil Service employees, had about 190,000 members dispersed across fifty states and forty other countries. In lengthy testimony AFGE spokesmen cited numerous flaws in the Hays Bill: it would remove about 10,000 jobs from the competitive classified merit civil service system; by substituting a rank-in-man arrangement, it would eliminate the "equal pay for equal work" principle established by Congress in the Classification Act; through the regulations for selection-out it would make seniority on the job a cause for removal rather than an asset for retention; it would extend to all career employees in the three agencies the State Department's practice of selection-out of competent officers with tested experience to permit management to recruit and promote new and favored individuals; it would confirm the department's practice of using confidential appraisals (the Development Appraisal Report) as a key factor in performance evaluation and promotion; it would permit no appeal from selection-out even though there were cases, reported by Congressman Hays, in which the department's judgment was too harsh; it would introduce favoritism, conformism, and a corrupting concentration of power destructive of both employee rights and the public interest; it would cause a disruptive competition for survival to replace the cooperation and confidence currently seen among employees; and it would permit continued intervention and manipulation by top management and politicians under the cover of secrecy (adapted from p. 206).

The focal point of the AFGE attack was the requirement that former Civil Service staff would be subject to selection-out. The vehemence of the reactions to this point was strongly conditioned by the recently introduced Development Appraisal Report (DAR). Early in his testimony the first AFGE witness, Thomas G. Walters, stated:

In the last year a startling, dangerous, secretive personnel procedure has been developed in the Department of State. Until last year the performance rating report was the normal report in the Department of State. But in 1965 the so-called development appraisal report was written on all Foreign Service employees and made applicable to Civil Service officers in GS-9 and above (p. 80).

We have been informed it was developed in the very top echelon of the State Department and the people who make the surveys and determine these 10 percent of the people [the bottom group—candidates for selection-out] are never permitted to see this until the report is ready for the selection-out process, and then someone, I presume in Mr. Crockett's office, has authority to look at this and to fix it up to where the employee can be selected-out even though his ratings have been good (pp. 85-86).

Walters, who was special assistant to the President for legislation of AFGE, drew an explicit connection between the DAR and the Hays Bill:

There is too much novelty, too much arbitrary power, too much danger in this recent personnel development, and we are afraid that worse things might happen in the future if HR 6277 is passed (p. 87).

It would appear to me that we are somewhat approaching a dictatorial setup in this particular agency to give one man, whoever he might be, the power to have this little secret document where he can pull it out and work on it and fix it up or have somebody else do it and then select a guy out and move him on down the road. I think we are just moving in a dangerous direction (p. 91).

USIA lodge 1812 of the AFGE took a slightly more differentiated stand, opposing the Hays Bill but strongly endorsing the integration of USIA officers into the Foreign Service. Bernard Wiseman, lodge president, defended the latter provision on the grounds that it would give USIA career officers more prestige and status and would facilitate their overseas work. On the other hand, Wiseman was adamant and bitter in his opposition to a "foreign affairs personnel octopus in which the careers of some 30,000 employees would be determined in secrecy by a handful of mysterious manipulators under their own rules and without opportunity of appeal or review" (p. 160). In his view the Hays Bill was nothing but an administrative coup by Crockett and his associates. Its real purpose was "to enable State's management to hire and fire at will: to promote, sidetrack, move around, or shelve as management sees fit; to select in, select up, and select out, under its own rules and under its own interpretation of those rules" (ibid.). And, like MOP, the Hays Bill—widely regarded as Crockett-inspired —suffered from guilt by association with other management reforms underway in the State Department. In Wiseman's words:

Mr. Crockett has also introduced a MUST [Manpower Utilization System Technology] program to eliminate job classifications . . . Such lumping together destroys professional specialization and permits management to shuffle officers around like computer cards which will be used for the shuffling of assignments (p. 161).

This theme—that Crockett and his minions were dehumanizing the State Department and acquiring increased control over the resulting robots—came up in various guises throughout the hearings.

The Government Employees Council (AFL-CIO), a group of unions representing postal and wage board employees, opposed not only the selection-out provision, but also the removal of veterans' preference rights and the reduction of positions under the Civil Service. Nathan Wolkomir, president of the National Federation of Federal Employees, likewise submitted a letter repeating several of the objections raised by the other unions.

## Veterans' Organizations

The veterans' organizations, particularly the Veterans of Foreign Wars (VFW) and the Disabled American Veterans (DAV), were no less intransigent in opposing the Hays Bill. Understandably, their *bête noire* was the provision that Civil Service employees moving into the Foreign Service system would no longer be protected by the Veterans Preference Act. In essence this act granted preferential treatment to veterans both in initial appointment and in retention when there were reductions in force. Such preferences were not granted to employees covered by the Foreign Service Act, mainly because of the practical difficulties of applying them to a rank-in-man system. Under the Hays Bill they would also not be applicable to employees entering the expanded foreign affairs personnel system.

The distinctive arguments advanced by the veterans' groups were basically emotional appeals to preserve a time-honored practice and to think of "our boys." This excerpt from a statement submitted by Andy Borg, commander in chief of the VFW, conveys the flavor of the testimony:

As I have travelled through this nation and to the far corners of the world, the questions I hear today have a familiar ring to them. They are the same questions as servicemen and their families have asked in years and in wars gone by. I think these questions, which are concerned for the future of the veteran, have more pertinency today than for some time because only a relative few are commanded to serve their nation today (p. 143).

Francis Stover, the principal spokesman for the VFW at the public hearings, drew the expected connection to the Hays Bill:

HR 6277 would create the absurdity for a veteran coming back from Vietnam. If he stops at the Interior Department on Virginia Avenue, he will be told, "Yes, the fact that you have served your country, you get 5 or 10 points, and so forth, depending on what status you are in." But if the veteran who served in Vietnam goes a block or a couple of blocks farther to the State Department and knocks on the door, they will say "I am sorry, son, your Purple Heart doesn't count here" (pp. 144-45).

Stover's lengthy prepared statement also replayed the full gamut of objections raised by other groups, including the evils of selection-out, the concentration of power in the State Department, and the alleged undermining of the merit system. His conclusion: "This bill has few compensating features. It is virtually all bad" (p. 154).

The Disabled American Veterans, in a written statement, joined in the same refrain. At its most recent national convention the DAV had adopted a resolution "that the National Commander, the National Legislative Officers, and the Congress be called upon to oppose any efforts to weaken or reduce benefits provided veterans by the Veterans Preference Act and to defeat any attempts to convert such measures into law." The Hays Bill was obviously such an attempt. The DAV was also indignant at the implied slurs on the competence of the Civil Service heard during House debate on the bill: "The proponents of the bill would have us believe that the present system is one of general ineptitude" (p. 308). The reference was to the argument that the existing staff could not handle foreign affairs assignments, and probably to the comments made about the near-impossibility of dismissing a Civil Service employee.

Veterans' organizations carry considerable weight with legislators, partly because of their sheer numbers and wide dispersion, partly because of their association with evident patriotic causes. It was to be expected that congressmen and senators would not take their opposition lightly. Senator Frank Carlson of Kansas, a member of the Gore subcommittee who said practically nothing during the hearings, made a point to insert in the record letters from VFW and DAV representatives. Similarly, Howard Cannon, a highly influential senator, wrote to Senator Fulbright expressing strong opposition to HR 6277. His stance was based "on the proposal here to break faith with the commitment of the government to honor its obligations toward our former servicemen" (p. 259). It was apparent from the hearings and related correspondence that few senators wanted to take on such formidable opponents over a bill with virtually no political payoff.

## Senator Hickenlooper

In a curious political equation, Senator Hickenlooper became to the Civil Service and veterans' organizations what Senator Pell was to the Foreign Service Officer Corps. In their questions and statements both men echoed the concerns of the respective interest groups, but added ammunition growing out of their intimate involvement in the subject. And it is perhaps not coincidental that the style of operation correlated remarkably well, with Hickenlooper following the head-on approach of civil servants and Pell adopting the more roundabout tactics of the FSOs.

Hickenlooper was generally regarded as the leading subcommittee expert on the USIA. His remarks and questions reflected a latent concern with protecting this agency from the encroachments of the State Department and at the same time maintaining an effective dispersion of power across the foreign affairs agencies. While many of his statements did not fit easily into "for-against" categories, it was clear from the outset that he was not enthusiastic about the Hays Bill. His greatest worry was an expansion of the size and power of the State Department. Addressing the question of the USIA integration, he stated:

I know 700 isn't a very big colossus. Neither is a small foot in the door, but that foot in the door is sometimes the "open sesame" to a lot more, and as the Chinese say, "A journey of a thousand miles begins with a first step." This is not necessarily the first step, but it is one of several that are moving—gradually moving—toward an expansion of the whole State Department complex (p. 18).

The Hays Bill seemed a much larger foot in the door:

I have a genuine fear, and I have said it before, that by this legislation . . . we will create such a gargantuan situation over there that it will run the whole American Government. And it will put unconscionable directive power over the personnel of so many of these people who vitally affect our foreign affairs in one officer, that is the Director, whomever he may be, I again want to say I am not referring to Mr. Crockett as an individual (p. 132).

Hickenlooper thus took essentially the AFGE position that the bill would increase the arbitrary authority of the State Department, and particularly the deputy under secretary for administration. Throughout the testimony he also gave clear evidence of favoring the existing system of agency structure in foreign affairs, rather than any consolidation, even at the level of personnel regulations: "You have got the separate agencies doing specialized work, and it is very difficult to clarify, at least in my mind, why they should not keep on doing their specialized work" (p. 215). The senator displayed a common congressional attitude that the best structure for interdependent agencies is the one that happens to be in force at the present time. Whatever its irrationalities, it is the most easily understood and, in the case of foreign affairs, carries with it a system of checks and balances preventing the takeover of American government by the State Department.

### Foreign Service Officers

In the Hays Bill debate, as in every other effort at foreign affairs reform during the 1960s, the FSO corps responded with an enigmatic but ultimately negative stance. Part of the problem in this case, as well as in the MOP changes, was the perception that the reforms had been "sprung" on the Officer Corps without due consultation. An FSO who had served on the board of the American Foreign Service Association at the time later reported that "Crockett did an end run with Hays on this bill. The Foreign Service wasn't informed."

Beyond these procedural questions there was little in the Hays Bill to enchant the Foreign Service. Crockett's testimony that "actually this has nothing basically to do with Foreign Service Officer Corps" (p. 57) was accurate law but poor psychology. The FSOs correctly saw the USIA integration and the expanded personnel system as a threat to their own elite status. The Hays Bill would have placed reserve and staff officers as well as former Civil Service employees on an equal administrative footing with the Officer Corps. While Crockett took pains to point out that the concept of an elite career service would be preserved, the legislation itself and the bulk of the testimony left little doubt that democratization was afoot.

Perhaps characteristically, and certainly unlike the Civil Service unions and the veterans' organizations, the FSO opponents chose to lobby behind the scenes rather than at the hearings. Not a single active or retired officer appeared before the subcommittee to support or oppose the legislative package. The only one who did come forth was a selected-out officer who took up the Civil Service cudgels against selection-out. This glaring lacuna did not go unnoticed by the subcommittee members. Senator Pell remarked:

I am very surprised that no Foreign Service officers or retired Foreign Service officers have chosen to come up and asked to speak. I am informed that everybody who has asked to be heard has been put on the witness list. I have heard all kinds of grumblings from the Foreign Service about this bill, received private letters and I really am surprised at the lack of gumption that is shown by this fact.

If they are against it, as they say they are, why don't they come up and say so, but not grumble, and actually it takes no courage if they are retired (p. 131).

But, Senator Hickenlooper responded, "I know of a few Foreign Service officers who say it would be their neck if they came up here and dared to testify against what was the announced and ordered policy of the top office" (ibid.).

As the comments by Pell and Hickenlooper made clear, the FSO corps was lobbying against the legislation, albeit not in public. In December 1965, former ambassador Ellis Briggs, a prominent defender of the integrity of the Foreign Service, wrote to Senator Fulbright:[3]

As the new session approaches, I write to applaud the reluctance of the Committee on Foreign Relations to endorse the [USIA integration].I have no bias against USIS. It contains many good people . . .Their bloc transfer would . . . weaken the Foreign Service.

It is my hope that you and your colleagues will continue to oppose each and every step which would weaken our Foreign Service, impair its morale, or corrode its efficiency. The proposal to blanket seven hundred and sixty USIS personnel into the officer corps of the Foreign Service would perform all three of those disservices to our Government.

Other key members of the Foreign Service made personal visits or wrote privately to senators on the Foreign Relations Committee to express their disenchantment.

As the official lobbying group of the Foreign Service, the American Foreign Service Association (AFSA) held the potential for considerable influence on this legislation. Although the FSOs remained the dominant bloc in this organization, AFSA's success also required

[3] This letter was contained in the Senate files on HR 6277, but not printed in the report prepared by the Foreign Relations Committee. USIS (U. S. Information Service) is the correct designation of the foreign offices of the USIA.

attention to the concerns of the Foreign Service reserve and staff officers, a sizable part of the membership. One positive response to these concerns was a relatively unequivocal letter of support for the USIA integration measure. The FSOs apparently could tolerate a step that would expand but not destroy the elite corps.

AFSA's reactions to the Hays Bill were much more complex. The FSOs on the board objected not only to the substance of the measure, but to their lack of participation in its drafting. Several complained that the bill was kept under wraps until it was too late for AFSA to mobilize opposition. At the same time, AFSA wanted to give at least the appearance of cooperation with the administration and did not wish to alienate its own constituencies who favored the bill. The result, according to one participant, was a board meeting at which the FSO members shook their heads over the measure and decided to send a letter that was ostensibly favorable, but that contained as much latent opposition as possible. It is worth quoting this letter, which is a masterpiece of circumlocution:

(1) Subject to the comments which follow, the Board of the Association supports the concept of the single Foreign Service personnel system ... The Board favors flexibility of administration and believes that the rigidities arising from the present dual personnel system should be corrected. We must point out, however, that flexibility is a management tool; it is a means to overcome present deficiencies; it is not an end in itself ...

(4) Those sections of the bill which have engaged the major attention of the Board are ones of broader import where policy decisions under authority granted by the bill are left for administrative determination in the future. Particular attention has been focussed on provisions which will have long-term and broad effect on the concept and nature of the Foreign Service career. The Board has examined these provisions within the context of the needs to develop a uniform personnel system for the three principal agencies involved, while ensuring the maintenance of excellence in the foreign affairs field and encouraging the best qualified candidates to continue to apply for both domestic and foreign service...

(9) ... Recalling the personnel problems over the last ten years resulting from the Wristonization program, the Board must point out that a new large scale integration into the FSO Corps would have an important bearing on the composition, class distribution and career prospects of the present FSO Corps (pp. 308-311).

Given that the drafting was done by officers who pride themselves on lucid prose, section (4) can only be construed as deliberate obfuscation designed to convey antagonism masquerading as ambiguity. According to our board informant, the letter as a whole was intended to damn with faint praise—which it did.

*Senator Pell*

Claiborne Pell held a unique position within the Foreign Relations Committee and the Gore subcommittee on foreign affairs personnel matters. Himself a career FSO from 1945 to 1952, he thereafter maintained a vital interest in issues affecting the Foreign Service. This background, coupled with the general disinterest in personnel questions shown by Foreign Relations committee members, added weight to Pell's opinions and comments within the committee. As Carl Marcy, the committee's chief of staff later explained, when the Hays Bill and similar legislation came up, other members would turn to Pell and say, "Well, Claiborne, what do you think about this?"

Although Pell made various conciliatory gestures toward Crockett during the hearings, the bulk of the evidence suggests that he was opposed to the Hays Bill from the beginning.[4] In the hearings on the USIA integration proposal he inserted a statment in the record which included the following points, among others:

Since World War II, the unfortunate Foreign Service has been organized and reorganized, diluted, undiluted, and rediluted. . . At the middle and upper echelons, the Foreign Service administration sat on its hands at that time [immediate postwar period] and the provisions for war manpower lateral entry were very sparsely used. The result of that inaction was the Wristonization program a few years later when the pendulum was swung too hard and when many people were willy nilly brought into the Foreign Service who should not have been. . .
I submit that the way to achieve this ever better Foreign Service is to leave it alone for a while to develop its own *esprit de corps*. I also believe that the Foreign Service itself should be small and immensely capable and competent. . . But I would hope that there would be no

---

[4] Early in the hearings he remarked: "Mr. Crockett, as you know I have been thinking of this problem for some time and I have a great admiration for your own judgment and ability and I have been trying to convince myself it is a good idea. I still haven't got myself convinced. I still have an open mind" (p. 21).

more wholesale injection of people into the Foreign Service because the effect on the Foreign Service morale is profound (pp. 22-23).

Elsewhere in his comments and questions Pell took the FSO position that both the USIA integration and the Hays Bill would result in a "dilution" of the Officers Corps or further unnecessary scrambling. This exchange between Pell and Crockett is particularly instructive, revealing deep attitudes on both sides:

*Senator Pell.* The trouble with the poor Foreign Service, what makes them unhappy, they get reorganized.
*Mr. Crockett.* I am glad you feel sorry for them. I don't feel sorry for them. We have given them a good deal in the last 5 years. They never had it so good; so I don't feel sorry for them (p. 65).

In Crockett's view, Pell was the self-appointed protector of the virginity of the Foreign Service, defending it against rape by the administrators. Pell is a good example of the special-interest actor who can quickly move to the front stage of a drama and change the expected course of the plot. His role did not end at the hearings.

### Senator Fulbright

As chairman of the Senate Foreign Relations Committee, J. William Fulbright was potentially a key figure in the Hays Bill debate. When the legislation was first proposed for consideration, he seemed agreeable enough. But in 1965 and 1966, as the United States became further mired in Vietnam and the conflicts between the Foreign Relations Committee and the Johnson administration escalated, his attention shifted to matters of greater urgency than personnel reforms. Crockett commented in a 1971 interview:

At one time[Fulbright] was a strong supporter of the whole concept and despite his disagreement with Secretary Rusk over policy I was naive enough to believe that he would support the reform. But the word that all the "insiders" carried to me was that "there will be no Foreign Service legislation until the President and the Secretary [Rusk] fulfill the needs of this Committee." And when all the cards were on the table, it is my opinion that it was indeed this attitude by Senator Fulbright (and no doubt supported by most of his Committee) that did indeed defeat this reform. It was a victim of the times—caught in the crossfire of deeper and hotter issues.

This may have been an accurate assessment of the senator's overall attitude toward the legislation and the State Department, but our research shows that in the final act Fulbright was not directly responsible for the demise of the Hays Bill. By all accounts the legislation was already in critical condition upon arrival at the full Foreign Relations committee.

## Finale

At the conclusion of the public hearings in April 1966 it was clear that support for the Hays Bill in the Gore subcommittee was virtually nonexistent, while opposition was strong. Despite the case made by administration witnesses and prominent citizens, the reforms found not a single taker in the subcommittee. Senator McCarthy seemed uninterested, Senators Gore, Lausche, and Carlson indifferent to hostile, and Senators Pell and Hickenlooper firmly opposed. In a note to Senator Fulbright dated July 21, 1966, Gore wrote that there was "very little support for the proposals before [the subcommittee]." The Hays Bill was damaged goods.

The action from this point on was led by Senator Pell. In a note to Gore he revealed his plan for legislative euthanasia:[5]

Although the Administration is still officially committed to supporting the package of HR 6277 and the USIA nominations, I have been assured, unofficially, that the plan encompassed by these amendments together with letting the USIA nominations die in committee is acceptable as an alternative if the original administration proposals are unacceptable.

On August 18, 1966, the bill was ordered reported with amendments to the full Foreign Relations Committee. On August 30 it was ordered reported with amendments to the Senate. On September 15 Pell introduced a motion in the Foreign Relations Committee to table both the Hays Bill and the USIA integration. Its passage marked the end of major attempts to restructure the foreign affairs personnel system.

[5] Memorandum contained in Senate files on HR 6277.

# 9 • Why Bureaucracy Stays

Once hierarchy and rules take root in the federal system, many parties become interested in their preservation. Whatever its origins, whatever services it does or does not provide, and whatever the "rational" justification for its continued existence, an administrative agency will usually be able to mount substantial opposition to basic change in its structure or operation. Both President Johnson and President Nixon found, for example, that Congress was decidedly unenthusiastic about wholesale mergers of executive departments. Johnson's plan was to create a superagency embracing the Departments of Labor and Commerce. Early in his administration, Nixon came forth with an even more ambitious proposal to reorganize and consolidate existing cabinet departments. Both efforts died of congressional strangulation.[1] The most notable exception to this pattern is the massive change program initiated by President Truman under the Reorganization Act of 1949. Building on the recommendations of the first Hoover Commission, Truman introduced forty-one reorganization plans, most of which were approved by Congress. This was the only successful effort of its kind in the past sixty years.

The pattern of conservatism seen with macroscopic change applies to less ambitious efforts such as the O area reforms and the Hays Bill. The garden variety of executive reorganization consists of an internal reshuffling of agency structures by political appointees attempting to consolidate or gain control of their own units. Such efforts typically dissipate as the appointee moves on to greener pastures, becomes co-

[1] It might be added that both plans, in the judgment of fairly dispassionate observers, made little administrative sense on their own terms. The point here is that "administrative sense" is typically not the major criterion by which reorganizations are judged in Congress.

opted by his subordinates, or stumbles on the hurdles erected by Congress or the career employees. The U. S. experience with both large and small reorganizations thus reveals an entrenched resistance to bureaucratic change, and a tendency for amputated limbs to grow back.

This chapter reviews the manifold and interlocking forces that work to hold established bureaucracies in place. If there is a single theme to the discussion, it is that organizational structures in the federal bureaucracy respond to many interests other than administrative rationality. The homage paid in word and statute to the gods of efficiency and economy may, in Freudian fashion, compensate for flagrant neglect in deed. Both in their origins and in their continuation, executive agencies show the influence of organized interests, personal whims, political brokerage, and sheer bureaucratic inertia.

## Unfreezing, Changing, and Refreezing

For present purposes it is helpful to view organizational change as taking place in three stages: unfreezing, changing, and refreezing (cf. Schein, 1969; Kelman and Warwick, 1973). *Unfreezing* involves the initial opening of a system to change. In practice, this means identifying and overcoming the initial resistances to change—those personal and social conditions supporting existing structures and behaviors. *Changing* demands that the system be moved to a new state with different attitudes, structures, and behaviors. Finally, *refreezing* is the process of integrating the new patterns into the knowledge, attitudes, and behavior of the members and the surrounding sociopolitical structures. It requires that change be generalized and stabilized so that it does not melt under the heat of everyday existence.

The remaining discussion considers both internal and external obstacles to organizational change in the public agency. The central argument is that external obstacles, such as the appropriations framework used by Congress, operate primarily at the level of unfreezing and changing, while internal obstacles have their greatest impact on the possibility of refreezing.

## External Resistance

The major external barriers to change are congressional orientations, agency ownership patterns, statutory bureaucracy and system-
wide rules, pervasive interagency linkages, and interest groups. The
salience of these factors can be illustrated by the efforts at foreign
affairs reform in the 1960s, as well as by other examples.

### Congressional Orientations

Members of any organization gradually develop perspectives
toward their work that make some courses of action appealing and
others unattractive or even invisible. Congressmen and senators are
no exception.

Considerations of power normally outweigh any other factor,
including administrative efficiency, in congressional reactions to
bureaucratic change. Harold Seidman (1970, p. 37) puts it well:

Executive branch structure and administrative arrangements are not
matters of mere academic interest to members of Congress. Organization or reorganization of executive agencies may influence committee
jurisdictions, increase or decrease the "accessibility" of executive
branch officials to members of the Congress, and otherwise determine
who shall exercise ultimate power in the decision-making process.

In the Hays Bill debate it is significant that Senator Hickenlooper was
much more concerned about the liabilities arising from a gain in State
Department power than about the gains in economy and efficiency
that would result from the merger of personnel systems. The theme of
power-grabbing raised by the American Federation of Government
Employees and by the veterans organizations also struck a resonant
chord among the senators.

An immediate source of congressional resistance to even thinking
about change is the twelve-month appropriations framework. Many
legislators come to view this as the longest possible time span for
considering agency operations. Hence when administration officials
arrive with elegant proposals showing the benefits of a reorganization
over ten or twenty years, the discussion may fall outside the operating
perceptual boundaries of the audience. The Hays Bill further suggests
that the salience of this year compared to the future will be increased if

there are loud cries of opposition from aggrieved groups. Typically, the future beneficiaries of a reform are not around to applaud its virtues, while the casualties are close at hand. Abstractions such as "the public interest" are poor stand-ins at any time. As Gawthrop (1969, p. 258) observes, "Congress as the authorizing body is simply not geared—intellectually, temperamentally or structurally—to adapt to an innovation design of the executive branch. Individual congressmen and congressional committees are almost exclusively conditioned to respond to current and immediate needs."

Another reason for congressional wariness about bureaucratic change is the tendency of members to deal with agencies more at the level of operations than of policy. As the size of the federal bureaucracy has increased, Congress has exercised its responsibility for oversight mainly by parceling out agencies and pieces of agencies to committees. Because of the complexity and abstractness of the policy issues at stake, legislators serving on these committees often are more comfortable talking and thinking about such subjects as expenditures and staff size than intangible issues such as the values underlying policy. This tropism toward the concrete is reinforced by the widely shared and largely accurate belief that one gains power in Congress by specializing in some realm of operations (cf. MacNeil, 1963), and by the growth of staff bureaucracies within the committees themselves. Seidman (1970, p. 39) observes: "Growth of a congressional bureaucracy and the institutionalization of committees have deepened the moats dividing the fiefdoms and accentuated the innate disposition of the Congress to concentrate on administrative details rather than basic issues of public policy."

The addition of two or five or twenty professional staff members to a committee means just that many more individuals whose own organizational culture will, on the whole, reward them for attention to operating detail. Moreover, both the legislators and their staff build up significant personal relationships with the career officials in the operating bureaus. Despite the separation of powers, bureaucrats in one branch become the natural allies of bureaucrats in another. It is hardly surprising, therefore, that both legislators and staff are most uneasy about any changes disrupting the terrain of their daily work—the existing agency structures and the resulting sets of interpersonal relationships.

Congressional resistance to unfreezing is particularly strong in the case of proposals for major executive reorganizations. Avery Leiserson (1947, pp. 71-72) traces this reaction to both psychological and institutional factors:

The Congressional predisposition to oppose executive reorganization is certainly general enough to justify designating this limitation as psychological. But the limitation even extends to the institutional process through which the Congressman has gained his position as the representative of his district. This process conditions him to making up his mind to emphasize certain factors that belong to a special order of political judgment. His sense of familiarity in dealing with matters of organization depends upon primarily personal factors, such as favorable impressions made by particular personalities, his experience in securing "cooperation" in appointments and getting information from particular administrative officials, and his identification with policies uppermost in the minds of politically important groups in his constituency . . . To him, arguments for lessening the Congressional leverage over specific agencies in which he is interested—particularly on such abstract grounds as the desirability of administrative unity, flexibility, planning, coordination, or consistency (of all things)—are either meaningless or else imply a degree of self-immolation that subverts the very reasons for being in Washington.

Another problem, Leiserson argues, is that congressmen tend to see proposals for changes in agency structure as battles between warring bureau chiefs or struggles among interest groups. Given this perception, they are inclined to choose sides on bases other than administrative rationality.

### Agency Ownership and Sacred Territory

Because of the strong legislative authority of Congress over executive agencies, the various House and Senate committees and subcommittees can often claim de facto ownership of a given agency or bureau. Depending on the relation between the agency leadership (including career officials) and Congress, this situation may work for or against change. Most often it works against.

Several different congressional committees hold mortgages on parts of the State Department. At the time of this study ownership of the strictly administrative parts of the department (Foreign Buildings, Budget, Personnel, Operations, Communications) fell to the House appropriations subcommittee chaired by Congressman John Rooney. Although Rooney had wide powers of intimidation throughout the department, particularly through the annual appropriations hearings, his actual control over administrative operations was relatively loose. Partly for this reason and partly because of his friendly relations with the Rooney subcommittee, Deputy Under Secretary Crockett enjoyed a fair amount of freedom in 1965 to unfreeze the O area. Rooney's attitude seemed to be, as long as it saves money, cuts bureaucracy, and doesn't raise too much hell with the rest of the department, go ahead. Crockett later said specifically that there were no objections from Rooney to either the concept or the implementation of his reforms.

The picture changed dramatically with the nondiplomatic functions housed in the O area. The most notable case was the Bureau of Security and Consular Affairs (SCA) and its largest division, the Passport Office. The control pattern for SCA grew out of its origins in the Immigration and Nationality Act of 1952, a measure designed to give Senator McCarthy direct influence in the department. This bill established the bureau in the State Department and charged it with handling security operations as well as monitoring passports and visas for "loyalty" and "subversion." The security arm was later removed from SCA and given an independent office. Following the mood of the times, Congress assigned jurisdiction over SCA to the House Committee on Internal Security and the Senate Internal Security Subcommittee of the Committee on the Judiciary. In 1965-66, primary ownership was held by the House committee, under the chairmanship of Congressman Michael A. Feighan.

This control pattern affected the 1965 reorganization of the O area at two points. First, in 1965 Crockett attempted to streamline the SCA superstructure, thereby eliminating the position of its administrator, Abba Schwartz. According to Crockett, this effort was applauded by Feighan. Neither he nor Senator James Eastland, chairman of the Senate Judiciary Committee, had any sympathy for Schwartz, the most visible liberal in the State Department. When the reorganization plan was announced, however, it was immediately interpreted by congressional and other liberals as a conservative coup to oust Schwartz. The issue drew coverage in the national press and stirred debate in Congress. These developments coupled with Schwartz's own resignation forced Crockett to abandon the plan.

Second, Crockett had orginally hoped to apply his concept of decentralized management to the Passport Office. He decided not to move in this direction, however, because of potential congressional opposition. Frances Knight, the director, not only maintained cordial relations with Feighan and Eastland, but had the support of the airlines, the travel industry, the traveling public, and other influential elements in the Washington bureaucracy. Crockett commented in a 1971 interview:

Frances Knight is an excellent example of "sacred territory" that could not have been reorganized except under the most favorable congressional circumstances, i.e., when the Secretary of State had no problems with any powerful committees and therefore would not need their help or fear their wrath.

But during the Rusk years this was never to be the case. We had the Otepka case[2] and the Schwartz case on our plates (two people items) and we were constantly in trouble with both the Senate Foreign Relations and the Senate Internal Security Committees on policy issues. So we could never have done a [reorganization] in these areas—and in some other areas of State—for the same reason.

Hence a major barrier to unfreezing, and a crucial prop for existing structures, is the perception that a change effort will be thwarted by mortgage holders in the agency's power setting.

Sometimes a reorganization plan will run aground on jurisdictional disputes between two or more committees, or ambiguity about which committees should be called into play. During testimony on the Hays Bill, one of the opponents argued that the scope of the personnel reforms was so extensive, and the implications for federal personnel systems so momentous, that the legislation really should be considered by congressional bodies other than the Senate Foreign

---

[2] Otto Otepka, a division chief in SCA, was accused by the State Department of leaking confidential information on "security risks" to the Senate Internal Security Subcommittee and was suspended from his position. The suspension triggered an outburst from Senator Eastland and his supporters in Congress, who demanded a full investigation. In the interim Otepka was assigned to an obscure position, seemingly to remove him from sight.

Relations Committee. Similarly, while the Agency for International Development is normally under the jurisdiction of foreign affairs committees, any reorganization of its activities in the field of agricultural commodities (for example, Food for Peace) would spill over into the territory of the agriculture committees. At one point, in fact, these latter committees blocked a move by AID to transfer responsibility for handling surplus agricultural products from the Department of Agriculture to itself (Seidman, 1970, p. 43). As a further example, the difficulties of changing *any* executive branch actions on water resources are now legendary (cf. Maass, 1951). The rivalries among the Army Corps of Engineers, the Bureau of Reclamation, and the Soil Conservation Service are outdone only by the jurisdictional squabbles among their congressional patrons.

### Statutory Bureaucracy and System-wide Rules

A further obstacle to the unfreezing of governmental bureaucracy consists in administrative structures embedded in federal statutes and therefore unable to be changed without legislative concurrence. A distinction is often made between unitary or essentially single-purpose agencies, such as the National Aeronautics and Space Administration (NASA), and complex, "holding-company" departments such as Health, Education, and Welfare (HEW). The latter are organizations that have drawn together a number of constituent units, some of which may have their own statutory bases. From the standpoint of change, a critical feature of such agencies is that senior executives may not have the legal authority to modify the internal structure of the statutory subunits. Change requires congressional assent—a scarce commodity in general when it comes to reorganizations, and doubly so when the subunits connect to significant interest groups. By contrast, heads of unitary agencies usually have the legal power to change organization structures under their authority.

Because this point is basic to an understanding of the federal system, and because it has received little attention from writers on organization theory, a few examples are in order. One of the primary aims of Truman's Reorganization Act of 1949 was precisely to move upward to department heads the authority previously vested by statute in subordinate agencies. Truman obviously wished to break the old pattern of decentralized power in the interest of promoting greater managerial flexibility on the part of the secretaries and the President. Congress approved some but not all of these plans and has shown a comparable ambivalence since that time toward control at the top.

Despite the overall aim of promoting flexibility, some of the reorganization plans submitted by Truman maintained statutory recognition for certain departmental subunits. Reorganization Plan No. 2 of 1949 contained the following provisions for the Department of Labor:[3]

Section 1. *Bureau of Employment Security.* The Bureau of Employment Security of the Federal Security Agency, including the United States Employment Service and the Unemployment Insurance Service, together with the functions thereof, is *transferred as an organizational entity* to the Department of Labor (emphasis added) . . .
Section 3. *Federal Advisory Council.* The Federal Advisory Council . . . is hereby transferred to the Department of Labor and shall, in addition to its duties under the aforesaid Act, advise the Secretary of Labor and Director of the Bureau of Employment Security with respect to the administration and coordination of the functions transferred by the provisions of this reorganization plan.

It is apparent that even with the amplified authority of office, the Secretary of Labor could not have abolished or greatly reorganized the Bureau of Employment Security without congressional approval. Along similar lines, the Reorganization Plan for the Department of the Interior (1950) provided for two officials below the Secretary: the Assistant Secretary of the Interior and the Administrative Assistant Secretary. Presumably these positions could not have been abolished, as in the MOP reorganization, without legislative assent.

More recently, in the Omnibus Crime Control and Safe Streets Act of 1968, Congress gave further evidence of its incurable tendency to impose organizational structures. This bill established the Law

[3] This and the other reorganization acts submitted by the President and not disapproved by Congress appear in the U. S. Statutes-at-Large, the yearly volumes of laws passed by Congress. The reader who wishes to scan them further will find them grouped together in numerical sequence following the public laws and preceding the private laws.

Enforcement Assistance Administration in the Department of Justice and gave it certain law enforcement responsibilities. By being specific about such responsibilities, the Congress undercut the earlier Reorganization Plan for Justice which transferred to the Attorney General "all functions vested in other officers of the Department of Justice" (Seidman, 1970, p. 87). The bill also specified that no more than two members of the "Administration" should belong to the same political party. The implications of such detailed specification of organization structures for administrative reorganizations are apparent. And:

> More important . . . than the direct vesting of duties in bureaus are the numerous congressional expectations with respect to the way they shall operate. For example, if the Secretary of Agriculture were to contemplate uniting all farmer-oriented programs into one line of control from Washington to the local offices, he would find among other things that Congress has prohibited regional offices for the Farmers Home Administration, has prescribed a system of state co-operation for the Soil Conservation Service, and is committed to a system of farmer committees for administration of the functions of the Agricultural Stabilization and Conservation Service. He would probably conclude that it was better to leave the conservation functions which the three agencies have, and other related functions as well, under separate administration than to seek amendment of the several pieces of legislation related to each (Redford, 1969, p. 75).

The combined weight of politics and law provides a heavy anchor for existing bureaucracy.

Parallel limitations on administrative discretion arise from system-wide standards, rules, regulations, and monitors in the executive system. For one, the tenure protection provisions of the Civil Service system make it very difficult as well as risky for a senior executive to use the threat of dismissal as a lever of change. The time and effort required to carry a dismissal through the web of appeals procedures makes it a costly alternative, and one that can boomerang against the superior if it fails. In the Hays Bill hearings, where this question came up, Senator Gore remarked: "In fact, most of the heads of agencies tell me it is so much trouble to get rid of an incompetent, it is easier just to put him on a desk someplace and give him nothing to do and let him stay on the payroll and hire somebody else to do the work" (Senate

Committee on Foreign Relations, 1966, p. 89). Representatives of the American Federation of Government Employees objected strenuously to this charge. But they had little to say when Senator Gore pointed out that in the Department of State, which had several thousand Civil Service employees, only about two per year were removed in accordance with Civil Service Commission regulations. And quite apart from legal protections for job tenure, the informal connections developed by many career employees may raise the political costs of dismissal to intolerable levels.

A reorganization plan may also be stymied because the new system requires extensive changes in job descriptions, a matter falling under the general jurisdiction of the government-wide Civil Service Commission. The position classification system works as follows. The Civil Service Commission, after consulting the agency in question, defines the classes into which individual positions must be fitted. The agency, under the decentralized classification system in operation since 1949, is responsible for relating its specific jobs to these classes. The Civil Service Commission retains ultimate authority over agency classification actions and exercises this control through a periodic inspection or audit of agency decisions. The commission not only may change an agency's classifications, but may, as an ultimate sanction, withdraw its authority to classify positions. Employees may also appeal agency classifications to the commission, which on review may side with the employee or make other adjustments.

These broad ground rules are highly germane to any reorganization program involving Civil Service employees. First, despite the existing decentralization of authority to agencies, it is likely that the CSC would not stand by idly if a reorganization involved the creation of many new positions or the reclassification of more than a few others. Second, to protect itself against subsequent criticism, the agency itself might wish to consult the CSC about its actions before the fact. It was clear from a study of the Department of Labor[4] that the department's

---

[4]This unpublished study was conducted by the Center for Research on Utilization of Scientific Knowledge of the Institute for Social Research at the University of Michigan. Marvin Meade, a collaborator on this volume, was one of the investigators.

classification division was careful to check major decisions, particularly at the level of GS-13 to 15, with the CSC before implementing a classification action. Third, in any major restructuring one would expect a number of disgruntled employees to appeal agency decisions, thus subjecting the reorganization to a partial CSC review. While the system-wide powers of the CSC certainly do not prevent reorganizations, they are another negative factor to contend with.

Still, our own research suggested that bureaucratic mountains are not immovable. The earlier review of the O area reforms showed quite clearly that major changes in bureaucratic structure can be made under optimal conditions. The major factor favoring Crockett's efforts was that the MOP reorganization dealt mainly with Foreign Service Officers and Reserve Officers, neither of whom are covered by the Classification Act. A distinctive feature of Foreign Service personnel systems is the principle of rank-in-man, rather than rank-in-position as in the Civil Service; this provides greater latitude not only in assignments but in organizational change. In an interview in 1970 we asked Crockett about the extent to which his reforms were facilitated by the fact that they involved mainly Foreign Service staff. He replied:

Yes—to some extent it may have made it easier to reorganize because the Foreign Service is a more mobile, flexible group because of the fact that they, like the military, carry their job grade on their person (it's theirs) while in the Civil Service the person's grade is geared to the position he occupies.

So, we could abolish jobs quite freely when they were held by Foreign Service people and not hurt people personally but when (if) the same happened to Civil Service people they could have been badly hurt personally.

I don't believe the Civil Service Commission would have actually vetoed the proposals, but there would have been more and more problems—for example—just moving the people from job to job would have required more bureaucracy because of the grade-salary relevance.

Summarizing his experiences with both statutory changes and the Civil Service classification rules, Crockett concluded on a note of moderate optimism:

*But*—this [Civil Service red tape] could be used more as an excuse than as a reason. Sure it's difficult—but still possible if the top man is willing to put up with the pain and make the effort. It's a real possibility for any agency . . .

Yes, there are some statutory problems but these can always be surmounted if the previous situation [political difficulties] could have been cured. But sometimes this very situation exists *because* of the existence of the above condition. They work hand in glove.

In other words, astute opponents of change can use an existing statute, such as that governing the Bureau of Security and Consular Affairs in the State Department, as a cudgel to beat down undesired reforms. If the fears of the opponents could be allayed, the laws themselves could be changed with little fanfare.

## Interagency Linkages

Anthony Downs has written (1967, pp. 165-166) that the more deeply a reorganization penetrates within a bureau, from superficial alterations of daily routines to the deeper levels of internalized values and missions, the greater the resistance encountered. The present research suggests an added hypothesis dealing with breadth rather than depth: *In the federal bureaucracy the greater the number of organizations bound to an agency in an interdependent system, the greater the potential resistance to organizational change.*

The Hays Bill illustrates this principle. The proposed reforms touched the interests of several personnel systems,[5] including the Foreign Service Officer Corps and the Civil Service system, and of numerous agencies, especially the State Department, the Agency for International Development, and the U. S. Information Agency. For different reasons (see Chapter 8), and in different ways, the FSO corps and the Civil Service unions strongly opposed the measure. AID and USIA, on the other hand, endorsed the reforms through statements from senior officials. Nevertheless, Senator Hickenlooper, who assumed the role of informal overseer of USIA, attacked the bill on the grounds that it would weaken this agency and confer excessive power

[5] For present purposes we shall treat personnel systems as organizations, although they are really suborganizations within an agency or cutting across several agencies.

on the State Department. The Departments of Commerce, Agriculture, and Interior, all of which are involved in foreign affairs and staffed mainly by Civil Service personnel, were also sources of muted backstage opposition. The strength of the resistance to change increases geometrically if the proposed reorganization involves shifts in operating responsibility as distinct from internal personnel reforms. The continuing battles among the water resources agencies mentioned earlier provide a case in point.

## Interest Groups

Rational administrative theory to the contrary, nothing is more characteristic of the federal bureaucracy than exchange relationships between agencies and interest groups. The Department of State is quite exceptional in having no significant domestic constituency providing favors to and drawing benefits from the bureaucracy. Some agencies, such as the Departments of Commerce, Agriculture, and Labor, were set up with the patent aim of responding to the respective clientele groups. Others, including the Tennessee Valley Authority, were established mainly for operational reasons but gradually became locked into interest groups (cf. Selznick, 1949). The significant point here is that, whatever the historical evolution of exchange and dependency relations, once established they will have enormous implications for the maintenance of established bureaucracy.

The Hays Bill case is a pallid example in the full spectrum available. Although the veterans' organizations were not, strictly speaking, clientele groups for the State Department, AID, and USIA, they exercised tutelage for their own constituents over these and all other agencies. Thus when a bill came forth removing the hallowed right of veterans' preference in hiring and firing, the Veterans of Foreign Wars were quick to defend the existing pattern. However eloquently set forth by Deputy Under Secretary Crockett and the Herter Committee, the concept of managerial efficiency simply had no meaning to such single-purpose interest groups. They attacked the Hays Bill with all the ammunition that could be mustered.

The full flowering of clientele resistance is seen in such areas as banking, agriculture, water resources and other "pork barrel" fields.

Harold Seidman provides numerous examples in his penetrating study of government organizations:

The American Bankers Association through the years has successfully blocked efforts to consolidate bank supervisory and examining functions in a single federal agency. The division of responsibility among the Comptroller of the Currency, the Federal Deposit Insurance Corporation, and the Federal Reserve Board is viewed by the ABA as "wholly in keeping with the broad principle that the success and strength of democracy in America is largely due to the sound safeguards afforded by the wisely conceived checks and balances which pervade our composite governmental system." The system is defended because banks retain the option of changing their Federal supervisors and thus gaining "some possible relief from unduly stringent examinations" (1970, p. 17).

Each of the agencies dispensing federal largesse has its personal lobby: the Corps of Engineers has the Rivers and Harbors Congress; the Bureau of Reclamation the National Reclamation Association; the Soil Conservation Service, the National Association of Soil and Water Conservation Districts. The Department of Agriculture's precedent in organizing its own support organization, the Farm Bureau, has been followed by many other agencies.

These groups are very jealous of the special relationship with their Government sponsor. Interlopers are not treated kindly. Programs which may dilute the sponsor's single-minded concern with their interests are vigorously opposed (ibid., p. 127).

A point made by the bankers is perhaps the key to the pattern described: the fractionation of power across numerous overlapping agencies provides checks and balances in the relation between government and governed. Put more politically, such an arrangement not only gives interest groups a better chance to make their influence felt with one agency, but allows more latitude for playing off rival agencies against one another. It is for this reason more than any other that clientele and other interest groups are so little impressed with reorganization plans premised on the desirability of clean lines of authority and reductions in the cost of government. Oddly enough, the lobbies for the latter interests are poorly financed and have few allies within the bureaucracy.

**Internal Resistance**

In public agencies as in all organizations there is also a variety of internal sources of resistance to unfreezing. Foremost among these are the agency's "sunk costs" in established programs, processes, and patterns of behavior. A significant change in the State Department's performance evaluation system might require not only the printing of new forms and the discarding of thousands of old forms, but costly retraining of supervisory personnel and selection boards, a new system of information handling and storage, and—most difficult of all—a modification of the attitudes and behaviors of all concerned. The Agency for International Development has run up against all of these problems, as well as others, in its recent efforts to overhaul its performance evaluation system.

However, in most agencies the greatest impediment to lasting change is not unfreezing but refreezing. The politically appointed agency director often has a honeymoon period providing a fair amount of freedom to undo and redo existing structures. However, such efforts typically break down when it comes to refreezing—integrating the new structures and procedures into the surrounding organization and into the attitudes and behaviors of the permanent employees. A critical factor in this process is the ambivalent relationship between political appointees and career officials.

## Leadership Discontinuity

Studies of corporate organizations show that a shift in top leadership can be a strong stimulus for change (Gouldner, 1954; Guest, 1962). The present study also demonstrated that the senior leadership of the O area in the State Department had a fair amount of freedom to change organizational structures. Deputy Under Secretary Crockett introduced dozens of changes, some rather substantial, both in the O area and in other parts of the department. In a strange way, Crockett's successor Idar Rimestad also acted as a change agent by restoring O to its pre-1965 structure. William Macomber, who followed Rimestad, likewise used the considerable leverage of his position to revamp limited sections of O and the department. It is common in Washington to have a burst of reorganization as a new secretary, under secretary, agency director, or other official takes over. Such changes, however, are usually superficial and ephemeral. In the short run they may unfreeze and overtly change the organization, but over time the failure to provide adequate "jelling" leads to their dissipation.

The most powerful force working against the consolidation of change is the limited tenure of political heads. The labyrinthine patterns of intra- and interagency relationships together with the persistence of forces hostile to change means that stabilization requires time. Even after the initial obstacles to unfreezing are overcome, the interval between the implementation and the completion of the changes will often be more than a year. In the O area reorganization changes were still being made at the time of Crockett's resignation in 1967, more than a year and a half after the starting date. Mosher (1967) shows that it is not at all unusual for governmental reorganizations to go on for three or four years, or more. And, in our terminology, this period refers only to *changing*; refreezing requires much longer.

By comparison, a study of 1,000 political executives appointed between 1933 and 1965 shows a mean tenure in office of about two years (Stanley, Mann, and Doig, 1967). Under secretaries and assistant secretaries typically lasted twenty-four months, with 57 percent serving less time. Politically appointed senior administrators thus are not in office long enough to provide for the institutionalization of their changes. The desire of their successors to be creative, assertive new brooms (or, as in the case of Idar Rimestad, tried and trusty old brooms) further shortens the life-span of a reorganization. These cycles of succession account in good part for the constant juggling and reshuffling of units, positions, and rules in federal agencies.

Looking back on his own efforts at change after a four-year absence from Washington, William Crockett concluded when interviewed in 1971:

The rotation of top officials in State (as in any agency or organization) does produce casualties to programs left by an outgoing official, especially if the program is either difficult to carry out, controversial, or in trouble. This is just one of life's realities and one that we should all be aware of in developing change plans. If we can't command the time frame to get it in place then we should think carefully about starting it in the first place. At least this is the way I feel now, but I frankly didn't even think of this matter at that time.

Crockett was not unusual in assuming that the most effective, if not the only, tool needed to promote change was the power of appointive office. This assumption is built into the entire Washington ethos, and is rapidly communicated to the fledgling appointee.

## Career Officials: Sitting Tight

The permanent impermanence of the top agency leadership breeds suspicion, wariness, and passive resistance at the middle and bottom levels. Veteran career officials with a high survival quotient look askance at the "Johnny-come-latelys who don't know a damn thing about what's going on around here." They are particularly contemptuous of appointed heads who come in to "shake up the place," a plentiful breed. Sometimes they are able, within a few months, to socialize the new man into the works and pomps of the agency. The reformer may even become the most ardent defender imaginable of the viewpoints of the career service. If the veterans have no luck on that route, they can protect their interests by tactics ranging from artful sabotage to surface compliance. Possessed of a well-developed actuarial sense, they know that it will not be long before this particular madness is over.

The efforts by the Kennedy and Johnson administrations to restore the primacy of the State Department in foreign affairs show traces of quiet sabotage by career employees. On March 4, 1966, President Johnson issued an executive order (National Security Action Memorandum, or NSAM, 341) directing the Secretary of State to "assume responsibility to the full extent permitted by law for the overall direction, coordination and supervision of interdepartmental activities of the United States Government overseas (less exempted military activities)." This directive established two types of interdepartmental committees: the Senior Interdepartmental Group (SIG), which included State, Defense, AID, USIA, the Chairman of the Joint Chiefs of Staff, and the Special Assistant to the President for National Security Affairs; and five Interdepartmental Regional Groups (IRGs), with agency membership paralleling the SIGs but with the main focus on regions such as Latin America and Africa. Within the State Department, country directors were part of the overall effort to improve foreign affairs coordination. Replacing the former officer directors in the regional bureaus, they were expected to take line responsibilities for one or more countries, and provide staff support to the SIG and IRG groups.

The overall reform program suffered from numerous drawbacks, most of which have been documented by William Bacchus (1974b) and several of which are common to the cases discussed in this volume. The system was developed by General Maxwell Taylor without adequate consultation with those who would be involved; Secretary Rusk, who was generally skeptical of committees, was not personally committed to the effort and lacked real authority to control the actions of other agencies; President Johnson, despite the formal support given in NSAM 341, preferred informal techniques for dealing with key foreign policy issues; Under Secretary Ball also was not an active promoter of the concept, partly because of his own plans to leave the department; his successor, Nicholas Katzenbach, failed to call meetings of the SIG and seemed generally unimpressed with the whole notion.

It was at the staff level within the Department of State that the resistance of the Foreign Service was most in evidence. Despite frequent complaints about being by-passed by the military and other agencies, the country directors and other key Foreign Service staff members in the new system did not capitalize on the opportunities provided for bureaucratic entrepreneurship. William Crockett, during a 1970 interview, described their stance in these terms:

The opposition to this new function was more apathetic than vocal and came from three groups, i.e., the Regional Bureaus, the other Foreign Affairs agencies, and the Foreign Service. One of the *most* effective, least risky, and most difficult-to-combat types of opposition is the "do nothing" variety. A leader can cope with direct confrontation, he can take hard action against outright insubordination, and he can handle groups that misuse or overuse their authority. But it is tough to deal with a whole group which *underuses* its authority. It's hard to get at the issues when a group simply doesn't do the job in the full sense of its potential and possibility. This is the way these three groups reacted to this new concept and since there was no actual *product* that the failure to act failed to produce, it was very hard to fault a group on the theoretical basis that *if* they had done more (taken action), "something" might have resulted.

I do not charge either the Foreign Service or the regional bureaus with a conspiratorial motive for their lack of action. They simply, for perhaps many reasons, didn't make the plan work nor did they try.

The 1965 reorganization showed similar signs of covert resistance. Under the decentralized management system in the O area, the former supervisors of operating programs were to strip themselves of all line authority and become "cone coordinators." Our research showed that, among the five individuals involved, compliance with this model was minimal in two cases, partial in one, erratic in another, and reasonably complete in only one case. The first two superiors simply did not believe in the applicability of decentralized management to the State Department. Furthermore, they were confident that Crockett would be leaving before long—and they were right. Hence their response was adherence to the more observable features of the new system, such as having managers prepare written program statements, but inward temporizing. Interestingly, some of the liberated managers reacted in the same way. They went through the motions of autonomous decision-making, but resented the reorganized structure and longed for their old cages. Crockett attributed their cautiousness to "human frailty"—an excessive need for the comforts of hierarchy. But their resistance may have been rooted in the belief that the reorganization would not last beyond Crockett's term, and that he would be succeeded by a more traditional administrator. As already noted, their fears proved to be well founded. This experience underscores the critical importance of refreezing in organizational change and the difficulty of attaining it in a system marked by constant rotation at the top.

## Organizational Conflicts and Tensions

Conflicts among subunits of the same agency further reduce the possibility of unfreezing, changing, and refreezing. The main difficulty posed by internal strife is that a proposed change is evaluated more on strategic grounds than on its own merits. In an atmosphere of battle, warring bureaucrats find it hard to think about the overall welfare of the agency, much less abstractions such as "the public interest." The greater the organizational tensions and the greater the impact of change on the contending parties, the more likely it is that a change program will become a bureaucratic battlefield. Even if the proponents are able to overcome initial resistance and implement some of the proposals, their efforts ultimately may be frustrated because refreezing is inhibited by the various tensions.

The effects of organizational conflicts and friction were apparent in the various change programs undertaken by the State Department in the sixties. The department was split by long-standing and cross-cutting cleavages: the Foreign Service vs the Civil Service, the regional bureaus vs the functional bureaus, the substantive specialists vs the administrators, and others. But the most frequent and powerful pole of resistance during this period was the Foreign Service Officer Corps. The difficulties of producing change in an atmosphere of suspicion are exemplified by the running struggle between the Foreign Service and the department's appointed leadership.

The prime reason for Foreign Service resistance was its elite status and guild structure. The Department's Task Force on Creativity commented:

> The Foreign Service has traditionally prided itself on being a kind of elite corps . . . Foreign Service Officers constitute, in their isolation from the main currents of national life (an isolation in part forced on them by the very nature of their profession), a kind of caste. They tend to be resistant to ideas from the outside. As one officer put it, "the Foreign Service Officer believes that his is an arcane craft which people on the outside cannot hope to understand." We listen carefully and politely but seldom change our views (U. S. Department of State, 1970, p. 311).

While retaining this elite image, the service has also felt itself under attack from various quarters: McCarthy in the 1950s, the rising class of administrators, competitors in other agencies, and the department's own political leaders. The result, in the eyes of even sympathetic observers, was a garrison mentality viewing all organizational change with hostility.

For its part, the political leadership of State in the 1960s was heavily laden with outsiders showing little understanding of the service. By their behavior and statements, which sometimes contained ill-concealed scorn for the FSO corps, the political appointees reinforced the already strong feelings of distrust and animosity in the career service. Some made it plain that they expected little creativity, progress, or initiative from a tired, defensive, and hidebound Officer Corps. Acting on these premises, the top leaders at State usually failed to involve the service in plans and programs for change. In the familiar cycle of the self-fulfilling prophecy, the FSOs dug in their heels. As one well-placed observer remarked, they reacted with a "very sensitive, protective, suspicious, defensive and closed attitude toward people, ideas, suggestions, innovations, etc., which in any way had impact upon areas which they perceived as being detrimental to their own vital interests, or areas which they considered of their primary ownership." Actions by the administrators, such as Crockett, produced counterreactions, such as superficial compliance and antipathy, in the Foreign Service. The service typically responded by clinging more tightly than ever to the core element in its professional self-definition: the traditional concept of diplomacy. And this was precisely what the political leaders were trying to change. The defensive reactions, of course, simply confirmed the initial impressions of the political leadership and widened the cleavage between the service and the department as a whole. This chain of events reduced the possibility of creative outputs from the State Department, reinforced its image as a "fudge factory" and a "bowl of jelly," and further undercut its bargaining position in the interagency setting.

## Administrative Orthodoxy and Organizational Goals

The management philosophy and organizational goals in a public agency comprise a final source of internal resistance. Most federal agencies are guided by managerial values emphasizing hierarchical and semiautocratic organizational structures with heavy emphasis on accountability. These values define the set of questions of basic concern to administrators and also set limits on the possibilities of change.

A strongly entrenched traditional view has several implications for organizational change. One is that officials working in the system may not even consider the possibility of major change. Indeed, they may feel that the hallmark of the federal system is its permanence. Moreover, if there are changes involving drastic departures from the traditional model, they are likely to be suspect from the outset. The more they depart from accepted principles of management, the more likely are they to meet with skepticism. Several respondents in our study took pains to point out the irrelevance of "new management theories" to an agency such as the State Department. Supervisors will be particularly resistant to changes involving greater participation in decision-making, greater openness in communication, and other aspects of participative management. While these sources of resistance are common to many organizations, they are fortified in the federal system by the widespread acceptance and deep internalization of the orthodox view.

A more subtle source of resistance arises in agencies dealing with broad, intangible goals. The problem is epitomized in a remark attributed to Dean Rusk: "Organization seldom stands in the way of good people and seldom converts mediocrity into excellent performance." This emphasis on the primacy of people over organization can undercut both the initiation and the consolidation of change. Such a philosophy is found most commonly in an agency, such as State, where objectives are broad, performance is difficult to measure, and there is a career service priding itself on personal qualities. The agency may then place a high premium on the personal characteristics required to achieve its mission: vision, mental acuity, and experience buttressed by a broad, generalist view of the world. Organizational forms and procedures are seen as strictly ancillary items that can safely be relegated to the "pants pressers."

Agencies working with less abstract goals and more stable programs may, on the other hand, be less concerned with people and more with administrative structures. Interest in the latter will rise if it can be shown that organizational changes produce measurable improvements such as more rapid processing of applications from welfare clients, lower unit costs in highway construction, or a reduction of overruns in the development of military hardware. Efforts at major change in the first type of agency will stumble on the belief that improved effectiveness requires better people rather than different structures. Groups such as the Foreign Service may see reforms like MOP and the Hays Bill as at best useless tinkering and at worst a power play by the administrators. As Senator Pell remarked during the Hays Bill debate: "I submit that the way to achieve this ever better Foreign Service is to leave it alone for a while to develop its own *esprit de corps* . . . My thought is that there should be a central core of highly skilled, articulate and educated Foreign Service Officers who would be assisted in their work by specialists in various categories" (Senate Committee on Foreign Relations, 1966, p. 23). By contrast, in the second type of agency the gap between "substance" and "administration" is likely to be smaller, and the legitimacy of administrative change correspondingly higher.

Beyond the level of agency operations, personalism is rampant in three sectors crucial to bureaucratic change: the White House, the Congress, and the senior political appointees. What this means in practice is that key officials or legislators will, perhaps for personalistic reasons, give their general benediction to organizational reforms, but continue to follow their accustomed patterns of decision-making. Thus President Johnson, the author of NSAM 341, appeared to throw his full weight behind this attempt to restore coordination in foreign policy. Yet,

President Johnson, for his part, continued to use the "Tuesday Lunch" and other informal techniques for important decision-making. As a politician who had little feel for organizations because "he dealt with people," he was disinclined to say, "let the SIG handle this problem." While he accepted the NSAM system as something that might be useful, he did not push it once it had been created (Bacchus, 1974b, pp. 273-274).

Harold Seidman points to a similar mentality in the Senate, from which Johnson moved to the vice presidency:

Whatever its other virtues as a breeding ground for Presidents, the Senate is a poor school for executives and managers. The emphasis in a legislative body is on individuals, not institutions or organizations. Legislators do not think in institutional terms, except when some immediate constituency interest is threatened (1970, p. 65).

Both at the highest levels of government and within agencies it is striking how often positions and issues are defined in personal terms. It was not accidental that in the Hays Bill hearings as well as in the wake of MOP many spoke of a power play by Crockett and his assistants. The personalization of government at all levels must, therefore, enter as a major term in any equation accounting for bureaucratic persistence.

### Summary

Numerous forces converge to hold bureaucracy in place once it becomes part of the federal system. The phenomenon of bureaucratic persistence is related to three facets of organizational change: unfreezing, changing, and refreezing. Resistance to change at all three points can be traced to extra-agency as well as intra-agency sources. The most powerful external sources of resistance are the orientations of members of Congress, including a twelve-month appropriations framework and a tendency to deal with agencies mainly at the level of operations; the pattern of agency ownership by congressional committees and subcommittees; the fact that some agency structures are embedded in federal statutes; system-wide rules, regulations, and standards, such as those administered by the Civil Service Commission; the interdependency of agencies in the federal system; and tutelage or exchange relationships between agencies and interest groups. These external barriers operate primarily at the level of unfreezing and changing.

The internal obstacles, on the other hand, have their greatest impact at the stage of refreezing or stabilizing a change program. These include the discontinuity of leadership arising from the limited tenure of political appointees, resistance from career employees, organizational conflicts and tensions, and the managerial philosophy and organizational goals of an agency. Personalism can also serve as a barrier to bureaucratic change.

# Part IV  Conclusions

# 10 • Bureaucracy, Organizations, and Organizational Change

This study underscores the need for a fundamental redirection of theory and research on bureaucracy, organizations, and organizational change. All three fields suffer from a constriction of theoretical perspectives and an overly narrow data base. Sociologists and social psychologists typically have built their theoretical edifices on the empirical foundations of those organizations to which they had the most ready access: factories, schools, universities, insurance agencies, hospitals, prisons, unions, and voluntary associations. The study of governmental organizations generally has been left to specialists in public administration, a field that until recently has shown little interest in broader theories of organizations and bureaucracy. To make matters worse, sociologists have, on the whole, treated Weber's conceptualization of bureaucracy as a sacred legacy to be interpreted but never radically changed. As a result, our theoretical understanding of public organizations, and therefore of the full range of organizations, remains seriously limited. The following conclusions are offered in the hope of broadening the base and widening the horizons of organizational research.

## Bureaucracy

The study of bureaucracy has lived far too long on the intellectual capital of Max Weber. Through no fault of this seminal theorist, the Weberian model has almost become an obstacle to a fresh look at bureaucratic structures. As is well recognized, Weber's conception of bureaucracy was far from comprehensive; historically and culturally specific, it carried more than faint overtones of admiration for the Prussian military organization. One glaring limitation is its inability to handle the variety of organization-environment interactions inherent in the existence of a U. S. federal agency. Given Weber's overarching concern with rationality and efficiency in organizational design, it is understandable that he paid little heed to such antirational factors as constituency influences, bargaining alliances, and internal conflicts.

Sociological research on bureaucracy, unfortunately, has become so wedded to the dimensions spelled out in Weber's ideal type that the role of the political environment has received scant attention. The work of Peter Blau and his associates demonstrates both the heuristic value and the conceptual limitations of the Weberian model. Blau (1968, p. 454) writes:

A theory of formal organization . . . seeks to explain why organizations develop certain characteristics, such as a multilevel hierarchy or decentralized authority. To furnish these explanations requires that the characteristics of organizations are not taken as given, but the conditions that produce them are investigated.

Over the past two decades Blau and his students have mounted an impressive research program to test the interconnectedness of organizational characteristics. The epitome, and perhaps the outer limit, of this approach is *The Structure of Organizations* by Blau and Schoenherr (1971). Using a massive correlational analysis and other statistical techniques, the authors explore the systematic interdependence of organizational characteristics in fifty-three U. S. employment security agencies.

As valuable as this kind of research may be for an empirically based theory of organizations, it is lopsided in its coverage of issues. The overriding concern is with the effects of one organizational property, such as size, on others, such as internal differentiation. The section on organizational contexts covers only such easily measurable environmental properties as population size and the percentage of foreign born in the surrounding community. Politics scarcely rears its head at all in this book, probably because the underlying theory is concerned almost exclusively with impersonal, structural forces. The result is an exhaustive analysis of organizational structure, and an almost total neglect of the politics of bureaucratic design in the federal system. Except for some background material that does not enter into the analytic discussion, one would hardly know that employment security agencies are subject to both state and federal intervention. Shifts in federal regulations, for example, might have more profound effects on the structure and operation of these units than many of the variables given explicit consideration. Admittedly, these agencies are almost unique in their administrative structure and are removed by geography and by mission from mainstream Washington bureaucratic politics. But even these distinctive qualities might have been noted as important qualifications on the generalizability of the data, particularly to Washington-based executive departments and agencies.

One notable exception to the general pattern of inner-directed research on bureaucracy is the study by Pugh, Hickson, Hinings, and Turner (1973) on the context of organizational structures. In a well-designed cross-sectional analysis of fifty-two work organizations, the authors explored the relations between internal organizational structure and several contextual (environmental) conditions, including origin and history, ownership and control, size, charter, location, and dependence. While their research deals only with work organizations, it provides a useful model for future quantitative research. They found, for instance, a correlation of 0.64 between impersonality of ownership and the concentration of authority. "To a considerable degree this relationship is due to the fact that government-owned, and therefore impersonally founded, organizations tend to be highly centralized" (p. 67). This finding, which derives from a sample of British organizations, is consistent with our interpretation of hierarchy in the State Department.

Much of the existing research on organizations, including the studies by Blau and Schoenherr and by Pugh and his colleagues, suffers from the usual limitations of cross-sectional and aggregate data analysis in establishing causal connections. A correlation of 0.60 between the number of employees and the number of hierarchical levels may mean that greater size leads to more hierarchy, greater hierarchy to increased size (an interpretation consistent with Parkinson's Law), or that both hierarchy and size stem from some other unspecified condition such as communications overload. Blau and Schoenherr have gone to great lengths to determine the independent as well as the joint influence of key variables, but their efforts do not resolve this core problem of interpretation. Our follow-up of the O area reforms, moreover, suggests that the origins of bureaucracy in the State Department are complex and not readily encapsulated by variables such as size, number of divisions, and span of control.

A significant and unexpected conclusion of our research is that the bureaucrat can be an important source of bureaucracy, whether in origination or preservation. Once again the lenses of conventional wisdom may have filtered out a basic phenomenon of organizational life in the public agency. In the usual paradigm the bureaucrat is portrayed as the product of the organization — its creation rather than its creator. He is socialized, hypnotized, or victimized by the agency, but never builds the structures that shape him. We argue instead for a two-way influence pattern. On the one hand, the reward system of an agency such as State, and the socialization pattern of which it is a part, breed caution, limited discretion, and low risk-taking. These qualities in turn lead the employee to seek clearances and to refer even minor decisions "upstairs" for action. This pattern at the lower and middle levels of an organization creates bottom-up pressures for hierarchy and rules. Limited discretion and low risk-taking also work to prevent debureaucratization by instilling a fear of added responsibility and of direct exposure to the top. The O area reforms revealed instances of both short- and long-term resistance to liberation from the shackles of the old hierarchy.

What should be done to move the study of bureaucracy from the present dead center of inner-direction? The most fruitful step would be a coordinated series of case studies systematically exploring the effects of both internal characteristics and organization-environment interactions across a representative selection of public agencies. No agency, of course, is ever "representative" of any other, but it should be possible to choose a sample of public organizations that provides reasonable variation of such conditions as interest group penetration; control by congressional committees; and complexity, uncertainty, threat, and dispersion in the operating environment. To the extent that the key variables can be quantified, so much the better. Nonetheless, the fact that a critical condition, such as interest group influence, remains spongy and qualitative should not remove it from the analysis. For some agencies such swampy variables as "effectiveness of director's relations with congressional committees" may carry as much weight as size, span of control, and other easily measurable conditions.

It would also be crucial in the research mentioned to introduce a longitudinal dimension including, in particular, attention to the unique history of each agency. The experience of the State Department strongly indicates that the tensions, conflicts, assaults, and critical incidents of the past are essential to an understanding of contemporary organizational structure. We would assert without qualification that any analysis of bureaucratization in this setting that did not include consideration of the McCarthy period and Wristonization would be seriously incomplete and distorted. Public agencies more than most remain subject to the vicissitudes of political history and the whims of powerful individuals.[1] To exclude such factors on the grounds of unquantifiability would be to accord measurement a primacy it does not deserve. The next step, in short, is to wed the qualitative and historically attuned case study with representative coverage and quantification.

The critic of the model of bureaucratization developed in this book could properly argue that its major empirical base, the Department of State, is atypical of the federal bureaucracy and that therefore the model is of limited or unknown generalizability. As noted in the preface, we plead guilty as charged, but do not agree that the

---

[1]In this connection Harold Seidman (1970, p.118) observes:
Organization structure may provide clues to dimly remembered public controversies and catastrophes. The Forest Service might well be in the Interior Department today if the historic dispute between Secretary Ballinger and Gifford Pinchot had not left conservationists with a nearly pathological distrust of the Department. A collision of two commercial airliners over the Grand Canyon brought about the removal of the Federal Aviation Agency from the Department of Commerce. . . President Kennedy wanted a Southerner to administer the Community Relations Service and enforce the public accommodations laws and mainly for this reason gave the job to Secretary of Commerce Luther Hodges, who was from North Carolina.

limitations of coverage invalidate the central arguments made. The State Department is indeed atypical, as are all agencies, but it also shares many core features with other organizations in the executive system. In fact, one need not walk very far in Washington to hear comments to the effect that whatever agency one happens to be in is somehow distinctive and cannot be the subject of generalization. Lacking the range of data suggested earlier, the best that one can do at this stage is to show the distinctive features and make appropriate qualifications in the overall theory.

The characteristics listed below are exceptional in the federal system, and may increase bureaucratization in the ways indicated:

—The *rank-in-man system* tends to heighten bottom-up pressures for bureaucracy by increasing the salience of fear in performance appraisal and promotion. Career progression and selection-out loom larger when the employee is promoted on the basis of personal qualities and individual accomplishments rather than, as in the Civil Service, by changes in position. The rank-in-man system is also more prone to overstaffing than the Civil Service system, especially when there are cutbacks in positions.

—The *security emphasis* in the State Department is unquestionably greater than in most agencies with the exception of the FBI and the CIA. This emphasis derives not only from the inherent requirements of diplomacy and national security, but also from the furor raised about Foreign Service loyalty during the McCarthy period. To the extent that security precautions generate rules (see Chapter 5) and hierarchy, the State Department, the CIA, and the FBI may be more than normally inclined to bureaucracy.

—The *multiplicity of personnel systems* in the same department, as discussed in Chapters 5 and 8, creates heavy demands for hierarchy and rules, not only for the sheer administration of personnel operations, but also for umpiring the disputes and perceived inequities that are endemic to such an arrangement. These demands would be greatly reduced in an agency staffed exclusively with Civil Service personnel.

—The *complexity, uncertainty, threat, and dispersion* of the department's operating environment are all greater than normal in the federal system. This situation, coupled with the emphasis placed on written communications, creates pressures for hierarchy in the manner indicated at the end of Chapter 7.

—The department's high degree of *interdependence with other agencies* and its relatively sharp *separation of policy and administration* heighten the demands for interagency concurrences as well as the volume of communications. The implications for bureaucracy were noted in Chapters 5 and 7.

Some would also say that the ethos of the State Department is strongly affected by the self selection seen in the Foreign Service. After reading an earlier version of this manuscript, an official of the Office of Management and the Budget remarked: "The Foreign Service attracts people who want to be somebody rather than those who want to do something." While this assertion receives some support from both casual observation and serious research, one must be careful about accepting such statements as accurate reflections of organizational character. Once again, if the observer travels a bit farther in the bureaucracy, he or she will hear comparable remarks about the farm-boy origin of employees in the Department of Agriculture or the Western orientation (and often background) of officials in Interior, not to mention the Irish Catholic stereotype of the FBI agent. Nevertheless, it is true that even the Foreign Service regards itself as "different," if only because of its unique mission.

Before making too much of the atypicality of the State Department, one would do well to reexamine the characteristics it shares with other agencies: congressional control and oversight, rotation of political appointees, system-wide rules and monitors, accountability to the White House and to the public, interest group pressures (albeit of limited scope), alliances between career officials and external actors, and so forth (see Chapter 4). Given that all of the distinctive factors noted earlier operate to increase hierarchy and rules, bureaucracy in the State Department would appear to be overdetermined. If these factors were pared away, the pressures for bureaucracy stemming from the overall organizational system would still be strong. Still, we would be the first to concede that the only way to determine the impact of agency-specific and system-wide forces is to launch the broad program of organizational analysis previously suggested.

## Organization Theory

Despite their ubiquity, size, and pervasive impact on national and international life, federal executive agencies have received scant attention in organization theory. (By this we mean systematic attempts to set forth the basic structures and underlying dynamics of organizations as such.) Mosher (1967, p. 475) is still correct in his criticism that "the more general works on organization tend to summarize, synthesize, generalize, hypothesize, and theorize, largely on the basis of studies in non-public settings." There is no shortage of books and articles that purport to explain organizational behavior on a universal basis and even offer prescriptive statements based on such "general theory." But as of the time of writing there is not a single general work on organization theory that pays systematic attention to the distinctive features of the public bureaucracy and makes a serious effort to incorporate the findings of the many case studies reported in the literature of public administration. Even at a lower level of generality one can still count on two hands the studies that have systematically applied social scientific theory to organizational behavior in government agencies. Most noteworthy are Selznick's (1949) study of the TVA; Kaufman's (1960) analysis of the U. S. Forest Service; Blau's (1963) research on an employment and a law enforcement agency; Mosher's (1967) interpretation of numerous cases of governmental reorganization; Mott's (1972) search for correlates of organizational effectiveness in NASA and other units; and the extensive work of Blau and his colleagues on various government agencies (Blau, Heydebrand, and Stauffer, 1966; Blau and Schoenherr, 1971; Meyer, 1972). Also of great value, although not explicitly theoretical, is Harold Seidman's (1970) overview of the dynamics of federal organization. Beyond these analytic works are several dozen autobiographical, anecdotal, or otherwise descriptive accounts of managerial experiences or the operation of specific agencies. One of the better works in this genre is *Space Age Management* by James Webb (1969), former head of NASA. This last set of works provides ample raw material for theoretical analysis, but does not itself directly address issues of organization theory.

Partly as a result of this limited empirical coverage and partly because of the narrowness of the conceptual models used, organization theory is heavily biased toward internal structures and processes. The bulk of research still focuses on such conditions as size, functional complexity, supervisory structures, and employee motivation. Of late there has been greater attention paid to organizational environments, but usually in ways that do not apply particularly well to the public agency.

A critical omission in this regard is the effect of political control and influence on the internal structure and operations of an organization. The Watergate and related impeachment hearings of 1973 and 1974 brought out dramatic evidence of political tampering with such agencies as the Internal Revenue Service and the Central Intelligence Agency, as well as many other incidents of White House pressure on the bureaucracy. Yet one can even now read through thousands of pages of "general theory" on organizations without encountering a single reference to such external influences. For example, an otherwise useful book by David Silverman entitled *The Theory of Organisations* (1971) almost totally disregards the political environment in the conceptual framework proposed.

Ironically, even some of the studies concerned explicitly with public agencies have adopted a predominantly internal focus. Mott (1972) addresses the question of organizational effectiveness in NASA with little reference to that agency's relations with Congress, the aerospace industry, and other critical parts of the environment. Yet Webb, in his managerial memoirs, underscores the significance of precisely such extra-agency factors in NASA's success. The studies by Blau and his associates, as noted earlier, also treat the political environment as a negligible factor in organizational behavior. Admittedly, this internal orientation may be quite appropriate to the specific research questions addressed and to the parts of the agencies studied. In NASA Mott worked mainly with the Office of Administration, where the problems of internal efficiency could be highly important. Nevertheless, it is difficult to imagine that even there the relations between NASA and congressional committees did not influence the unit's efficiency and effectiveness. Similarly, it could be that the agencies studied by Blau and his colleagues were so far removed from the mainstream of political action as to be insulated from environmental pressures. It is equally plausible, however, to argue that these authors focused mainly on internal factors simply because their guiding organizational theory assigned no explicit influence to the environment. From the accounts presented in these and other studies it is difficult to know if environmental pressures were considered and rejected, or never considered at all.

The present study has shown numerous ways in which organization-environment interactions can affect bureaucratic growth and persistence as well as other aspects of organizational behavior:

(1) Controllers, particularly the legislative and appropriations committees of Congress, can exert *direct* control over agency operations by granting or not granting funds for certain kinds of activities, by granting or failing to grant legislative authority for specific agency operations, by creating new organizational structures within an agency or preventing change in existing structures, and in other ways. Controllers may *indirectly* affect agency operations through their demands for the accountability of ranking officials in the agency, through shame or embarrassment of these officials in public hearings, through tepid endorsement of agency proposals requiring legislation, and through similar influence mechanisms.

(2) Alliances between career officials and controllers may undercut the de facto, if not de jure, line authority of politically appointed agency heads. Of particular importance are the working relations between career civil servants and the chairmen of congressional committees and subcommittees. The presence of these relationships may lead the appointed head to use bureaucratic means of bolstering his authority, or they may encourage various kinds of sabotage by the career officials below him. Similarly, as demonstrated by Crockett's attempts to extend MOP to the Bureau of Security and Consular Affairs, such alliances may prevent debureaucratization or other kinds of change.

(3) The interdependencies among agencies in the executive branch create a demand for concurrences, coordination, and extensive communication among the agencies involved. These conditions in turn increase the volume of messages flowing through a single agency and produce demands for accountability and centralization of message handling.

(4) The White House, as the focal point in the executive branch, may bring on an escalation of decision-making and information

handling in an individual executive agency by demanding instant information on sensitive matters from senior officials in that agency.

(5) The managerial orthodoxy found in the executive branch as a whole may provide a positive model for organizational structure and operations in an individual agency and a strong barrier to change in agencies attempting to depart from this model. Crockett's experience with his superiors in implementing debureaucratization suggests that a federal executive agency cannot be a free agent in determining its own styles of management.Developments in one department will almost certainly be subject to comments by others, and may also draw the attention of Congress and other controllers. The same situation applies even more clearly in the case of system-wide rules and regulations on hiring, firing, purchasing, and similar matters.

(6) The complexity, uncertainty, threat, and dispersion of the agency's operating environment may influence internal structure and operations in several ways. First, a high degree of complexity, uncertainty, and threat creates pressures for extensive reporting to maintain adequate surveillance of the environment. As discussed in Chapter 7, extensive reporting leads to a high message volume and consequent strains on message-handling capability. Second, uncertainty combined with threat creates both internal and external demands for the accountability of senior officials and for the centralization of message handling. Third, considerable dispersion of the operating environment may lead to a heavy reliance on written communications, a situation which further increases the message volume. When, as is the case in the State Department, dispersion is accompanied by a large number of field stations (embassies and consulates) operating in widely different circumstances, there will be strong pressure within the organization to standardize or rationalize responses to these diverse situations.

Several steps should be taken to redress the balance between internal and external factors in organization theory. First, and most basic, we must have a more adequate typology of influence relationships between the organization and its power setting. Some promising leads are found in the work of Thompson and McEwen (1958) on organization-environment interactions in goal setting. The processes described—competition, bargaining, co-optation, and coalition—are fundamental, but do not cover the range of transactions seen even in the State Department. A more thorough model would have to include direct legislative and budgetary control, intimidation, oversight, mutual accommodation, and other relationships discussed in this and earlier chapters. Also promising is the more recent literature on "bureaucratic politics" (Allison, 1969, 1971; Neustadt, 1970; Halperin, 1971; Allison and Halperin, 1972), although the writings in this tradition seem little concerned with generic organizational processes. The time now seems ripe for the systematic integration of the latter approach with theories growing out of the sociology and social psychology of organizations.

The second suggestion is almost identical to that made for the study of bureaucracy: a comprehensive analysis of organization-environment interactions across a broad spectrum of agencies. The model proposed here emphasizes, for example, the internal effects of complexity, uncertainty, threat, and dispersion in the operating environment. While our conclusions seem persuasive for the State Department, we recognize the limits of hypothesis testing and model building with a single organization or set of related organizations. Ultimately the only way to determine if complexity and threat have the effects postulated here is to compare the internal structure and operation of agencies marked by high, medium, and low complexity and threat.

Third, future studies of public organizations should comment explicitly on the role of environmental factors, if only to note their lack of influence. One of the prime drawbacks of existing comparative studies of organizations is an overemphasis on the similarities among the units of comparison and a neglect of key differences. Mott (1972) reports data on the following organizations: NASA; an anonymous public agency; the Financial Management Office of the Department of Health, Education, and Welfare; and ten community general hospitals. He also uses limited amounts of data from the present study of the State Department. Now there are clearly sound reasons for testing hypotheses about organizational effectiveness across a wide range of organizations; indeed, a general theory will ultimately require precisely such testing. But there is also abundant evidence to suggest significant variations among these organizations in the extent to which internal operations are dependent on the environment. The community general hospital, while certainly not impenetrable, seems more immune to direct political influence and more under the control of "professionals" than either NASA or the State Department. Mott's analysis simply does not provide enough information for the reader to make an independent assessment of the role of the environment. The same is true of the studies by Blau (1963), Blau and Schoenherr (1971), and Meyer (1972). Although an investigator cannot hope to do everything in a single study, the issue of environmental dependence seems critical enough to deserve explicit comment in future analyses of public agencies.

### The Dynamics of Organizational Change

Following the path of organization theory in general, analyses of the dynamics of organizational change have typically adopted an internal focus. The dominant approaches in this field can be distinguished by relating them to the classification suggested by Barnes (1967): (1) *what* is to be changed—people, technology, or structures; (2) *who* is to be changed—key executives, middle-level managers or supervisors, lower-level subordinates, or all of these; and (3) *how* change is to be achieved—the specific methods and strategies to be employed.

At the level of *what* is to be changed, some writers have conceived organizational change primarily as a process of modifying individual characteristics, such as perceptions, motivations, and behaviors. The underlying assumption of this approach (cf. McGregor, 1960) is that the creation of a more effective organization requires modifications of attitudes and behavior among key individuals in the system, such as managers. Other authors, such as Chapple and Sayles (1961) and Leavitt (1965) have focused less on individuals and more on processes and structures in the organization. Hence, rather than changing attitudes, values, and beliefs, an intervention may attempt to reshape the structure of power and authority, the pattern of communications and decision-making, or the system of rewards and recognition. This was the basic model followed by Deputy Under Secretary William Crockett in the 1965 reorganization of the O area. Still others have explicitly tried to relate personal and structural conditions by showing the impact of organizational structure on individual motivation, commitment, and self-realization (cf. Golembiewski, 1964; Argyris, 1962).

Considerations of *who* is to be changed derive from one's definition of the main sources of organizational effectiveness. Those who begin with essentially elitist assumptions will direct their efforts at the top levels. Those who emphasize the role of employee attitudes, worker satisfaction, and similar mass qualities will prefer to spend their time at lower levels in the system. In short, where the change agent enters the system and where he concentrates most of his efforts will depend in good part on definitions of the problem to be solved and conceptions of the weight carried by the different actors in the system.

Beginning with the work of Kurt Lewin (1951), a large part of the literature on organizational change has been concerned with the question of *how*. The emphasis on process has led to a search for strategies of change that are applicable across a wide variety of organizational settings. One of the earliest and most widely used approaches was sensitivity training (cf. Argyris, 1964). Departing from several basic assumptions about *who* and *what* should be changed, in its earliest applications sensitivity training was geared to producing greater understanding on the part of managers and sometimes middle-level employees about their impact on others. Although this point was often not explicitly articulated, the underlying assumption was that improved self-understanding among managers and other key officials in an organization would lead to more effective work relationships and ultimately to improved organizational performance. A related approach, which has been widely applied in industrial organizations, is the "managerial grid" developed by Blake and Mouton (1964). Another strategy for inducing awareness of problems and a desire for change involves periodic data collection about morale and other salient qualities of the organization, followed by feedback of the data to "families" of organization members. These groups then assume responsibility for further analysis and interpretation of the findings, and for deciding on what directions of change, if any, are indicated (Mann, 1957). More recently a variety of approaches to organizational change have been incorporated and codified under the general rubric of organization development (OD). A comprehensive OD program might now involve sensitivity training with key members as a preliminary step, data collection and feedback, problem-solving sessions focused on immediate issues in the organization, group confrontations, and other activities (cf. Beckhard, 1969).

Our point is that the available general discussions of who, what and how in organizational change are largely based on experience in nonpublic organizations. This observation in itself would be of little consequence if there were empirical or presumptive evidence that the same models could be applied directly in public settings. This study, and particularly the experience of the 1965 reorganization of the O area, suggest that such is not the case. Specifically, the evidence points to several critical features of the federal executive agency which may impinge on the process and outcome of a change program.

*External Factors*

The most significant implication of this study for organizational change concerns the limits imposed by the agency's power setting. The following incidents, reported in previous chapters, illustrate these limits:

— Crockett was unable to eliminate the position of Administrator of the Bureau of Security and Consular Affairs essentially because of political opposition. The admininstrator in 1965, Abba Schwartz, interpreted the administrative streamlining as a plot by his enemies in the department and in Congress to remove him. When Schwartz and his supporters mobilized congressional opposition to the reorganization, Crockett's efforts were forced to a halt.

— Crockett also concluded that it would be impossible to reorganize the Passport Office of the Bureau of Security and Consular Affairs "except under the most favorable congressional circumstances, i.e., when the Secretary of State had no problems with any powerful committees and therefore would not need their help or fear their wrath." The major source of opposition was the political

[197]

support that the director of the Passport Office, Frances Knight, had built up in Congress.

— The Hays Bill, a measure designed to produce a unified foreign affairs personnel system, was defeated for several reasons related to the power setting of the State Department: opposition from a senator who, as a former Foreign Service Officer, saw the integration as a dilution of the service; opposition from the American Federation of Government Employees and other associations, who saw the bill as an encroachment on the Civil Service; tepid support from the chairman of the Senate Foreign Relations Committee, who wanted better cooperation from the Secretary of State on questions related to Vietnam; and effective lobbying by the Foreign Service with their supporters in Congress.

— After the 1965 reorganization was underway, Crockett reported pressure from his superiors to reduce some of its more controversial features, particularly the large span of control for the deputy under secretary. Apparently one reason for this pressure was the fear that controversy brought on by internal change would arouse congressional opposition at a time when the department was deeply embroiled in difficulties arising from Vietnam.

— An associate of Deputy Under Secretary Idar Rimestad reported that criticisms of the Argyris Report during hearings of the Rooney subcommittee reinforced his determination to restore the O area to a more traditional, hierarchical structure.

These examples provide clear evidence that the who, what, and how of organizational change in the federal government must be evaluated in light of the agency's political environment. To launch a reorganization or development program without explicit attention to the power setting is self-defeating.

### Internal Factors

Various features of the internal environment of the executive agency are also sufficiently different from nonpublic organizations to warrant careful analysis. Foremost among these is the discontinuity of leadership at the top of the organization. We argued in Chapter 9 that the constant rotation of politically appointed leaders, whose average tenure is about two years, works against the consolidation of organizational change. Hence, even though an enterprising leader such as Crockett might unfreeze the system and actually effect change, the effort would often be submerged because of leadership change followed by new reorganizations.

Closely related to the problem of discontinuity at the top is the tendency of lower-level career employees to build their own defenses against change. Veteran officials accustomed to a change in top leadership every two or three years will be most reluctant to modify their own attitudes and behavior in order to facilitate change imposed from the top. Moreover, if they feel threatened by the change, they can easily sabotage it by tactics ranging from the mobilization of opposition in Congress to doing nothing. The efforts by the State Department to restore its primacy in foreign affairs were deterred by a "do nothing" response by the Foreign Service. Similarly, some of the key officials involved in the MOP reorganization were most reluctant to change their accustomed ways of relating to subordinates, seemingly because of their belief that the new ways brought in by Crockett would not last. Finally, our research provides unmistakable evidence that even the best-intentioned change program may be paralyzed by internal conflicts and cleavages. While this point is regularly made in treatises on organizational change, we would note one distinctive feature of the executive agency. This is the very real possibility that an internal power contender, such as the Foreign Service in the State Department, can seek outside allies to reinforce its position in the fray. Because of the high degree of permeability of the federal agency to outside influence, what would seem to be essentially internal rifts can quickly escalate into confrontations between one part of the agency and significant actors in the power setting outside.

*The Participation Hypothesis*

Our analysis further leads us to question the sometimes facile advocacy of employee participation in decisions about change. Briefly, both laboratory and field experiments are often cited to support the view that change will be most effective when the individuals affected participate in decisions about its substance and methods

(Coch and French, 1948; Morse and Reimer, 1956). The reasoning behind this approach is quite simple. Members of an organization are less likely to resist change and more likely to understand it and see it as their own if they take part in decisions about change. Some would go further and say that participation not only improves employee attitudes toward change, but contributes to the quality of the decisions. made. The arguments in favor of this approach are so familiar as to deserve little comment.

Generalizing from his analysis of numerous cases of governmental reorganizations, Mosher (1967) cites several inherent obstacles to participation in large public organizations.

"The first of these arises simply from *size* and the mechanical difficulty of bringing into effective participation some hundreds or thousands of individuals who may be affected by a decision" (1967, pp. 519-520). Mosher quite properly notes that the data base for much of the discussion about participation has been the small, face-to-face group. Serious questions of generalizability thus arise in applying such findings to agencies with thousands of employees.

The second obstacle is hierarchy.

Hierarchy appears to be an inevitable and essential ingredient of all sizeable administrative organizations. Officers at whatever level (except perhaps at the very apex) derive their authority from one or more superiors and are in some degree responsible to them for actions of their subordinates. Under such conditions, any substantial sharing of power by a leader with his subordinates involves a certain amount of risk to himself unless he has strong confidence that they will propose and take actions that he can defend before his superiors. Complete reliance upon participative decision [sic] might not only undermine his position with superiors; it could also erode the respect and posture of leadership he holds among his subordinates (ibid.).

The third problem is the scatter of power in making and carrying out decisions. Mosher's comments on this point are supported by our analysis of the 1965 reorganization.

This is partly a matter of hierarchy. . ., partly of law (in a nation built on the concept of division of powers), and partly of politics (which may and often does involve the actual or potential influence of political parties, clientele and interest groups, legislatures and their committees, and influential individuals, employee groups, and others).

The legal complexities of governmental reorganization are usually considerable and often tremendous. In agencies that are exposed to the public or to a significant clientele and that operate in controversial fields, political considerations are unavoidable. Seldom can a single official, no matter what his rank, order a major reorganization of his agency without facing the prospect of review, modification, or veto elsewhere (ibid.).

A corollary of this statement is that an official cannot share with subordinates a power that he does not have himself. The use of participation becomes particularly complicated when the decision at stake involves relationships with elements in the power setting. Very often employees at middle levels and lower in the organization are not familiar with the intricate negotiations involved between senior officials and outside controllers, such as Congress. It was quite evident, for example, that Crockett was able to move as far as he did precisely because he had paved the way through favorable relationships with Rooney and his subcommittee. Had he chosen to involve his subordinates in decisions about the MOP reorganization, their contribution on the essentially political features of the change program might well have been limited and perhaps even damaging. However, as Mosher points out (1967, p. 521), this situation is an obstacle to participation but does not prohibit it. Moreover,

the possibilities of organizational change are usually the result of events, such as changes in leadership, which render an organization temporarily pliable. They are customarily followed by a congealing period when significant change becomes increasingly difficult. The most propitious time for reorganization is soon after the spark, and a long delay for participative decision-making may dissipate the opportunity (ibid.).

The development of a modernized communications system in the State Department illustrates the apt use of crisis to accomplish change. For many months before the Cuban missile crisis senior administrators had been concerned about the antiquated communications system in the department and had studied the possibility of establishing new facilities. But nothing was done until the missile crisis. At that time the facilities quickly became overloaded and were unable to transmit important information about the crisis to U. S. embassies. After one particularly embarrassing incident, the senior administrators capitalized on the crisis atmosphere to obtain authorization for a multimillion dollar computerized communications system (Crockett, 1972). Had there been extensive deliberation within the department about the need for a new system, the type of equipment that would be most suitable, and the relation between this system and that of the CIA, the opportunity in all likelihood would have evaporated. This point relates directly to the power setting of executive agencies, where crisis is often the most powerful stimulus to change. If participation takes action beyond the stage at which crucial controllers, allies, and constituencies are anxious to "do something," the effort may be aborted.

A fifth barrier to participation arises from expectations about the proper behavior of superiors in the public organization. This is closely tied to our earlier discussion of managerial orthodoxy. The problem is

the executive's fear, sometimes well-grounded, of appearing weak, indecisive, and timid in failing to make decisions that are within his prerogative. This concern may apply to the opinions of superiors and outsiders who consider him the "boss" of his organization; it may apply to his own subordinates, to whom participation may signify lack of confidence or even incompetence, particularly where "command decisions" are customary. And it may appear to the executive himself to be a contradiction of his self-image as a leader (Mosher, 1967, p. 553).

In our study the problem of expectations arose most sharply in the case of Crockett's successor, Idar Rimestad. During a meeting in which we reported some of the findings of our research, Rimestad said that he could not tell the secretary that a given decision was the ultimate responsibility of one of his subordinates. He felt that the decentralized management system established through MOP entailed a degree of delegation that was unacceptable in a hierarchical system such as the State Department. If he was to be accountable to his superiors, he would have to exercise control over his subordinates.

A sixth argument against participation is that it provides an opportunity for influential subordinates to mobilize opposition to the proposed changes. In Mosher's cases "secrecy, which is the opposite of participation, was most frequently invoked where the organizational goals as perceived by the executive were obviously in conflict with individual and group goals of those who might participate" (1967, p. 533). Similarly, had William Crockett used extensive participation in planning for the MOP reorganization, the opponents of the program almost certainly would have used the occasion to rally internal and external forces against the effort. At the same time, when asked specifically about this point in a 1970 interview, Crockett commented:

I do believe that all of the programs which we attempted suffered because of our Theory X methodology and that whatever the cost of earlier and more extensive involvement might have been (e.g., a chance for opposition to mount forces, etc.)—that the probable success would have been enhanced by using it.

In short, a strong case can be made for employee participation in organizational change, but it must be made on its own merits in each situation. There is simply no basis for claiming that "tested theory" or "extensive research" support a recommendation of employee involvement in all forms of change. Much of the theory used to endorse participation was developed in settings other than public organizations, and some in laboratory settings that screened out even the normal complexities of organizational life. Both Mosher's cases and this study suggest that the value of participation will hinge on a variety of internal and external factors, including the precise nature of the change (for instance, programs involving highly sophisticated communications equipment vs a modification of the promotion system); the formal structure of authority and accountability; informal expectations about the proper behavior of superiors; the size of the organization; the costs of delay in losing external or internal support for the changes; the extent to which participation will provide opponents or rivals with an opportunity to mount opposition; the willingness of employees themselves to participate (something that cannot be taken for granted); the degree to which other organizations or actors are affected by or interested in the change; and the extent to which the organization's authority on the issue in question is shared with other agencies or controllers. From our observations there is as much danger in a reflexive invocation of Theory Y in organizational change as in a hidebound adherence to traditional managerial dogmas.

If there is a common denominator to the conclusions presented in this chapter, it is that the public organization should be taken seriously by students of bureaucracy, organizational theory, and organizational change, and studied on its own terms. It is not enough to pack a briefcase with concepts and measures developed in other settings, unload them in a public agency, and expect them to encompass all of the worthwhile reality to which they are exposed. Rather, like the anthropologist about to enter an unknown community, the student of public organizations would do well to assemble the available information about the agency and its power setting and arrive at no hasty conclusions about the applicability of existing theories and conceptual structures. With the study of bureaucracy and organizations enriched by the added insights to be gained in public settings, and the understanding of public organizations advanced by the analytic tools of organization theory, we may hope for a more exciting and better balanced subdiscipline of organizational studies.

# 11 • Is There Hope?

It would be fashionable to end this book on a ringing note of reform: "Cut positions—slash hierarchy—abolish rules—merge overlapping units—streamline the bureaucracy." Such pieties make good copy, but they would be totally insincere as policy recommendations from this study. If there is a single conclusion to be drawn from our observations, it is that a reorganization plan pegged only to considerations of rationality is doomed to failure. Even worse, it will often aggravate the very maladies it was designed to cure. Almost any significant change in the executive bureaucracy touches the interests and self-definitions not only of the employees involved, but also of related congressional committees, constituency groups, and interested publics. To treat a reorganization solely as an intra-agency matter is to overlook the fundamental values and assumptions undergirding the U. S. government.

Yet many citizens, including concerned congressmen and public employees, regard executive branch hierarchy, rules, and paperwork as both excessive and oppressive. Those at the bureaucratic bottom complain of job dilution, restricted authority, and too little scope for initiative. Those at the top, like Dean Rusk, curse the sheaves of memoranda sent up by buck-passing subordinates. Some on the sidelines, including congressional critics, decry the splintering of decision-making and the time wasted in interagency concurrences. The public at large weakly bemoans the expansion of the federal bureaucracy, the rising costs of government, and a growing sense of immersion in red tape. And so on in the familiar cycle of complaint and inaction.

Is the problem of excessive bureaucracy really hopeless, or are there avenues for significant, if limited, change?

Two paths to reform are almost certain to be counterproductive. The first is debureaucratization by decimation. Its advocates typically plead for the President, the Congress, or "someone" to cut positions, merge agencies, or otherwise reduce bureaucratic size. *The Foreign Affairs Fudge Factory* (Campbell, 1971) offers proposals along these lines for the State Department:

Size is the first problem to attack and bureaucratic surgery is the answer. State might adopt a Five Year Plan of abolishing functions and reducing personnel, designed to trim the 7,000 man Department of today by 50 percent or more, to a new ceiling in the low 3,000s (p. 230).

Cutting functions should also include reducing the number of chains of command in State. Nine of the present bureaus headed by assistant secretaries. . . could be usefully abolished, leaving a total of seven (p. 231).

The policy bureaus contain a "buried administrative factor" of 20 to 30 percent, since that many administrative liaison officers work in the executive directors' offices of nonadministrative bureaus. These latter offices could be eliminated with a saving of perhaps as many as 400 to 500 positions. The "housekeeping" side of administration could then be centralized under the assistant secretary for administration, responsible and responsive to the Secretary of State and the other six assistant secretaries (p. 234).

And how is this massive reduction in scale to be accomplished? Campbell claims that the methods "need not simulate those of an unsettling purge" (p. 231). The only step that meets this criterion, however, is normal attrition of about 10 percent per year. The remaining methods would indeed be interpreted locally as a purge:

Incentives for early retirement should be continued to ease over-population in the senior ranks, along with a more serious application of selection-out to low performing Foreign Service officers. At least the lower 5 percent, or 160 officers per year, could be *eliminated* [emphasis added] . . . Cutbacks can also come in the Foreign Service "reserve officer" category. Of the 750 "FSRs" now serving in

Washington as temporary specialists, an estimated 250 or one-third of the total are congressional patronage jobs (p. 231).[1]

For a Secretary of State willing to study the problem, its solution would seem almost childishly simple. He has only to prescribe a fixed number or percentage of promotions and forced retirements each year, in accordance with a long-range plan designed to achieve whatever balance among ranks and ages he thinks desirable. He might order the Foreign Service selection boards, for example, to eliminate the lowest-ranking 5 percent of all officers, about 160 per year (p. 252).

As the author himself says, these proposals are "almost childishly simple." Why, then, are they certain to fail? Our research on a much less grandiose reform program in the same organization suggests a number of obstacles to Campbell's battle plan.[2]

One problem is that the entire effort would be interpreted as a plot by the Foreign Service to strengthen its hold on the State Department. If Crockett's reforms were seen as a coup by the administrators against the Foreign Service, Campbell's bureaucratic surgery would be regarded as just the reverse. It is scarcely accidental that most of the amputations would be in the functional bureaus, which are to be collapsed into one, in the O area, and in the administrative sections of the regional bureaus. Campbell, in fact, makes no secret of his desire to restore the primacy of the Foreign Service. It is not difficult to imagine the scenario that would develop if this proposal were taken seriously. The administrators, the functional bureaus, and the Civil Service, an overlapping set, would establish battlements within the department and begin lobbying with their allies and friends on the Hill. The Foreign Service would do the same, but this time with less chance of success than with the Hays Bill. Because more controversy is generated by changing than by preserving the status quo, the odds would be against them.

[1] The author does not indicate how he would identify those whose jobs originated from patronage—or whether the origin of their jobs, as distinct from present performance, would be the only criterion for dismissal. Nor does he seem to recognize that the congressional "patrons" may have some interest in the matter.

[2] We regret having to offer these criticisms when Mr. Campbell, a former Foreign Service Officer, will not be able to respond. Shortly after the publication of his book he died of cancer at the age of thirty-one.

Forced retirement and increased selection-out would also work to decrease risk-taking, increase conformity, and otherwise fortify the bottom-up pressures for bureaucracy. A prime reason for the avoidance of initiative in the Foreign Service is a high fear of selection-out coupled with a performance appraisal system providing little discrimination among candidates in the middle range of excellence. Campbell's proposal for eliminating "low performing officers" assumes that this system provides valid and reliable information on performance. But the testimony of many raters and ratees is to the contrary. In their view the widespread "inflation" of ratings and the positive bias in prose narratives leads evaluation panels to seek out single unfavorable incidents in the officer's record. If the present system produces conformity, one can imagine the effects of a sudden increase in selection-out.

Further, a drastic reduction in the total size of the State Department might have the ironic effect of a proportional increase in bureaucracy. Massive cuts in personnel or increases in selection-out will lead to even less risk-taking and to a search for organizational defenses against a hostile environment. A reduction in risk-taking will mean that more and more decisions are referred to superiors for approval, with a consequent strain on their information-handling ability. At the same time the battered bureaucrat will seek out other means of protecting himself against the threat of dismissal. One might be more sharply defined rules about "proper" behavior. Another might be a heightened demand for management positions, on the hypothesis that managers or administrators are more durable than ordinary bureaucrats. There is anecdotal evidence to suggest that in agencies such as NASA, which have experienced an overall reduction in size, there was a proportional increase in management positions. Such a development would be doubly ironic in a reform movement aimed at eliminating administrators. In short, a reduction in size, particularly when effected by slash and burn tactics, may set in train a per capita expansion of hierarchy, rules, and administrative positions.

A second change strategy that also seems of dubious value is top-down debureaucratization from within the organization. This was essentially the model followed by William Crockett in the O area reforms, and is the prototypical method in the federal government. The core limitations of this approach were stated in Chapter 9: the failure of institutionalization or refreezing growing out of the impermanence of the appointed leadership; bureaucratic counter-attacks launched by career employees and their external allies; and the tendency of top-down efforts to destroy initiative and to generate defenses at the lower levels of the organization. Looking back in a 1970 interview at the 1965 change program, Crockett reflected on what he would do differently:

In hindsight I guess I would do a number of things differently and maybe be a lot more successful with a lot fewer changes.

While I have no changes I would make with "content" I would start a great many fewer undertakings which had to be done simultaneously. I would try to develop a better priority of issues and a better ordering of them so that the results of doing one would be an action-forcing process for doing the next and so on.

Too many problems facing me too constantly sapped my strength and prohibited me from pursuing hard enough on any one item when the need was met. So I would be more cautious (smart) about what I started—and when.

Secondly, I would be more patient with the process—I would involve a great many more people and groups—all of the interested constituencies from the inception of the problem and try to make it *their problem* for *their solution*. I thought that I knew all of the problems and had all the answers (which I probably did) but this attitude doesn't elicit much broad support. I met my needs—not theirs.

Thirdly, I would have started earlier ensuring that my personal assistants and those responsible for change also worked through the participative mode instead of "the boss wants so and so to be done" mode. I suspect that there was much of this by fine, loyal subordinates who fell into this trap as a means of getting things done for me!

The last comment documents once again the critical importance of the *total* attitudinal system within which change takes place. Even the best Theory Y intentions at the top may be rapidly subverted when subordinates slip into the traditional Theory X methods of the surrounding organization.

We have now rejected debureaucratization by decimation on the grounds that it will either fail outright to accomplish its goals or, if it succeeds numerically, will increase the already strong pressures for hierarchy and rules among the survivors. We have also rejected top-down debureaucratization because the changes produced, even when accomplished in a benignly patriarchal manner, are not likely to last and may foster defensive bureaucracy. It might thus seem that both change from the outside and reform from the inside are hopeless. While we see little possibility of far-reaching change given the existing values served by bureaucracy, and while we hold no brief for any gimmick promising instantaneous results, there does seem to be room for a moderate reduction in bureaucracy. Any successful reform program, however, will have to be positive in orientation, respect those affected in the bureaucracy, be geared to long-term rather than short-term objectives, give due recognition to the linkages between the executive system and Congress, and otherwise take account of the distinctive features of the federal system. The following principles are consistent with our research on foreign affairs agencies, and would seem to have broader applicability in the executive system:

(1) The key point for initiating a debureaucratization effort is *within* the agency. This may seem an odd suggestion given the earlier documentation of the self-protective tendencies within the State Department. Nevertheless, if change is to be made and, more important, if it is to endure, it must have strong roots within the agency. For reasons that should now be clear it is threatening and ultimately counterproductive to direct appeals for change to external agents, such as Congress or the White House. They can force an agency into reduced size by budget cuts, or they can shuffle its lines of authority, but they cannot themselves remove the conditions beyond size that favor tall hierarchies and elaborate systems of rules. Put simply, you can lead bureaucracy to slaughter but you can't make it shrink.

(2) There will be little commitment to reduced bureaucracy until the employees within the agency perceive hierarchy and rules as a problem *for themselves.* As long as bureaucracy is perceived to be someone else's problem, employees will not only be uninterested in change, but will actively oppose reforms initiated by outsiders. The

Hays Bill case study shows that employee associations such as the American Foreign Service Association and the American Federation of Government Employees will not sit by idly if a reform program threatens their interests.

(3) In attempting to foster a sense of the problem the promoters of change must immediately involve all significant internal constituencies. The topmost officials must participate not only to provide internal legitimacy but also to prepare the way for gaining the approval of outside controllers and constituencies. The fact remains that in most agencies the task of external diplomacy falls most heavily on the senior leadership, both career and appointed. Still, important as the top may be, the program must also develop a broad base of support in other sectors of the agency. The change agents must be particularly conscious of the rivalries and organizational cleavages within the system and take steps to ensure that the program is not overly identified with any single power contender. In the State Department it would be fatal to have a debureaucratization program billed as the major initiative of *either* the Foreign Service Officer Corps *or* the Management (Administrative) Area. Such identification would quickly touch off all the protective mechanisms reviewed in this book. In other words, it is essential to identify all of the various potential constituencies on an issue, and to involve them not only at the stage of implementation but also in problem identification and overall diagnosis. The experience of the O area reforms suggests that participation only at the stage of solutions may be too late.

(4) Following an adequate involvement of all relevant internal groups, there should be a careful, collective diagnosis of the problem. The importance of this step cannot be overemphasized. John Franklin Campbell (1971), for instance, attributes many of the bureaucratic pathologies in the State Department to excessive size. His prescribed treatment, therefore, is a drastic reduction in positions. But Campbell mistakes a symptom for the more basic causes of organizational ineffectiveness. Our own diagnosis would place much stronger emphasis on the power setting and on such internal and changeable factors as the reward system and the fear of selection-out from a prestigious career service.

External consultants may be helpful in aiding diagnosis, provided that they understand the system, take it on its own terms, and do not project onto it interpretations arising from other kinds of organizations or solutions that fit their own brand of competence. It is hard to disagree, for example, with many of the points raised by Chris Argyris (1967) in his interpretation of the "living system" of the State Department. At the same time, Argyris could be criticized (and has been within the department) for failing to consider the larger organizational system of State. One suspects that his diagnosis, which is mainly inner-directed, is based more on his work with business organizations than on a thorough analysis of the agency at hand. And, whatever the accuracy of the diagnosis, there is a natural tendency for agency employees to resent and reject critical interpretations made by outsiders. From our observations at the time, the reactions to the Argyris Report showed an odd blend of resentment and admiration—resentment because of the bad press created by an outsider, yet admiration for his honest exposure of hidden truths about the Foreign Service culture. In a more recent management reform program (cf. Marrow, 1974) the department relied heavily on internal task forces to complete a self-study, but also called on various consultants, including the author. From all indications this broad-based participation conferred much greater internal legitimacy than the Crockett reform methods, although it did not guarantee widespread acceptance of the recommendations (see Bacchus, 1974a).

(5) Diagnosis should be followed by broad-based discussions about concrete alternatives for change. The successful completion of the diagnostic stage can often lull participants into thinking that significant change has been accomplished, or will be brought about automatically. Here again, consultants can be useful in formulating action alternatives, but should not be allowed to dominate the discussion or to push through the "right" solutions.

(6) At an appropriate point in the deliberations the proponents of debureaucratization should set out to enlist the support of key controllers, allies, and constituencies outside the agency. Exactly when this point is will depend on many circumstances, including the likely sensitivity of the changes and the pattern of relationships

between agency actors and outside groups. In some cases it would be sensible to involve interested congressmen and senators and their staffs from the very beginning. More often, perhaps, the critical stage of involvement would be when the reform plan has passed the pure discussion stage, so that the outsiders feel that participation is not a waste of time.

The development of external support and the defusing of potential opposition will typically require extensive lobbying by the senior leadership, including the secretary and under secretary, and by members of the career service(s) who enjoy more permanent relationships with congressmen, interest groups, and other influentials. It would also be ideal to have employee associations and unions, such as the American Federation of Government Employees, build support within their own ranks. One of the problems likely to be raised by a debureaucratization program even in one agency is the fear that it will set an untoward precedent for other organizations that may not desire such changes. Or, as happened in the Hays Bill debate, one interest group, such as the veterans' organizations, will see in the new personnel policies a threat to their own privileges, which could easily spread further. The close connection between agencies working in the same domain, including foreign affairs, must be recognized at all times. In short, the effective implementation of change requires considerable sensitivity to the system-wide ramifications of the measures proposed.

(7) To avoid the liabilities of leadership rotation, the program should have a strong coordinating and monitoring body including more than one senior political appointee. In the State Department as presently constituted two obvious candidates would be the deputy secretary and the deputy under secretary for management. The committee should also have representatives from the upper echelons of the career employees and from the other key groups in the organization, including the secretarial and clerical staff.

With all of these requirements it is highly unlikely that large-scale efforts will be undertaken to reduce bureaucracy in the federal system. This comment does not reflect a boundless pessimism, but rather a recognition of the enormous inertia of established structures and, related to it, the many and varied needs served by hierarchy and rules.

At a broader level, any lasting solution to the problem of needless bureaucracy will require a revamping of existing relations between the Congress and executive agencies. The examples reported in this book and many others leave little doubt that at the operating level, as distinct from their origins in the Constitution, the legislative and executive branches are bound together in a bureaucratic symbiosis. So long as congressmen define themselves and are defined by significant others on the basis of their relations to executive agencies, it is virtually meaningless to speak of debureaucratization on just one side of the relationship. The efforts at foreign affairs reform in the 1960s revealed that some of the strongest opponents to bureaucratic change were members of Congress who preferred known chaos to uncertain rationality. Until the Congress takes steps to reduce the balkanization of power within its own bailiwick, it is improbable that much will be done about the executive bureaucracy to which it is tied.

Another macroscopic shift that would improve the climate for a streamlined bureaucracy is an improvement in public attitudes toward the bureaucrat. There has been entirely too much stereotyping of public employees as parasites on the body politic, and of governmental positions as barnacles on the ship of state. Bureaucrats, whether Foreign Service Officers, Civil Service employees, or members of the armed services, are human beings, with much the same motivation for security and self-esteem as the rest of the population. Viewed in context, their efforts to protect their jobs or to buffer themselves against the caprice of political employees seem neither irrational nor nefarious, even when the cost is surplus bureaucracy. Some of their coping efforts also show a level of resourcefulness hardly associated with Parkinsonian incompetence. Frederick O'Riley Hayes, Director of the Budget under Mayor Lindsay in New York and formerly of the U. S. Bureau of the Budget, has independently come to similar conclusions:

We are not likely to learn much about bureaucracies or about changing them if we persist in considering the problem in terms of musty and outworn cliches. The bureaucracy is a social system with its own articulated rules of behavior, whether explicit and written or implicit and understood. It is made up of human beings, much like you and I, in fact, rather superior in average education, in intelligence, and in general competence.

This is not to say that the bureaucrat—or more particularly the senior bureaucrat—does not have limitations, nor that the bureaucratic social system is not an obstacle to movement. It is, however, an argument for understanding the character of both the social system and the bureaucrat—and, inferentially, for treating the bureaucrat as a human being.

The typical senior bureaucrat in the City of New York, as in the Federal Government in Washington, has worked for the government for twenty years or more, not uncommonly thirty years or longer. In New York he will most usually be self-made with origins in the lower middle class or even among the poor . . . He is intelligent, ordinarily perhaps in the top 5% of any representative sample . . . He is, in truth, a virtuoso in the operation of whatever bureaucratic system he is engaged in—and the worse the system's characteristics, the more that they are compensated for by his virtuosity (1973, pp. 19-21).

In sum, the public itself and its elected representatives are powerful sources of hierarchy and rules in the federal system. So long as bureaucrats remain a handy scapegoat for public frustration, they are unlikely to relinquish the comforts of a layered structure bedecked with regulations. If the nation wishes to reduce bureaucracy, it must cease beating the bureaucrats and involve them in the process of creating a less threatening, less cumbersome, more satisfying, and ultimately less expensive work environment. This study also suggests that the process of change is intimately related to the product. Reforms involving decimation of agencies or other meat cleaver tactics only serve to vindicate the inveterate fears of the bureaucrats and to bolster the protectiveness of their congressional allies. In the end, the development of a more efficient, humane, and effective public bureaucracy is best accomplished by humane methods.

Appendix
Bibliography
Index

# Appendix
# Biography of a Research Project

## by Donald P. Warwick

Discussions of research methodology in the social sciences customarily stick to the facts, detailing the guiding theory (if any), the data collection techniques, and the methods of analysis. Reports on surveys usually suggest that the study was executed with clockwork precision, save for a few recalcitrant respondents and unavoidable delays in data processing. Few accounts provide insight into the living process of social research, the halts and starts, politics, conflicts, and frustrations that enter into almost any complex field study. Unless there is an obvious windfall of serendipity, it is seen as faintly disreputable to admit that all did not go according to a foreordained plan. Studies by organizational researchers are particularly anomalous in this regard. While we sagely counsel others to pay heed to "the human side of enterprise," we often report our own work as if it had none.

This is a study which, in its earliest stages, seemed the very model of the modern organizational survey. It was commissioned and paid for by the agency to be studied, so that problems of access were likely to be minimal. The interview schedules were drawn up with the help of some of the best methodological minds at the University of Michigan's Institute for Social Research. The research team was able to draw a precision sample from available lists, and met with excellent cooperation from respondents. Despite a few refusals here and there, the overall response rate and the quality of the data were better than in many comparable studies. And yet almost none of the statistical data appear in this book, mainly because the numbers became increasingly irrelevant to an understanding of the engines of bureaucracy in the State Department.

The following account tells how the study came about, how the data were collected during the survey stage, and why, over a period of eight years, the analysis took an entirely different turn from its original direction. Also of interest are the organizational context of the survey and the politics of research in a sensitive agency. As the account is a personal one prepared by a participant in the events described, it can make no claims to disinterested objectivity. It should, nonetheless, not only lay out the methodological background of the interpretations, but also yield substantive insights into the culture and power setting of the State Department.

**Origins**

The remote origins of the study lie in a sweeping effort undertaken by the Department of State in the mid-1960s to improve its managerial effectiveness. Short-lived though it was, this program was significant in being the first large-scale application of organization development and sensitivity training to a federal executive department. The prime mover behind the reforms was Deputy Under Secretary for Administration William J. Crockett. Entering office in 1963 with a reputation for bureaucratic boat-rocking in overseas missions, Crockett lost little time in tackling the rigidities of the Administrative (O) Area and the department at large. He sought help from external advisers in universities and business and by 1965 had assembled a working committee of some fifteen experts on management and organizational behavior. The most active were Alfred Marrow, chairman of the board of the Harwood Manufacturing Company; E. Edgar Fogle, vice president of the Union Carbide Corporation; F. A. L. Holloway, president of Esso Research and Engineering Company; Chris Argyris of Yale University; and Warren Bennis of the Massachusetts Institute of Technology. Marrow, Fogle, and Holloway formed a core group that met frequently with Crockett. Argyris and Bennis later played an active role in the change program that emerged. Out of the discussions came the program known as Action for Organization Development and identified by the acronym ACORD.

This effort began with three key activities:

(1) A series of sensitivity training sessions (T-groups) called "Laboratories in Executive Development." Their aim was to promote such qualities as trust, openness, confrontation, and collaboration among departmental employees, especially Foreign Service officers. These exercises were carried out under contract with the National Training Laboratories in Group Development (NTL) and normally used the format of off-site "stranger" groups. The list of trainers read like a Who's Who in T-groups: Argyris, Bennis, Charles Ferguson, Robert Tannenbaum, Charles Seashore, and others.

(2) Team-building and problem-solving activities. The typical session involved an ongoing work unit in the department (such as the accounting office), was held off-site in Virginia or Maryland, and lasted two or three days. Where sensitivity training aimed for changes in individual attitudes and behaviors, these techniques sought to identify emotional and other blocks to effective work relationships, and to deal with them. This sphere was also the responsibility of NTL, which joined forces with the internal staff of ACORD.

(3) Management by Objectives and Programs (MOP). This effort (see Chapter 3) was handled by Crockett and the ACORD staff.

When it became apparent that MOP had created as well as solved problems in the O area, a fourth activity was added: an outside evaluation of the reorganization. In July 1966, representatives of ACORD approached the Institute for Social Research (ISR) at the University of Michigan about the possibility of taking on the evaluation. Earlier there had been some preliminary discussions between ACORD, NTL, and ISR about a joint research and organization development project, but these broke down over differences in approach between the two potential contractors. As a result of these discussions and other contacts with the department, Rensis Likert, then ISR director, and other staff members were sufficiently familiar with the change program to move quickly on a contract. The document was drafted in August and signed in September 1966, with a deadline of June 1967.

### The Organizational Survey: 1966-67

Within two weeks ISR was able to assemble the core research staff, most of whom were already on its payroll. My own appointment as project director was rather fortuitous. In July 1966 I had returned to Ann Arbor from a two-year assignment with the Michigan Survey Research Center in Peru. The project there was carried out under contract with the Agency for International Development, a subsidiary of the State Department. This experience had given me considerable exposure to the structure and operations of the department and had whetted my appetite to learn more. Although my specific plans on returning to ISR were to work on questions related to social change and national development, when I was asked by Likert to head the State Department project I replied quickly and enthusiastically in the affirmative. The more I learned about the MOP reforms, the more intrigued I became with the fundamental questions that they raised about organizational change. And, like many of my colleagues at the time, I was more than mildly interested in the internal operations of the State Department, which was regularly in the news because of the Vietnam War.

My immediate collaborators were Dr. Allen Hyman, former deputy mayor of Philadelphia and a Ph.D. in public administration, and Marvin Meade, also trained in that field. We very quickly recruited Theodore Reed, a graduate student in sociology with a strong interest in formal organizations. We were joined at various points, particularly in designing the questionnaires and interview schedules, by Stanley Seashore and Donald C. Pelz, as well as others on the ISR staff. Rensis Likert also consulted with us regularly throughout the survey stage.

Both the Michigan study and the NTL effort were formally part of the ACORD program, itself under the Office of Management Planning (OMP) in the O area. The director of OMP was Richard Barrett, a special assistant to Crockett. John E. Harr, a political scientist who had served as a staff member to the Herter committee on foreign affairs reform, served as program manager of ACORD during most of the research. Two members of his staff, Walter Hobby and Raymond Walters, were specifically responsible for liaison with the ISR project.

We spent most of September familiarizing ourselves with the structure of O and the State Department and clarifying the expectations for our research. During this period and throughout the study we received invaluable help from Barrett, Harr, Hobby, Walters, and other members of ACORD. We saw Barrett less often than the others, but he did agree to two interviews and offered occasional comments as he passed through the ACORD offices. Early in the month all of those mentioned, together with Charles Seashore (the NTL coordinator), Hyman, Meade, and myself, joined in a wide-ranging discussion of the origins and aims of MOP, the goals of the ACORD program, and the most appropriate strategy for our research. Barrett gave a lengthy commentary on the development and results of MOP, emphasizing that Crockett (whom we had not yet met) wanted an honest evaluation of the changes as well as practical suggestions for improvements.

From these and related discussions the following strategy emerged. We would begin by interviewing those most directly involved in the reorganization, the program managers. The specific questions to be covered would be worked out by the research team, building on our own observations and hypotheses as well as joint discussions with the ACORD staff. Later the evaluation would move to the clients of O programs, both within O and in the bureaus.

While the Michigan study was building up speed, the NTL effort and other O reforms were moving ahead at full gallop. Sensitivity training sessions were held nearly every week, consultants came in for team-building and problem-solving sessions, and "Barrett's Shop" seemed to sire another organizational innovation every fortnight. Toward the end of September John Harr suggested that it might be useful for me, as project director, to become more familiar with the NTL activities. He asked specifically if I would like to attend one of the T-groups scheduled in the coming weeks. Because of the way the question was put, I did not feel that I was being put under pressure to sign on. Since even then sensitivity training was a source of controversy in the department, and at the same time one of the key ACORD activities, I decided that it would be instructive to join in one of the laboratories. So in early October I packed my bags for a session in Easton, Maryland.

The experience proved useful not only in understanding the NTL approach, but also as a basis for substantive insights into the State Department. Though I was the only member, aside from the group leader, who was not from the Foreign Service, I was able to join in as a full participant. I was not and am not an enthusiast for this type of group manipulation, but within the limits of my own resistances entered into the spirit of the exchanges. One incident during the week seemed particularly revealing about the Foreign Service ethos. For the first three days a financial officer from a European embassy sat through the soul-baring discussions without saying a word and with visible signs of discomfort. During one of the recreation periods I struck up a conversation with him and found him much less reticent than his group behavior had suggested. When I finally asked how he happened to be at Easton, he said that his superior had heard of the laboratories through the departmental grapevine and thought that it would be "good for him" to attend one. In a culture where a strong suggestion from above amounts to an order, this man felt that he had no alternative but to fly to Maryland. The group pressures mobilized to force him into participation also belied the leader's initial comments to the effect that joining in would be strictly voluntary. Other incidents, such as the sight of normally rather guarded Foreign Service officers "cradling" each other (two persons rocking a third back and forth in their arms) at 3:00 A.M., did not shed particular light on organizational culture, but may have contributed to the subsequent backlash against sensitivity training within that culture.

## Collecting the Data

Most of October and November went into designing an interview schedule for the program managers. These were about forty executives, typically on the top rungs of the Foreign Service or Civil Service ladders, whose positions had been removed from the traditional O hierarchy. It was clear from the outset that our assessment of the effects of MOP would not be a clean, before-after study of organizational change. We were called in a year after the major changes had been made, so that no "before" measures could be taken, and a search through the files uncovered no data that could serve as a substitute. Even had we been invited in at the beginning, political considerations probably would have made it nearly impossible to collect the necessary information. The hurriedness and secrecy in the planning of MOP as well as the very real dangers of political sabotage from within or from the outside would have precluded the possibility of a pre-change survey. In retrospect, given the difficulties of obtaining hard measures of performance or almost anything else except expenditures in the State Department, I doubt whether a set of "before" measures would have contributed substantially to our understanding of the reorganization.

The content of the program manager questionnaires derived from two main sources: the objectives of the MOP reorganization itself, and earlier research on organizations at ISR. As is true in most evaluation research, the goals of the intervention set the dominant directions of data collection. Much of our time in Ann Arbor was spent devising items to measure change in the program managers' autonomy and job involvement, the efficiency of communication between organizational units, and the other dimensions outlined in Chapter 3.

We were also free to include some questions related to our own professional interests, particularly if they bore at least a tangential relationship to the outcomes of the reorganization. At ISR there was an informal understanding that all studies in the broad area of organizational behavior would include a series of semistandard items on job satisfaction and supervisory styles to permit subsequent comparisons across different types of organizations. We included a modified version of this series, as well as a few other questions suggested by our emerging hypotheses on the structure and operation of the State Department. Only later did it become apparent that the implicit model of organizations underlying the "Michigan" questions missed some of the overriding influences on bureaucratic behavior in the State Department. Even if we had entered the scene with a more adequate conceptual model of the public organization, for reasons to be noted it is doubtful that we could have greatly expanded the scope of the questionnaires used to evaluate MOP.

From the outset we were much concerned with the perceived legitimacy of the study within the department and the practical question of access to respondents. We knew from our first visits that State was an organization exuding security consciousness, and we had heard enough horror stories about the McCarthy purges to know that some respondents might still be suspicious of interviews. To develop a better sense of the situation, we began with a few exploratory interviews. These were arranged by Walter Hobby and Raymond Walters with managers considered to be cooperative and well-informed about the impact of MOP. A bit to our surprise, there were (with one exception) no problems of access, and the discussions proved to be frank and informative. Even managers who had grave doubts about MOP and the ACORD program in general accepted the legitimacy of our research because of the introductions from Hobby and Walters. Paradoxically, the hierarchical structure of the State Department worked in favor of both initial access to respondents and frankness in their replies. A call from the ACORD staff told the individual that ours was an official study commissioned by the department, and requested cooperation. The same message was communicated by office directors to their subordinates at staff meetings. While one might initially expect information produced through such channels of legitimation to be bland and evasive, it most definitely was not. The cautious managers quite properly wanted to be sure that the interviewers had been duly cleared by the system and were not investigative reporters in survey researcher's clothing; once they had such assurance, they did not hesitate to speak candidly. This conclusion is supported by the abundance of critical comments quoted in the text, and many others not included.

The one exception occurred early in the study when we tried to set up an exploratory interview with a manager in the Office of Security. In this case one of the Michigan researchers called, rather than a member of the ACORD staff.

The employee's instant response was, "I not only don't want to talk with you, I don't even want you to tell anyone that you called me." Later, after the office director explained the research and recommended cooperation, the same man agreed to be interviewed and spoke critically about a variety of subjects. There was no evidence that he was coerced into participation, since we made it clear that nonparticipation would also remain confidential. Rather, following a deeply ingrained bureaucratic tradition in the department, one that was doubly prominent in the Office of Security, he seemed to want iron-clad guarantees that conversations with outsiders would not be held against him. His concern was undoubtedly accentuated by the furor touched off by the Otepka case, which was a very live issue at the time of this study and directly involved the Office of Security (see Chapter 9).

Gradually, according to reports reaching the ACORD staff, word circulated through O that this was an objective study and that the Michigan staff could be trusted not to reveal confidences. The project's image for objectivity was consolidated during a data feedback session held with the program managers in January 1967. The purpose of the meeting, run jointly by Michigan, NTL, and the ACORD staff, was to present our preliminary findings on the positive and negative effects of MOP. I opened with a detailed presentation of the results gathered from the first round of interviews with the program managers, most of whom were present. Then the NTL staff used this information to stimulate a wide-ranging discussion of problems, successes, and possible solutions. Candor was facilitated by the presence of considerable negative data, and by the absence of Crockett and the cone coordinators. During this session it became clear that the Michigan study was not being used as a whitewash for Crockett's mistakes, and that the feelings and suggestions of the program managers were being taken seriously. A larger feedback session, attended by Crockett, his successor-designate, the cone coordinators, and the program managers, was held about two weeks later. This had comparable results for candor but, as we shall see, less happy implications for continuation of the study. Both meetings also proved useful as a source of supplementary information about the reorganization and the State Department more generally. Such sessions are especially valuable in giving the researcher a qualitative sense of the validity of interpretations based on quantitative data.

Although access proved no problem, we found that a ticket to an interview could not be treated as a fishing license. The managers were cooperative and some were quite intrigued with the study; they were also very sophisticated and politically wary. With their wits and suspicions sharpened by a decade and a half of external assaults on the State Department, they kept a keen eye on the survey process. Once we explained the purposes and scope of the research, they held us and themselves to the implied boundaries of data-

\g. A few wide-ranging questions in the exploratory interviews were ....u with raised eyebrows or comments such as, "How does this relate to your study?" Such experiences prompted a critical look at the manifest content of the survey items and at the ways in which they might be misperceived. The result was a set of questionnaires with a slightly more narrow focus than we would have preferred, but which raised no objections ever to reach us.

The first series of program manager interviews was completed in December 1966, with more to come in February and March. Also in December we taped a lengthy discussion with William Crockett and interviewed the four cone coordinators. This was our first meeting with Crockett, who had been traveling with President Johnson much of the time since September. We found him to be extremely interested in the study and very willing to speak frankly about the background of MOP, its problems, and the fit between its accomplishments and its intended goals. The cone coordinators also were cooperative and candid in their reactions.

From January to May the study focused primarily on the internal and external clients of the reorganized programs and, toward the end, on the effects of MOP on the rank-and-file employees in O. To assess the impact of the reorganization on the client units, we devised a series of rating scales and open-end questions to be used with respondents who were well-informed about the flow of information and services from O. The greatest difficulty at this stage lay in conceptualizing the exact output or product of the various programs, divisions, and offices in O. With the exception of one or two "producing" units, most notably the Passport Office, there is simply no measurable product in O or, for that matter, in most of the State Department. In the end we turned to a set of rating scales asking for the informant's subjective impressions of the quality and speed of services provided by the respective O units and the efficiency of communication with those units. Once again, when the purposes and sponsorship were explained to the respondents, we had no difficulty in gathering the requisite information and in eliciting the critical reactions that abounded in the regional and functional bureaus. By May we had succeeded in interviewing almost every major administrative official, short of the assistant secretaries, in the department. The final stage of data collection involved a short questionnaire survey of a sample of some six hundred O area employees beneath the rank of program manager, division chief, or office director. The next three months were spent analyzing the survey data and preparing the final report, which was delivered to meet the extended deadline of August 1967.

### The Study in Jeopardy

William Crockett resigned in February 1967 and was immediately replaced by Idar Rimestad. Several events led quickly to Rimestad's disenchantment with the Michigan study. One was apparently the second feedback session noted earlier; he had attended, and found it not to his liking. His dissatisfaction was compounded when he read our preliminary reports, which were highly critical of certain aspects of the reorganization (criticisms, incidentally, with which Rimestad himself later agreed). According to Alfred Marrow, who met with him during this period, Rimestad had no use for a survey that gave employees an opportunity to vent their dislikes in such an open manner. Other evidence (see Chapter 3) suggests that he was also quite disturbed by some of the more controversial activities of ACORD, particularly sensitivity training. To complicate matters, the report by Chris Argyris, *Some Causes of Organizational Ineffectiveness within the Department of State*, was published almost on the day of Crockett's departure and left, like an unwanted child, on his successor's doorstep. If I remember correctly, the report was given added publicity by the appearance of Crockett and Argyris on a local television program. The upshot was that the Michigan project and several other ACORD activities came up for immediate and close scrutiny.

Not long afterward I was approached by Ralph Roberts, the senior budget official, about the possibility of cancelling the Michigan contract. Roberts made no mention of Rimestad's dissatisfaction, but his rather sheepish demeanor suggested that more was at work than the stated reasons of tight funds and alternate priorities. From a legal standpoint there was no barrier to canceling this or any other comparable contract, for all are written with a "boilerplate" provision allowing nullification by the government with fair notice and compensation. In this case the arguments seemed weak, since nearly all of the data had been collected, and Roberts did not appear entirely convinced of his position. After discussing the issue with Rensis Likert and other colleagues, I thought that it would be neither unfair nor unethical to use the government against Rimestad in a round of bargaining. I approached Roberts with three counterarguments: the study was almost complete, so that a cancellation at this stage would be wasteful; since over half of the budget had been spent and there would be settlement costs, the savings would not be so great as it might appear; and if the contract were broken, we would not be able to deliver a written report of any kind. I indicated that we were unwilling to rush through the data analysis or to sacrifice our professional standards in order to come up with an ad hoc, slapdash survey report.

Given the politics of monitoring in the federal government, I thought that the third argument might be persuasive. If we left without delivering a report, the General Accounting Office could well criticize Rimestad for spending $50,000 with no tangible results. This hunch proved correct. Roberts and I negotiated a settlement permitting completion of the study and at the same time providing for a savings of some $25,000 for the department. With the remaining funds we were able to complete the basic analysis and deliver a 220-page report.

### Politics on the Periphery

For the organization development/human relations movement a great deal was riding on the ACORD program. This was, after all, the first large-scale attempt to apply sensitivity training and allied techniques to the federal government, and one that involved some of the most prestigious practitioners in the field. If the techniques developed in the small-groups laboratory and in industry could be used to enhance organizational effectiveness in the federal government, applied behavioral science would have scored an impressive new triumph. And if the effort failed, it would be an unmistakable black eye for all concerned.

It is not surprising, therefore, that several leading social scientists associated with the organization development movement became ardent boosters and lobbyists for ACORD. The three who will be mentioned here (Marrow, Argyris, and Likert) were all consultants to the State Department at the time of our project, and all prominent students of organizations. Marrow and Argyris had long been involved in promoting sensitivity training, team building, and related approaches in business and industrial organizations; they were obviously convinced that the same methods could be applied fruitfully to government. From an intellectual standpoint Likert had less at stake in ACORD for, as he pointed out at the time, the changes introduced by Crockett did not follow his own prescriptions for participative management. In addition to advocating the need for solid research, his political role seemed to be limited to serving as a second line of support for Marrow and Argyris.

Alfred J. Marrow, one of the intellectual progenitors of ACORD, was by far its most active external booster (see the account in Marrow, 1974). In various ways he tried to build a constituency for the ACORD approach among Congressmen, senior government officials in other departments, and even the general public. His most visible effort was an article published in November 1966 in *Personnel*, a widely circulated journal of the American Management Association. Carrying the title "Managerial Revolution in the State Department," this twelve-page manifesto extolled in euphoric tones the marvelous transformations being wrought by ACORD. The opening paragraph (p. 2) captures the spirit of the discussion:

Unknown to most people outside the Department itself, and until now unreported in the national press, a managerial revolution has been underway in the U. S. Department of State—a revolution that is drawing on the experience of private enterprise and the research of behavioral scientists to make major changes in the operations of this large and complex arm of the government.

Regrettably, in his zeal to sell ACORD, Marrow provided a seriously distorted view of the Michigan study, which was described as follows (p. 6):

The fourth resource included a research team from the Institute for Social Research at the University of Michigan that (evaluated) the effectiveness of changes set up by the ACORD program. They observed the events that took place, recorded what was done, what happened, what was accomplished, and documented the program so that this model could be studied by other government departments and organizations that faced similar problems.

The difficulty lay in the use of the past tense. While our goals were roughly those described, in November 1966 we had "documented" nothing about the effects of ACORD. At that point we were still busy constructing the program manager questionnaire. The article continued (p. 7) with this précis of the effects of MOP:

A very encouraging picture emerged when State Department officials were interviewed on their experience with the new system. One of them graphically illustrated the improvement. Before the reorganization, he had to go through the following chain of command to reach the Deputy Under Secretary: Division Head, Office Director, Deputy Director of Personnel, Director of Personnel, Deputy Assistant Secretary for Administration, Assistant Secretary for Administration, Deputy Under Secretary. Now he reports directly to the Deputy Under Secretary.

The official pointed out that on any given issue one or more of the individuals in this chain would turn out to be overcautious and that at each level there were always staff people who had to be approached for clearances.

The source of these interviews was left ambiguous, but the earlier statement leaves the clear implication that it was the Michigan survey. In addition, the article nowhere even hints at the myriad problems with MOP uncovered when the research was actually done.

Marrow apparently sent reprints of this article to numerous influential members of government, including ranking civil servants. In December 1966 a colleague at ISR received a call from an acquaintance who was a senior official in the Department of Labor. He complained that the Marrow article, which had been sent to him, implied that the ISR survey had been completed, when he knew that it had just begun. He felt that the presentation of the results was quite misleading and that the article as a whole was more suited to publicity than to a report by a social science professional. Our colleague made clear, after checking with us, that the research had indeed just begun, and that we had had nothing whatever to do with the preparation of the article.

Another round of activities began when Crockett announced his resignation in January 1967. In this case Likert and, I believe, Marrow and Argyris, launched an informal campaign to convince him to stay on. Their feeling, which I certainly shared and communicated to Likert, was that the change program was not yet firmly enough rooted to be left to the vagaries of succession. Likert called Secretary Dean Rusk, whom he had known earlier, and urged him to encourage Crockett to reconsider. Rusk supported the idea in principle, but felt that since Crockett was resigning for personal and financial reasons and wanted to take a position with the IBM Corporation, little could be done. Likert told me that both Marrow and Argyris were making similar gestures of support.

After Crockett's resignation, Marrow and Argyris continued their efforts to win political backing for ACORD, which was in serious trouble. At this juncture Argyris had attracted considerable national attention for his report on the State Department. On February 20, 1967, the New York *Times* carried an editorial by Graham Hovey citing the Argyris study as evidence of the need for and the feasibility of change in the State Department. Argyris seized this opportunity to urge Rusk to continue the ACORD effort. In a letter dated February 21, and quoted here with his permission, he wrote:

The program that Bill Crockett began (ACORD), with careful nurturing could become the finest example of genuine change in a large governmental organization, initiated, guided, and successfully executed by members within the system. In addition, the program makes a modest beginning to induce people to take on more responsibility and take risks. Moreover, this program has within it the ingredients to provide a viable basis for establishing and integrating PP&B [Planning, Programming, and Budgeting], plus the other recommendations of the Hitch Committee into the living system of the State Department.

The progress of the ACORD project, and more important, of the attempts being made by high ranking Foreign Service officers to unfreeze the system and make it more effective could be greatly accelerated with some more visible support by you and others at the highest levels.

Drs. Alfred Marrow, Rensis·Likert, and I have been working together trying to be of help to the State Department to change its internal system. If you would find it convenient to meet with any one or a combination of us, we would appreciate the opportunity to inform you further about our work.

Because of some confusion in Argyris' files it is not clear if Rusk ever replied to this letter. It is clear, however, that Rusk was not particularly interested in the implementation of management reforms in the State Department. While he may have been committed in principle to the elimination of "layering" and gave Crockett fairly free rein in the latter's reform efforts, most of his energy in early 1967 was devoted to fighting external skirmishes related to Vietnam. From all indications he neither actively promoted ACORD nor did he object when the entire effort was gradually dismantled by Crockett's successor.

Except for the comments on Marrow's *Personnel* article, none of this discussion should be interpreted as a criticism of the support-building activities of Marrow, Argyris, and Likert. Each was perfectly within his rights as a citizen, and more so as an adviser, to press for management reform in the State

Department. The noteworthy point of these activities is rather the ease with which social scientists involved in governmental settings move from scientific or consulting to essentially political roles. I have noticed before, in myself and in others, a tendency for researchers to take on some of the attitudinal coloration of the organizations that they study. Psychologists surveying insurance companies sometimes come back sounding a bit like insurance agents, while sociologists delving into steel mills pick up some of the *macho* tones of that environment. Similarly, behavioral scientists dealing with governmental agencies may find it quite tempting to shed their normal defenses against organizational politics to become part of the power setting of the units in question. Such behavior is most likely when the researchers are simultaneously part of an organized movement to advance a certain mission or point of view, such as sensitivity training or participative management. There may be, in short, more of a resonance between the researcher and the research environment than we have been prepared to admit.

### Making Sense of the State Department

In August my colleagues and I were in the anomalous position of having completed an exhaustive study of an evaporating reorganization. While our contractual obligations had ended as of that date, as a matter of courtesy we scheduled a meeting with Rimestad and his staff in October to discuss the survey findings. At this point we were not fully aware of the degree of Rimestad's hostility to the Michigan study. I found him, on that first and last meeting, to be a gruff, flinty man, almost the personification of the virtues of the County Court House. His administrative style, from all reports, was emblematic of the managerial orthodoxy discussed earlier in the text. Rimestad made it very clear at the beginning of the session that he had no desire to use survey data as a basis for making decisions in O. After a few comments on the "dismal mess" he had inherited from Crockett he left the room, presumably to answer a phone call, and never returned.

In retrospect, I have two hypotheses about Rimestad's behavior. First, as a traditional bureaucrat he was convinced that a good manager doesn't need surveys to know what is going on in his own shop. Many of the problems with MOP were so obvious that survey data were superfluous, so that in this sense he was probably right. Some of the more subtle difficulties had also been pointed out in our oral presentation eight months earlier, to which, from all appearances, Rimestad had listened attentively. Second, he undoubtedly regarded the Michigan study as part of a larger Crockett legacy that he planned to scuttle. Hence the sooner he could be rid of it, the better. Given the cultural ethos and internal politics of the State Department, the value placed on objective information about attitudes was at that point markedly lower than the premium attached to the restoration of order.

Now came the dilemma about what to do with this research. We were perfectly free, on the one hand, to move ahead with publication. The contract stipulated explicitly that the study would lead to books or articles of scholarly interest.* The possibility of publishing the MOP findings was an attractive one, for we all felt that the survey had gone well and had produced some new insights into bureaucratic behavior. Yet several practical and intellectual considerations restrained us from this course. The most compelling was that the reforms whose origins and effects we had so diligently traced were beginning to fall apart. Even in the autumn of 1967 there were premonitory signs that a research monograph on MOP might soon have historical value only. I also had the nagging sense that we had missed or failed to conceptualize some critical events during the study. One of these was the string of references, heard through the survey, to Congressman Rooney: "They can't do this because Rooney will be furious"; or "Crockett got away with all of this because he and Rooney are buddies"; or "The only reason they picked Rimestad was, when all of the cards were sorted, his was the only one acceptable to Rooney." We knew, of course, who Rooney was, but at that time did not appreciate his broader influence—and that of his subcommittee—on the internal operations and mentality of the State Department. Another incident directly related to our research, but which we appreciated only in its journalistic context, was the Abba Schwartz case described in Chapter 3.

The paramount conceptual difficulty was that the research ground had shifted beneath us. We began the study asking, "Under what conditions is it possible to reduce hierarchy and rules in the federal government, and what personal and organizational effects do such reductions have?" By 1968 the more fundamental and interesting questions had become, "Why didn't Crockett's reforms stick? Why was Rimestad able to abolish ACORD and restore the old hierarchy, and why did he want to do so?" For a long while we simply did not have the conceptual tools to answer these and related questions in any systematic way.

The root cause was an excessively inner-directed view of organizations. We were not helped in our gropings by the prevailing approach to organizations at our home base, the Institute for Social Research. The Michigan school was and is strongly identified with a psychological emphasis, giving particular attention to the effects of different supervisory and management styles. The work of Rensis Likert, while heavily prescriptive, falls very much within this tradition. At the time of our study the groundbreaking book of Katz and

*One limitation was necessary to satisfy a cautious contract officer. This was the requirement that none of the results would be published, without permission from the department, within a year from the termination of the contract. We agreed to this on the grounds that it would be unlikely in any event that material would actually appear in published form before this period.

Kahn (1966) had just been published, but it had not yet had much impact on the design of organizational surveys. Moreover, while they combine a "systems" approach with the earlier Michigan concerns, their treatment of organizational environments is highly abstract and not particularly well attuned to the public agency.

Hence we came into the study well prepared to measure and analyze supervisory styles, job satisfaction, unit performance, leadership, and related intra-organizational problems, all of which were germane to the original research focus. But when the terrain shifted and other concerns came to the fore, we found ourselves with a very limited armory of concepts for attacking the public organization on its own terms. The challenge from 1967 to 1974 was to build on existing theory to develop a more comprehensive view of the State Department and the U. S. federal executive bureaucracy more generally.

In 1968 we decided explicitly not to publish the data in their original form, and to move ahead with a broader approach to the public bureaucracy. Although our efforts were aided by a grant from the James Marshall Fund, our communication problems began to mount. I had left Michigan in 1967 to take a position at Harvard University. In 1968 Marvin Meade moved to Kent State University and Allen Hyman to Wayne State University, while Theodore Reed continued his studies at Ann Arbor. Because of new administrative responsibilities Hyman was unable to participate further in the project. Meade, Reed, and I remained in contact by mail, but quickly discovered the limitations of that medium for collaborative research.

While in Washington for another purpose in 1968, I visited the State Department to inquire about the health of MOP under Rimestad. My initial contact was Howard Mace, a close adviser to Rimestad and an official with whom we had discussed our findings a year earlier. Mace brought me up to date on the post-Crockett changes, which had been numerous, and supplied the relevant documentation. He also mentioned a departmental reform movement being led by the American Foreign Service Association (AFSA) and suggested that I contact its leaders. In 1967 there had been a leadership coup in AFSA, traditionally a rather stodgy professional association, with the result that a slate of "Young Turks" had gained control of its board of trustees. Conversations with Lannon Walker, the new board chairman, and Charles Bray III, another key figure, proved highly instructive about "The Movement." Remembering my research interests, Bray visited me in Cambridge a month or so later during his campaign to win outside support for the AFSA reform program. I suggested then that AFSA pay particular attention to the role of promotions and to the overall reward system as factors impeding change in the department. In June 1969, when the reform movement was in full swing, Bray recalled this suggestion and asked me to prepare a position paper on performance appraisal and promotions. The resulting document was circulated widely within AFSA and eventually published in the *Foreign Service Journal* (July 1970).

Deputy Under Secretary William Macomber responded favorably to the AFSA initiatives and in 1970 established a series of departmental task forces to prepare a comprehensive management reform program. One of these dealt specifically with performance appraisal and promotions. Because of my earlier writings I was asked to serve as a consultant to this group; I also met briefly with the Task Force on the Stimulation of Creativity. These experiences, which included access to letters submitted by Foreign Service Officers on personnel matters, proved invaluable in amplifying my qualitative understanding of the State Department and in providing raw materials for Chapter 6 of this book.

By the summer of 1970 we felt ready to undertake an initial consolidation of the material accumulating since 1966. Earlier, Marvin Meade had drawn on his background in public administration and his research experience in another federal agency to draw up a statement on the distinctive characteristics of the public organization. Theodore Reed, in turn, had summarized the available literature on the history and organizational structure of the State Department. Since 1967 I had read widely in the field of public administration and had taught a graduate course on The Public Bureaucracy at Harvard. Drawing on all of these materials, as well as the draft reports from the Macomber task forces, I attempted a synthesis that would blend organization theory, the literature on U. S. federal executive organizations, and the material on the State Department. These efforts led to some conceptual progress, but at the same time revealed important holes in our understanding of the State Department and even of MOP. For example, my still inchoate view of the public organization's power setting raised new questions about why Crockett did and did not do certain things in the reorganization, such as why he failed to "MOP" the Bureau of Security and Consular Affairs.

Coincidentally, Crockett called me in late 1970 to inquire about the state of our research, my first contact with him since 1967. After his departure from State to take an executive position with IBM, he had moved to the Saga Corporation as Vice President for Human Relations—his position at the time of this writing. After we completed our conversation, it occurred to me that Crockett could be an invaluable source of additional information. I wrote immediately asking if he would be willing to help, and sent along a list of some twenty questions. Thus began a series of airmail interviews extending over the period of a year. The result was around fifty double-spaced pages of replies that add up to a very candid and highly revealing insider's account of organizational behavior in the State Department. Crockett also provided me with an assortment of other useful materials, including presidential memoranda and his own personal papers related to our concerns.

From the beginning I was concerned about the pitfalls in the relation between a research sponsor, such as Crockett, and an evaluation team, such as our own. The normal dangers of cooptation are magnified when the changes under study are controversial and rest heavily on the personal inspiration of the sponsor, as was true in this case. Also tipping the balance in Crockett's favor was his own personal charm, which was conceded by even his severest critics. He is a big, genial man with an easy smile on a disarmingly cherubic countenance—just the sort of sponsor for whom a researcher would like the results to come out "right."

Still, in our dealings with Crockett and ACORD several conditions worked in favor of objectivity. One was our own initial awareness of the potential for a problem, and our insistence that we have a free hand in designing the study. We made it clear to Richard Barrett and John Harr that we did not want to get into a situation where we could take only those measures which would cast MOP in the most favorable or least negative light. Fortunately, they and other members of ACORD agreed with this stipulation and shared our conviction that the only worthwhile evaluation was an honest one. Second, we did not meet Crockett until December 1966, a point at which many of the initial results had been collected. Hence the opportunities for personalism to come into play were greatly reduced. Third, Crockett himself insisted that the study be done as objectively as possible and that the results be disseminated outside the department. He did not conceal his disappointment when we found serious flaws in the reorganization, nor has he hesitated to quibble with this or that interpretation. Still, it is much to his credit that neither in this research nor in other projects touching on his reforms has he ever pressed for soft-pedaling any negative finding or expressed personal pique at interpretations that were less than flattering to his image as an administrator. In fact, after publication of the Argyris report some of his associates accused him of being possessed by a suicidal tendency to divulge damaging data. It is perhaps characteristic of Crockett that in his present position he has allowed the Stanford Business School to conduct a controlled experiment with work units to assess the effects of organization development programs. As he said in 1973, "I don't know what I'll do if they don't find any differences."

In 1970 I noticed that the *United States Government Organization Manual* once again listed the position of Assistant Secretary for Administration in the Department of State. As the restoration of this position—the highest abolished in 1965—was of obvious interest to our analysis, I immediately wrote to Deputy Under Secretary Macomber to inquire about the change. He replied very quickly with a clear, concise statement of his reasons (see Chapter 3). Early in 1971 we again corresponded about other changes in O, and he was most cooperative in sending memoranda and organization charts as well as his personal comments.

A further opportunity to understand the motivational problems of the Foreign Service arose while I served as consultant to the Agency for International Development (AID) in 1972 and 1973. My assignment was to advise the agency on a study of problems in its performance appraisal and promotion system. Although AID's personnel evaluations are independent of those in the State Department, many of the complaints heard among Foreign Service Officers in the latter were also endemic among reserve and staff officers in AID. Of particular concern were charges that promotions were based on personal relations with supervisors rather than on performance; that efficiency ratings suffered from gross inflation; and that, as a result of the previous conditions, the actual rankings of officers for promotions were irrational and unfair. In the summer of 1972 I interviewed many of the senior administrators in AID as well as a sample of Foreign Service Reserve Officers. In addition, I worked closely for several months with an internal task force charged with responsibility for developing a new performance appraisal system and, in early 1973, addressed an open meeting of AID employees on the findings of our research. Both the survey findings and the group discussions confirmed my initial impressions about the psychological consequences of the reward system prevailing in both AID and State (see Chapter 6).

The final round of information-gathering came in late 1973 as the result of a suggestion made by James Q. Wilson. After reviewing the penultimate draft of this book, Wilson recommended that we provide greater documentation on the Hays Bill case, which had received only cursory treatment. During a visit I had with him in California, William Crockett, who had been our main source on this topic, provided me with a list of other reliable informants. While in Washington for another purpose in December, I pursued these leads and in a few hours uncovered a surprising amount of information. The most helpful contact was Carl Marcy, chief of staff of the Senate Foreign Relations Committee. He supplied the lengthy committee document mentioned in Chapter 8 and steered me toward other sources, including a fascinating file of documents stored in the National Archives. As I worked my way through these materials in 1974, I realized that the Hays Bill showed important parallels to the MOP reorganization, and yet marked differences in the issues raised for a theory of public bureaucracy. It was at this point that I settled on the present organization of this volume.

In sum, this research biography has tried to document the tortuous evolution of a view of public organizations, and to lay out the varied bases for the interpretations offered. The analysis draws on many sources that are usually not explicitly identified: unstructured interviews with officials throughout the Department of State; questionnaires and rating scales administered to several hundred employees of that organization; my own two years of service as a contract employee of AID in Peru; personal observations by the authors in meetings at the State Department and AID; lengthy written interviews with William Crockett and more brief correspondence with William Macomber; letters submitted by Foreign Service Officers and others to the State Department's Task Force on Performance Appraisal and Promotions; hearings published by the House Appropriations Committee, the Senate Foreign Relations Committee, and other congressional bodies; unpublished documents contained in the National Archives and obtained from other sources as well; dozens of informal conversations with knowledgeable individuals; and, of course, published literature on the State Department and other federal agencies, much of which is not cited in the bibliography.

In the end we concluded that a qualitative, loosely documented, but broadly based interpretation of the central issues in public bureaucracy would be immensely preferable to a narrowly based quantitative analysis of the wrong questions. I am now convinced that any comprehensive study of organizational behavior in a federal agency, especially one that hopes to deal adequately with the political environment, must use the widest range of information possible. Perhaps one other lesson of this project is that the student of public organizations should not be too hasty either in publishing the results on a change program or in abandoning a study when the bureaucratic tides have shifted. In our experience a five-year perspective on organizational events was none too long.

# Bibliography

Albrow, M. *Bureaucracy* (London: Pall Mall, 1970).

Allison, G. T. "Conceptual Models and the Cuban Missile Crisis," *American Political Science Review* 63:689-718 (1969).

―――― *Essence of Decision: Explaining the Cuban Missile Crisis* (Boston: Little, Brown, 1971).

―――― and M. Halperin. "Bureaucratic Politics: A Paradigm and Some Policy Implications," *World Politics* 24:40-79 (1972) (suppl.).

Anderson, T. R., and S. Warkov. "Organizational Size and Functional Complexity: A Study of Administration in Hospitals," *American Sociological Review* 26:23-28 (1961).

Argyris, C. *Interpersonal Competence and Organizational Effectiveness* (Homewood, Ill.: Irwin, 1962).

―――― *Integrating the Individual and the Organization* (New York: Wiley, 1964).

―――― *Some Causes of Organizational Ineffectiveness within the Department of State* (Washington, D.C.: Center for International Systems Research, U. S. Department of State, 1967).

Attwood, W. "The Labyrinth in Foggy Bottom," *Atlantic* (February 1967).

Bacchus, W. I. "Diplomacy for the 70's: An Afterview and Appraisal," *American Political Science Review* 68:736-748 (1974a).

―――― "Obstacles to Reform in Foreign Affairs: The Case of NSAM 341," *Orbis* 18:266-276 (1974b).

Barnes, L. B. "Organizational Change and Field Experiment Methods," *in* V. H. Vroom (ed.), *Methods of Organizational Research* (Pittsburgh: University of Pittsburgh Press, 1967), pp. 57-111.

Barnett, V. M., Jr. (ed.). *The Representation of the United States Abroad* (New York: Praeger, 1965).

Beckhard, R. *Organization Development: Strategies and Models* (Reading, Mass.: Addison-Wesley, 1969).

Bendix, R. *Max Weber: An Intellectual Portrait* (Garden City, N. Y.: Doubleday, 1960).

_____ "Bureaucracy," *in* D. L. Sills (ed.), *International Encyclopedia of the Social Sciences* (New York: Macmillan and the Free Press, 1968), pp. 206-219.

Bernstein, M. *The Job of the Federal Executive* (Washington, D. C.: Brookings Institution, 1958).

Blake, R. R., and J. S. Mouton. *The Managerial Grid* (Houston, Texas: Gulf, 1964).

Blau, P. M. *The Dynamics of Bureaucracy* (Chicago: University of Chicago Press, rev. ed., 1963).

_____ "The Hierarchy of Authority in Organizations," *American Journal of Sociology* 73:453-467 (1968).

_____ and R. A. Schoenherr. *The Structure of Organizations* (New York: Basic Books, 1971).

_____, W. V. Heydebrand, and R. E. Stauffer. "The Structure of Small Bureaucracies," *American Sociological Review* 31:179-191 (1966).

Burnham, J. *The Managerial Revolution* (New York: Day, 1941).

Campbell, J. F. *The Foreign Affairs Fudge Factory* (New York: Basic Books, 1971).

Chapple, E. D., and L. R. Sayles. *The Measure of Management* (New York: Macmillan, 1961).

Coch, L., and J. R. P. French, Jr. "Overcoming Resistance to Change," *Human Relations* 1:512-532 (1948).

Committee on Foreign Affairs Personnel. *Personnel for the New Diplomacy* (New York: Taplinger, 1962).

Crockett, W. J. "Introducing Change to a Complex Organization," *in* R. Hacon (ed.), *Personal and Organizational Effectiveness* (London: McGraw-Hill, 1972), pp. 289-304.

Davies, J. P., Jr. *Foreign and Other Affairs* (New York: Norton, 1963).

Dill, W. R. "Environment as an Influence on Managerial Autonomy," *Administrative Science Quarterly* 2:409-443 (1958).

Downs, A. *Inside Bureaucracy* (Boston: Little, Brown, 1967).

Gawthrop, L. C. *Bureaucratic Behavior in the Executive Branch* (New York: Free Press, 1969).

Golembiewski, R. "Authority as a Problem in Overlays," *Administrative Science Quarterly* 9:22-49 (1964).

Gouldner, A. *Patterns of Industrial Bureaucracy: A Case Study of Modern Factory Administration* (New York: Free Press, 1954).

Gross, B. *The Managing of Organizations*, 2 vols. (New York: Free Press, 1964).

Guest, R. *Organizational Change: The Effect of Successful Leadership* (Homewood, Ill.: Dorsey, 1962).

Halperin, M. "Why Bureaucrats Play Games," *Foreign Policy* 2:70-90 (1971).

Harr, J. E.  *The Professional Diplomat* (Princeton: Princeton University Press, 1969).

Hayes, F. O'R.  Unpublished manuscript on experiences as budget director in New York City, 1973.

Hintze, O.  "Die Entstehung der modernen Staatsministerien," *in* O. Hintze (ed.), *Staat und Verfassung* (Göttingen: Vandenhoeck und Ruprecht, 2nd ed., 1908), pp. 275-320.

Hoopes, T.  *The Devil and John Foster Dulles* (Boston: Little, Brown, 1973).

Hoover Commission.  *Report on the Organization of the Executive Branch of the Government* (New York: McGraw-Hill, 1949).

Ilchman, W. F.  *Professional Diplomacy in the United States, 1779-1939* (Chicago: University of Chicago Press, 1961).

Jackson, H.  Committee on Government Operations, Subcommittee on National Security Staffing and Operations, staff reports and hearings, 88th Congress, *Administration of National Security*, pt. 2, 1965.

Katz, D., and R. L. Kahn.  *The Social Psychology of Organizations* (New York: Wiley, 1966).

Kaufman, H.  *The Forest Ranger—A Study in Administrative Behavior* (Baltimore: Johns Hopkins University Press, 1960).

Kelman, H. C., and D. P. Warwick.  "Bridging Micro and Macro Approaches to Social Change: A Social-Psychological Perspective," *in* G. Zaltman (ed.), *Processes and Phenomena of Social Change* (New York: Wiley, 1973), pp. 13-59.

Leacacos, J.  *Fires in the In Basket* (Cleveland: World, 1968).

Leavitt, H. J.  "Applied Organizational Change in Industry: Structural, Technological, and Humanistic Approaches," *in* J. G. March (ed.), *Handbook of Organizations* (Chicago: Rand McNally, 1965), pp. 1144-1170.

Leiserson, A.  "Political Limitations in Executive Reorganization," *American Political Science Review* 41:68-84 (1947).

Lewin, K.  *Field Theory in Social Science* (New York: Harper, 1951).

Maass, A. A.  *Muddy Waters: The Army Engineers and the Nation's Rivers* (Cambridge, Mass.: Harvard University Press, 1951).

McCamy, J. L.  *Conduct of the New Diplomacy* (New York: Harper, 1964).

McGregor, D.  *The Human Side of Enterprise* (New York: McGraw-Hill, 1960).

MacNeil, N.  *Forge of Democracy: The House of Representatives* (New York: McKay, 1963).

Mann, F. C.  "Studying and Creating Change: A Means to Understanding Social Organization," *in* C. M. Arensberg et al. (eds.), *Research in Industrial Human Relations: A Critical Appraisal* (New York: Harper, 1957), pp. 146-147.

Marrow, A. J. *Making Waves in Foggy Bottom* (Washington, D. C.: NTL Institute, 1974).

Meyer, M. W. *Bureaucratic Structure and Authority* (New York: Harper & Row, 1972).

Morse, N. C., and E. Reimer. "The Experimental Change of a Major Organizational Variable," *Journal of Abnormal and Social Psychology* 52:120-129 (1956).

Mosher, F. C. (ed.). *Governmental Reorganizations: Cases and Commentary* (Indianapolis: Bobbs-Merrill, 1967).

Mott, P. E. *The Characteristics of Effective Organizations* (New York: Harper & Row, 1972).

Neustadt, R. *Alliance Politics* (New York: Columbia University Press, 1970).

Parkinson, C. N. *Parkinson's Law and Other Studies in Administration* (Boston: Houghton Mifflin, 1957).

Pugh, D. S., D. J. Hickson, C. R. Hinings, and C. Turner. "The Context of Organization Structures," *in* W. Heydebrand (ed.), *Comparative Organizations: The Results of Empirical Research* (Englewood Cliffs, N. J.: Prentice-Hall, 1973), pp. 62-93.

Ransom, H. H. *Central Intelligence and National Security* (Cambridge, Mass.: Harvard University Press, 1958).

Redford, E. S. *Democracy in the Administrative State* (New York: Oxford University Press, 1969).

Rourke, F. *Bureaucratic Power in National Politics* (Boston: Little, Brown, 1965).

Rushing, W. A. "The Effects of Industry Size and Division of Labor on Administration," *Administrative Science Quarterly* 12:267-295 (September 1967).

Schein, E. H. "The Mechanisms of Change," *in* W. G. Bennis, K. D. Benne, and R. Chin (eds.), *The Planning of Change* (New York: Holt, Rinehart, and Winston, 2nd ed., 1969), pp. 97-108.

Schlesinger, A. M., Jr. *A Thousand Days* (Boston: Houghton Mifflin, 1965).

Secretary of State's Public Committee on Personnel. *Toward A Stronger Foreign Service* (Washington, D. C.: U. S. Government Printing Office, 1954).

Seidman, H. *Politics, Position, and Power: The Dynamics of Federal Organization* (New York: Oxford University Press, 1970).

Selznick, P. *TVA and the Grass Roots* (Berkeley: University of California Press, 1949).

Silverman, D. *The Theory of Organisations: A Sociological Framework* (New York: Basic Books, 1971).

Stanley, D. T., D. E. Mann, and J. E. Doig. *Men Who Govern: A Biographical Profile of Federal Political Executives* (Washington, D. C.: Brookings Institution, 1967).

Terrien, F. W., and D. L. Mills. "The Effect of Changing Size upon the Internal Structure of Organizations," *American Sociological Review* 20:11-13 (1955).

Thompson, J. D. *Organizations in Action: Social Bases of Administrative Theory* (New York: McGraw-Hill, 1967).

―――― and W. J. McEwen. "Organizational Goals and Environment: Goal-setting as an Interaction Process," *American Sociological Review* 23: 23-31 (1958).

Thompson, K. *American Diplomacy and Emergent Patterns* (New York: New York University Press, 1962).

Tout, T. F. *Chapters in the Administrative History of Medieval England,* 6 vols. (London: Longmans, 1920-1933).

U. S. Bureau of the Budget. "Measuring Productivity of Federal Government Organizations," *in* R. T. Golembiewski, F. Gibson, and G. Y. Cornog (eds.), *Public Adminsitration: Readings in Institutions, Processes and Behavior* (Chicago: Rand McNally, 1966), pp. 66-95.

U. S. Department of State. *Diplomacy for the 70's* (Washington, D. C.: U. S. Department of State, 1970).

U. S. Senate Committee on Foreign Relations. *Establishment of a Single Foreign Affairs Personnel System and Nominations of USIA Officers as Foreign Service Officers: Hearings Before a Special Subcommittee of the Committee on Foreign Relations* (Washington, D. C.: U. S. Government Printing Office, 1966).

Villard, H. S. *Affairs at State* (New York: Crowell, 1965).

Waldo, D. "The Development of a Theory of Democratic Administration," *American Political Science Review* 46:81-103 (1952).

Warner, W. L., P. P. Van Riper, N. H. Martin, and O. F. Collins. *The American Federal Executive* (New Haven: Yale University Press, 1963).

Warwick, D. P. "Performance Appraisal and Promotions in the Foreign Service," *Foreign Service Journal* (July 1970).

Webb, J. *Space Age Management* (New York: McGraw-Hill, 1969).

Weber, M. *The Theory of Social and Economic Organization,* A. M. Henderson and T. Parsons, trans. (New York: Oxford University Press, 1947).

# Index